China at the Crossroads

For Wang Xiaoqiang

China at the Crossroads

PETER NOLAN

polity

Copyright © Peter Nolan 2004

The right of Peter Nolan to be identified as Author of this Work has been asserted in accordance with the UK Copyright, Designs and Patents Act 1988.

First published in 2004 by Polity Press in association with Blackwell Publishing Ltd.

Editorial office:
Polity Press
65 Bridge Street
Cambridge CB2 1UR, UK

Marketing and production:
Blackwell Publishing Ltd
108 Cowley Road
Oxford OX4 1JF, UK

Distributed in the USA by
Blackwell Publishing Inc.
350 Main Street
Malden, MA 02148, USA

A catalogue record for this book is available from the British Library.

Library of Congress Cataloging-in-Publication Data
Nolan, Peter, 1949–
China at the crossroads / Peter Nolan.
     p. cm.
  Includes bibliographical references.
  ISBN 0-7456-3238-6 (alk. paper) – ISBN 0-7456-3239-4 (pbk. : alk. paper)
  1. China – Economic conditions – 1976–2000.   2. China – Politics and government – 1976–   I. Title.
  HC427.92 .N644 2004
  338.951–dc21
                                                     2003007751

Typeset in 10.5 on 12pt Sabon
by Graphicraft Limited, Hong Kong
Printed and bound in Great Britain by TJ International, Padstow, Cornwall

For further information on Polity, visit our website: www.polity.co.uk

Contents

[T]he disparity between our technology and our ethics is greater than it has ever been. [This] is mortally dangerous. . . . [I]n spite of his scientific and technological prowess, modern man, like primitive man, is not the master of the situation in which he finds himself. He has failed to master it because he has failed to master himself. . . . The individual self is alienated from the universal self by greed. This greed is a desire to exploit the universal for the individual self's purposes. The converse of greed is compassion. By practising compassion, the individual self can become the universal self actually. . . . It is hard to see how, in the atomic age, mankind can avoid committing mass suicide if it does not raise the average level of its behaviour to the level actually attained by the Buddha and Saint Francis of Assisi. . . . If mankind is not to destroy itself, it must now cleanse the pollution it has produced and must refrain from producing any more. [T]his can only be by co-operation on a world-wide scale. . . . [P]rivate competitive economic enterprise is condemning itself to death because all parties fail to restrain their greed. The ethical – or perhaps unethical – postulate of the ideology of competitive economic enterprise is that greed is a virtue, not a vice. . . . Unrestrained greed is self-destructive because it takes suicidally short views. . . . [I]n all industrial countries in which maximum private profit is the motive for production, the competitive economic system will become unworkable.

[T]he survival of mankind is more precarious today than it has been at any time since mankind established its ascendancy over non-human nature. . . . [T]he human race will be unable to survive unless it achieves political unification quickly. It is conceivable that the future unifier of the world will not be a Western or a Westernized country but will be China. . . . [F]or most of the time since the third century BC, [China] has been the centre of the world. Within the last five hundred years, the whole world has been knitted together by Western enterprise all except on the political plane. Perhaps it is China's destiny now to give political unity and peace not just to half but to all the world. . . . East Asia preserves a number of historical assets that may enable it to become the geographical and cultural axis for the unification of the whole world: [these include] the Chinese people's experience, during the last twenty-one centuries, of maintaining an empire that is a regional model for a literally worldwide world-state; the ecumenical spirit with which the Chinese have been imbued during this long chapter of Chinese history; the rationality of both Confucianism and Buddhism; the sense of mystery of the universe and the recognition that human attempts to dominate the universe are self-defeating, . . . the most precious intuition of Taoism; the conviction that . . . far from trying to dominate nonhuman nature, man's aim should be to live in harmony with it.
Arnold Toynbee, in conversation with Daisaku Ikeda, in Toynbee and Ikeda, 1989:
42, 128, 248–51, 264, 266, 330–1, 340 and 368

Do we expect China to meet the world's life and death demands? Will China make this attempt? If it attempts, will it succeed? We cannot predict the future, but it is already obvious that if China tries and fails, the prospect for mankind will be dim. . . . The world's unification is a way for mankind to escape suicide.

Arnold Toynbee in *Horizon Magazine*, Summer 1974

Preface

This little book was written in a relatively short period of time at the end of 2002 and early 2003. This short period was extremely significant in both Chinese and world history. The USA was trying to come to terms with 11 September, and preparing for war against Iraq. North Korea had announced it was re-starting its nuclear programme, in response to the USA's attempt to blockade its fuel supplies. By the time it was completed, the USA and the UK had launched a full-scale attack on Iraq.

In November 2002, China held the Sixteenth Congress of the Chinese Communist Party. This historic Congress announced a new Central Committee and elected a new Party General Secretary, Hu Jintao. The Congress took place at the end of a period of unprecedented growth of the Chinese economy. Alongside the extraordinary success of this development effort since the late 1970s, there were a wide accumulation of deep challenges for the new leadership.

The ideas in this book are the product of innumerable conversations with Dr Wang Xiaoqiang in the course of over ten years of research together. It was strongly influenced by our research on Guangdong province in South China during the Asian Financial Crisis.[1] It was written entirely by me, and I carry full responsibility for the content. However, it is not possible for me to separate my ideas from those of Dr Wang. I am immensely grateful to Dr Zhang Jin for constant discussion, advice and research assistance while writing this book. I am also greatly indebted to Dr Jiang Xiaoming for his deep concern and assistance at points of difficulty during the preparation of this book and in the course of other related projects.

Charles Curwen and Geoff Harcourt kindly encouraged me to turn this study from an appendix of another work into its current form as a free-standing book. Charles was kind enough to provide meticulous comments on the whole manuscript. I am grateful to two anonymous referees for their detailed and helpful comments. I am also grateful to John Thompson of Polity for his interest in the publication of this book, and to Justin Dyer for seeing it through the editorial process. Finally, I wish to thank Oxford University Press for their kind permission to reproduce the quotations from Arnold Toynbee that constitute the opening epigraph to the volume.

Introduction

This study examines the following question: is it possible for China to build a civilized, socially cohesive society over the next few decades, during what is still the early phase of China's industrialization, and during which time there will still be a huge rural reserve army of labour?

Will China be condemned to pass through a long phase of harsh political rule in order to meet the imperative of the accumulation process? If China fails to achieve a socially cohesive path of development, will the society and political structure remain stable? Does the fact that China is trying to industrialize at the beginning of the twenty-first century make this task more or less difficult? Is this task made more difficult by the fact that China faces numerous other deep development challenges, including a wide-ranging threat to the natural environment? Is it made more difficult by the fact that China faces a massive international relations challenge, notably in its relationship with the USA? What is the impact of the fact that China's large firms face a deep threat to their survival from the global giant firms headquartered in the high-income countries? Is this task more or less difficult in a huge country such as China, with a long history of economic development, possessing a highly sophisticated culture?

Since the late 1970s, China has enjoyed one of the most remarkable periods of economic growth ever seen. However, the country faces deep economic, political and social challenges as it moves into the next period in its development. These challenges include the vast extent of poverty and rapidly growing inequality; the challenge for Chinese businesses from the global business revolution; a deeply degraded natural environment; declining capabilities of the state; a comprehensive challenge in international relations; widespread corruption within the Chinese Communist Party; and extreme dangers in engaging closely with the global financial system, which were vividly exposed during the Asian Financial Crisis. The Chinese leadership is trying to deal simultaneously with the challenges of globalization, transition and development. No other country has ever faced such a set of challenges. There are no textbooks to guide China along this path. The responsibilities for the leadership are massive, because the price of failure is so huge. The possibility of social and political disintegration is real. Every effort of policy has to be directed towards avoiding this potentially catastrophic outcome.

There is intense debate among Chinese policy-makers, scholars and society at large about each of these issues. There is a wide sense that the country has arrived at a crossroads in its long journey away from the administratively planned economy. At a crossroads in the middle of nowhere the traveller cannot stay put. He can turn to the left, to the right, or even turn around and go home. The other option is to keep on in the same direction as the road he has come down.

Some people argue that China has no alternative but to accept that this phase of development will be characterized by a harsh political-economic order. They compare this with the phase of 'primitive capitalist accumulation' in Marx's *Capital*, Vol. 1. Few people dispute that the main task for China's policy-makers is to ensure social stability. Many people argue that the only way to achieve this in such a turbulent, challenging environment is through the exercise of harsh social control: the process of accumulation must come first or there will be no 'development'. Such arguments are typically supported with historical examples from early industrialization elsewhere.

Many people both inside and outside the country argue for a 'regime' change. They believe that the hard tasks that lie ahead can only be resolved with Western democratic institutions. Many people in this camp believe that the model for China to aim at is the USA, not the 'bankrupt' models of the European welfare states or 'quasi-socialist' Japan. Almost invariably, those advancing such arguments claim the authority of Adam Smith, who, they argue, demonstrated that the only rational way to organize the economy is through the free market. Frequently, it is asserted that China's long economic history provides a powerful object lesson for today's policy-makers: China's achievement in technical progress in medieval times was blocked from making further progress by a despotic state that prevented China taking the capitalist path that was followed in Europe.

They believe that the smaller the role for the state, the faster will China progress in the period ahead.

A third group, the 'new left wing', argues that the country has taken a fundamentally wrong turning by moving towards a market economy, increasingly integrated with and 'dependent' on the global economy. They believe that the country can only solve the growing tensions by reducing the country's reliance on international trade and capital inflow, and returning to the policies of the Maoist years, from the mid-1950s to the mid-1970s.

Another perspective is that China must continue along the path it has trodden for the past two decades, but adapt this approach to the fresh challenges that the country faces. For the past two decades, the Chinese leadership has been groping its way forward, away from the 'planned' economy of the Maoist period (Naughton, 1995; Wang Xiaoqiang, 1998). In the sharpest contrast to the reform path of the former USSR, China has been 'groping for stones to cross the river' (Nolan, 1995). China's approach was deeply influenced by the disasters that the country has experienced since the middle of the nineteenth century, not least the massive famine after the 'Great Leap Forward', and the great suffering during the Cultural Revolution. China's policy-makers were determined to avoid such policy-induced disasters. The process of reform has throughout been treated as a complex process of comprehensive 'system transformation', in which economic, social, political and psychological factors are considered as a seamless whole. Unlike the former USSR, China decided to address economic reform before considering political reform, though this was not inconsistent with making great efforts to improve the capability of the bureaucratic apparatus.

In economic reform, the watchword has been consistent experimentation before widespread adoption of a particular policy. Reform began in the countryside in the late 1970s and early 1980s with the system of contracting land to the individual household. It spread to the urban areas in the 1980s with the widespread introduction of the 'contract system' for individual enterprises. By the 1990s this had been replaced by a system of even wider enterprise autonomy, with taxation substituted for profit hand-overs to the state, corporatization and flotation of part of companies' equity on domestic and international stock markets. Controls over foreign investment were lifted slowly, and were followed by a surging tide of foreign direct investment (FDI) in the 1990s. By 2002, China was the world's largest recipient of FDI, and had over US$400 billion in accumulated FDI. Rural 'township and village enterprises' were allowed increased freedom in resource allocation, becoming a highly dynamic part of the economy in the late 1980s and early 1990s.

Market forces, including market-determined prices, and entrepreneurship gradually permeated the economy. Private business activity gradually was accepted and spread into all corners of the economy, though it was still not given formal protection. However, in July 2002, it was announced that private business people were eligible formally to join the Communist Party. At the Sixteenth Party Congress in 2002, Party General Secretary Jiang Zemin announced that citizens should be judged on their contribution to society and not penalized for their property holdings, a statement that was seen to provide 'support for the speedier development of legal institutions for protecting private property and the wealth generated by the emerging middle class of entrepreneurs' (*Financial Times [FT]*, 10 November 2002). Controls over foreign trade were relaxed slowly over the course of two decades, and given a final impetus by China finally joining the World Trade Organization at the end of 2001. Foreign exchange controls also were only slowly relaxed, and by 2003, the *renminbi* was still not convertible on the capital account.

China's incremental system reform produced outstanding results. By the time of the Sixteenth Party Congress in November 2002, China had decisively left one 'bank' of the river, that of the old Maoist system, but the 'other bank' was only dimly visible. At the end of 2002, at the Congress, a new generation of leaders was appointed, including a new Party General Secretary, Hu Jintao. In his first speech after being elected, he likened China's current situation to that facing the leadership under Chairman Mao at the end of the Civil War.

In March 1949 at the Second Plenum of the Seventh Central Committee of the Chinese Communist Party Mao Zedong made a highly significant speech outlining the tasks ahead. The victory over the Guomindang (KMT) was basically complete. The Party was entering a new phase in its development. Chairman Mao warned that it should guard against complacency, and realize that a long, arduous struggle lay ahead: 'To win countrywide victory is only the first step in a long march of ten thousand *li*. Even if this step is worthy of pride, it is comparatively tiny; what will be more worthy of pride is yet to come' (Mao Zedong, 1949: 374). The central theme of the speech was the need for the Party to find a path through the enormous tasks that confronted them in the face of great challenges both at home and abroad. In the same way, China now stands at a crossroads. It must grope its way forward in the face of these immense challenges, fully aware that there is a serious danger of system disintegration. This would be disaster for the Chinese people. It would render previous achievements meaningless.

In their search for a path forward, China's leaders are looking to the lessons from the country's own past, as well as to those from other countries, in order to find a way to build a stable, cohesive and prosperous society. This effort is of vital importance, not only for China, but also for the whole world.

Prologue
Groping for a Way Forward

Deng Xiaoping launches China's 'reform and opening-up'

The overall philosophy behind China's reform path since the death of Chairman Mao and the overthrow of the Gang of Four was established early on in the reform years. In 1978, the Third Plenum of the Eleventh Central Committee of the Chinese Communist Party set in motion the overall policy direction of 'reform and opening-up'. It began the process of rural reform which was to act as the guiding path for all subsequent reform. Even this first stage of China's system reform was to be a prolonged process of institutional experimentation. It was not completed until the high tide of 'contracting output to the household' swept across the whole country in 1983.[1] Each year, the crucial 'Document Number One' on rural reform summed up the results from the previous year, and indicated the way forward in rural reform in the year ahead. Deng Xiaoping was by far the most important figure in this process.

In June 1979 I was fortunate to be a member of a delegation from Oxford University, led by Neville Maxwell,[2] which was able to conduct first-hand research on the reforms that were just beginning in the rural people's communes. In the middle of this research, on 21 June, we were privileged to be granted a long interview with the Vice-Premier, Deng Xiaoping.

In the course of this interview he expounded his philosophy for economic reform. At this point he could have had no idea of the way in which China would change over the following decades. He had no grand blueprint for system change. What stood out from the key points in his exposition to us was the overall pragmatic philosophy of trying to 'seek truth from the facts', moving forward incrementally to see if the change in question was likely to produce good results for the whole mass of the Chinese population. The first, groping efforts at rural reform, which he outlined to us, were to prove representative of the approach applied to the whole process of system change, which is still under way in 2003. Each incremental reform helped to build a process of mutually reinforcing, positive feedback effects. Once China set out on this path, the process of cumulative causation created powerful 'path-dependent' effects, and it became harder and harder to shift the country off the development path it had established. The crucial part of this process was the starting point. It set the ball rolling in a particular direction. It established the overall philosophy and set up the pattern for the whole subsequent reform effort.

Some of the main points made by Vice-Premier Deng Xiaoping to our group at this, the very outset of the reform process, were as follows:[3]

> China is poor. Poverty cannot demonstrate the superiority of socialism. Our general aim is for everyone in society to become rich and prosperous. This will take a long time. Our overall method is to encourage the advanced to take the lead in becoming rich, so that the others can follow.

> Truth is to be found in practice (*shishi qiushi*). If we can achieve an increase in the average income of all Chinese people, then it will prove that our practice was correct. If our future experience proves that we have upheld socialism and prevented the restoration of capitalism, then it will demonstrate that our political practice was correct.

> When I visited the USA recently, I was asked the question: Won't this lead to the restoration of capitalism? However, all the profits gained from accumulation will go to the people because there is ownership by all the people, despite the differences of income among the people. Because we have all-people ownership, polarization will not occur. Therefore, a bourgeois class will not arise. In China very few people receive high salaries. My salary is the highest in China, but I am sure it is less than that of any of the foreigners here today. Moreover, such salaries will not be increased for a long time. China's economic policies and efforts to accelerate the Four Modernizations under the leadership of the Communist Party of China are based on four principles: socialism, the dictatorship of the proletariat, Marxism-Leninism and Mao Zedong Thought. Under these principles, the income and profits from economic growth will go to the collectives and the people.

We think it is a good thing that in certain people's communes there has been a marked increase in incomes. If a group of people's communes, say ten or twenty per cent, have become fairly well-off, then there is no need for the state to give them aid to increase their accumulation. . . . The state will then be able to concentrate its efforts on helping backward areas. In general, we should help some people's communes to get rich first, and then the state will help poor people's communes to become rich. Those that have taken the lead in getting rich will serve as a model for the other people's communes to become rich. Of course, inequality will exist for a long period of time, but 'rich' is a relative term, and we do not mean rich in the Western sense. I have seen two different production teams with similar natural conditions, one with an average per capita income of around 100 *yuan* and the other with just a couple of dozen *yuan*. The difference lies in the quality of management. Is it reasonable to ask the well-run people's communes to wait for the backward ones to catch up? Our policy throughout the country is to allow regions or people's communes that achieve high incomes thanks to good management to go ahead.

We are not afraid of such inequality. We can work out ways to prevent it. Generally, the basic thing is to retain the collective ownership. So far even the most prosperous people's communes, around Shanghai, have only around 300 *yuan* per capita income. Our policy is to encourage those with higher incomes to put more money into accumulation, buy machinery, diversify the economy and push their economy to a higher level.

The principle we are today following in the rural areas is exactly that of before the Cultural Revolution. The principle of 'distribution according to labour' was laid down in the 1950s. It is not a new thing. The Gang of Four destroyed these policies. This harmed the peasants' enthusiasm. No matter how hard they worked, under the Gang of Four, they still received the same.

China today is still very poor. There still are some problems at present for which there is no solution, but we will find one in the future. For example, today there is no income tax. If some day there emerges a marked inequality between collectives and individuals, we can introduce an income tax to correct the inequality. But today incomes are too low to warrant this. This is just one possibility. Other methods could also be used to correct this problem.

Poverty is not socialism. If socialism means poverty, where is the superiority of socialism? In the past decade we suffered greatly from excessive egalitarianism and ultra-left tendencies. The Gang of Four would rather have poor socialism than rich capitalism.

We also suffered from egalitarianism in the industrial enterprises, which caused great suffering. People earned the same pay irrespective of their work. Those enterprises that manage well should have higher incomes than those that manage badly. This will compel the enterprises that manage badly to improve their management. In the past, the enterprises making losses received the same income as the well-run, profit-making enterprises. We should not treat these two types of enterprises in the same way.

The success of 'groping for a way forward'

The outcome of China's reform strategy, initiated by Deng Xiaoping, has been the most explosive and long-sustained period of economic advance that the world has ever seen. Even the Asian Financial Crisis made no dent in China's forward momentum. Moreover, this growth has taken place in a vast country, with more than one-fifth of the total world population. Therefore, the significance of China's unprecedentedly successful development eclipses that of all other late-comer countries.

From 1978 to 2001, China's average annual growth rate of GDP per capita was 8.1 per cent, and its rate of industrial growth was 11.5 per cent, placing it at the top of the world's growth performance in this period.[4] When one considers the huge diversity of conditions of China's different regions, this was a remarkable performance. It went far beyond merely 'taking up the slack' from the inefficiencies of the Maoist period. No other former planned economy achieved remotely this performance. It went far beyond simply benefiting from the 'advantages of backwardness'. No other developing country achieved remotely this performance.[5]

By 2001, China had climbed to first place in the world in the production of a wide array of products, including cereals, meat, cotton lint, fruit, crude steel, coal, cement, chemical fertilizer and TV sets. It was the world's largest production base for a wide range of household appliances. In 2001, China produced 96 million electric fans, 60 million cameras, 41 million colour TV sets, 25 million mobile phones, 14 million household refrigerators, 14 million household washing machines, 11 million vacuum cleaners, 11 million household freezers and 11 million video recorders.

China's exports grew from US$18.1 billion in 1978 to over US$266 billion in 2001, an average annual growth rate of over 12 per cent. Its manufactured exports in the same period rose from US$9 billion to US$240 billion, an average annual growth rate of over 15 per cent. Manufactured exports' share in China total exports rose from 50 per cent in 1978 to over 90 per cent in 2001.

China had become the largest single focus for global firms' foreign direct investment. The total stock of FDI in the Mainland had reached US$395 billion in 2001, and US$452 billion in Hong Kong Special Administrative Region, totalling more than US$847 billion (UNCTAD, 2002: 311).[6] This combined total was significantly greater than that in the whole of Latin America and the Caribbean, which stood at US$693 billion in 2001. It greatly exceeded the stock of FDI in the rest of Asia, including East Asia (including Japan), Southeast Asia and South Asia, the total for which amounted to US$434 billion in 2001. It eclipsed that in the former USSR and Eastern Europe, which totalled just US$163 billion in 2001.

Even more importantly, this period of exceptional growth saw a comprehensive transformation of Chinese people's livelihoods. Real average per capita consumption of Chinese people rose by over 7 per cent per annum from 1978 to 2001 (SSB, *ZTN*, 2002). This achievement was all the more remarkable in view of the fact that the Chinese population grew by over 313 million people during the same period. Not only was the standard of living transformed during this period, but the early years of reform and opening-up saw the most remarkable reduction in absolute poverty that the world has ever seen. The World Bank estimates that the number of absolutely poor people in China fell from 270 million in 1978 (28 per cent of the total) to just 97 million (9.2 per cent of the total) in 1985 (quoted in Nolan, 1995: 14).

There are radically different interpretations of the causes and significance of this performance. At an international meeting held in Beijing in 2001, one Chinese economist delivered an impassioned speech. He said that although China had achieved a great deal in the previous two decades, if only the government would stop interfering in the economy, then the growth rate would be double or more that of the previous period. The statement was met with loud applause from the international business people attending the meeting. My own view is that the reason China has been so successful is that despite great strains and numerous policy shortcomings, the state has continued to play a critical role in maintaining social stability, resolving problems of market failure, regulating the distribution of income, wealth and life opportunities, and regulating the way in which China interacts with the global economy.

1

The Challenges to China's Economic and Political Stability

Can China Build a Sustainable and Civilized Modern Economy?

We have seen in the prologue to this study that China has achieved remarkable results in its social and economic development since the process of 'reform and opening up' was initiated by Deng Xiaoping over two decades ago. However, that same process has produced a series of formidable challenges for the entire system of political economy, coming from several directions at once.

Poverty and inequality

Behind almost every aspect of China's development process in the early twenty-first century lies the harsh reality of the 'Lewis model' of economic development with unlimited supplies of labour (Lewis, 1954).

China has a huge population of almost 1.3 billion, increasing by around 15–16 million people each year (SSB, *ZTN*, 2002). From 1990 to 1999, China's working-age population rose from 679 million to 829 million, an increase of no less than 150 million in less than a decade. Almost 70 per cent of the Chinese population still lives in the countryside. Employment in agriculture is stagnant (333 million in 1995, falling to 329 million in 1999). It is estimated that there may be as many as 150 million 'surplus' farm workers. This places a powerful constraint on the rate of growth of real incomes for low-skilled occupations in the non-farm sector (see below).

As the impact of the World Trade Organization (WTO) increases, pressures on rural employment will intensify. The main alternative source of rural labour absorption, the 'township and village enterprises' (TVEs), stagnated in terms of employment creation (at around 127 million employees) after the mid-1990s. The high-speed growth of the TVEs in the 1980s and early 1990s was based mainly on the rapid growth of small businesses in labour-intensive activities using simple technologies. In order to compete within the global value chain, the TVEs are being forced to increase labour productivity fast. The thousands of new enterprises established in the early 1990s faced increasing challenges from greater market integration. The unavoidable reality is that the level of rural underemployment will continue to rise rapidly in the early years of the twenty-first century.

The farm sector is continuing to grow at around 5–6 per cent per annum, and is investing on a large scale: the total power of agricultural machinery rose from 361 million kwh in 1995 to 489 million kwh in 1999 (SSB, *ZTN*, 2002). However, there is estimated to have been a 22 per cent drop in the prices paid to farmers between 1997 and 2002. The rate of growth of farm incomes has reduced, at best, to slow progress. Official data report average annual growth of farm income per capita of around three per cent in the late 1990s. However, many analysts estimate that rural incomes have stagnated, and some argue that they have even declined since the mid-1990s. For example, Chen Xiwen, Deputy Director of the State Development Research Centre, estimates that China's farmers 'suffered an average decline in income in 1998, 1999, 2000 and 2001' (reported in *FT*, 31 October 2002). Rural income distribution has become much more unequal: the Gini coefficient of rural income distribution is estimated to have risen from 0.21 in 1978 to 0.40 in 1998. The farm sector will face severe challenges in the face of the rise in imports within the WTO, and possible deterioration in the terms of trade for farm products. One recent study believes that within the WTO in the years ahead 'the prospects for most rural households are grim' (Qu Hongbin, 2002). The share of the rural population in total consumption has fallen from around 60 per cent in the early 1980s to just 42 per cent in 2001, while the share of the rural population in China's total population still stands at 65 per cent (Qu Hongbin, 2002).

In his valedictory speech as China's Premier, Zhu Rongji warned: 'Agricultural, village and farmers' problems relate to the overall situation of China's reform, opening and modernization. We cannot neglect them or relax at any time. If we do not change these conditions, they will severely damp farmers' enthusiasm to produce, undermine the foundation of agriculture and even threaten the overall health of the national economy' (quoted in *FT*, 6 February 2003).

There is no question that there was a massive decline in absolute poverty in the early years of China's rural reforms in the late 1970s and early 1980s (Nolan, 1988). However, there still are huge numbers of people who are absolutely poor in terms of international poverty lines. Moreover, recent estimates suggest that in eight out of twenty-nine provinces, the incidence of poverty rose significantly from 1985 to 1996 (Yao Shujie, 2002). The World Bank estimated that in 1995 there were 716 million people (58 per cent of the population) who had less than US$2 per day, and around 280 million who lived on less than US$1 per day (World Bank, *WDR*, 2001: 236). A large fraction of these are rural dwellers, or rural migrants to the cities. Official data for 2001 show that the average per capita income of China's 800 million rural residents is just US$290 (RMB2,366), or 80 cents per day (SSB, *ZTN*, 2002: 343). Within the total rural population, there were approximately 580 million rural dwellers (72.5 per cent of rural households) with less than US$360 per year (SSB, *ZTN*, 2002: 343).[1] In other words, the number of absolutely poor people is still huge, and may well be growing.

The massive growth of rural underemployment deeply affects the character of development in the non-farm sector. It provides intense incentives for rural–urban migration, and great downward pressure on non-farm wages in unskilled and low-skilled occupations. By 2002, there were around 150 million rural residents who worked in the urban areas without permanent urban residence qualifications. These were predominantly 'lumpen' labour, with limited skills. The rate of pay is simple to estimate, namely the equivalent of roughly US$1–2 per day, which is the price of 'lumpen' migrant labour throughout human history (at today's prices). Even in the fastest-growing region of China, the Pearl River Delta, there was no increase in the real wages of unskilled labour during the whole of the 1990s. There is great social tension in China's urban areas, with relatively large numbers of rural migrants on subsistence wages struggling for survival alongside the rising Chinese middle class and high income earners, working mainly in the foreign sector and in Chinese businesses within the value chain of the global giant firms.

The way in which wages are determined for 'lumpen' unskilled migrant labour is basically that vividly described by John Steinbeck in the *Grapes of Wrath* (1939), on the Californian fruit farms during the Depression:

> And the migrants streamed in on the highways and their hunger was in their eyes. They had no argument, no system, nothing but their numbers and their needs. When there was work for a man, ten men fought for it – fought with a low wage – If that fella'll work for thirty cents, I'll work for twenty-five. If he'll do it for twenty-five, I'll do it for twenty. No me, I'm hungry. I'll work for fifteen. I'll work for food.

Steinbeck graphically portrays the threat to social stability posed by huge numbers of migrants:

> In the West there was panic when the migrants multiplied on the highways. Men of property were terrified for their property. Men who had never been hungry saw the eyes of the hungry. Men who had never wanted anything very much saw the flare of want in the eyes of migrants. And the men of the towns and the soft suburban country gathered to defend themselves; and they reassured themselves that they were good and the invaders bad, as a man must do before he fights. They said, These goddamed Okies are dirty and ignorant. They're degenerate, sexual maniacs. These goddamed Okies are thieves. They'll steal anything. They've got no sense of property rights. The local people whipped themselves into a mold of cruelty. Then they formed units, squads, and armed them – armed them with gas, with guns. We own the country – we can't let these Okies get out of hand.

In early 2003, it was reported that in Qingdao municipality, there was a proposal to segregate public buses, dividing them between local residents and migrant workers (*South China Morning Post*, 5 March 2003).

Social tension in the urban areas has risen sharply with changes in the pattern of urban employment. China's state-owned sector is rapidly reducing the level of employment. Wang Wei, Deputy Director of the State Council Office for Reform of the Economic System, estimates that between 1996 and 2001, 30 million workers were laid off from state-owned enterprises (quoted in *FT*, 21 November 2002). Some researchers estimate that more than 48 million people are without work as a result of reform in state-owned enterprises.

Regular employment in the urban non-state formal sector increased from 21 million in 1995 to 35 million in 1999 (SSB, *ZTN*, 2000: 115), but this is far from sufficient to absorb the large numbers made redundant from the state sector together with the swelling number of new entrants to the workforce. By 1998, the urban unemployment rate had reached over eight per cent (UNDP, 2000: 58), and is likely to accelerate as the pressure produced by China's entry to the WTO begins to bite even more deeply into employment levels in state-owned enterprises. Moreover, in order to compete within the emerging global value chain, there is intense pressures on all types of non-farm enterprises to raise labour productivity and substitute modern IT systems for people. China's 'laid-off' (*xia gang*) workers at state-owned enterprises receive greatly reduced incomes compared to that which they were supposed to receive in regular employment. In general, the standard of living of laid-off workers has greatly reduced. The early years of the twenty-first century have witnessed numerous urban strikes and protests, often on a scale unprecedented since the 1920s. Even at Daqing, where laid-off workers in China National Petroleum Corporation received exceptionally favourable terms for lay-off pay, there were large protests in the years 2000/2. The UNDP's study concluded: '[T]he explosive increase in unemployment has become the most challenging issue in China's economic and social development' (UNDP, 2000: 58).

A further element in the rising social tensions in the urban areas has been the high-speed growth of FDI from global giant multinational firms. By 2001, as noted above, the accumulated stock of FDI had reached nearly US$400 billion (UNCTAD, 2002). This investment is creating clusters of modern businesses in relatively isolated areas within China's major cities, such as the new Beijing financial district, the Pudong Development Zone and numerous 'high-technology' parks across the country. These virtual 'Treaty Ports' are emerging as areas with a relatively high degree of *de facto* autonomy, and form a nucleus of relatively high-income employment for both Chinese and foreigners, isolated from the surrounding society. A rapidly growing group of China's highest income earners live in isolated, protected compounds. One can even see in the major cities the beginning of the 'helicopter' culture that is highly developed in Brazil's main urban centres. Instead of braving the traffic nightmare, top Brazilian business people use the helicopter as their preferred mode of short-distance transport. 'Helicopter taxi services' for the Brazilian elite are a booming business. This lifts them physically and psychologically away from the normal chaotic life of the mass of urban dwellers. The nature of class differentiation in China's urban areas is changing at high speed, and in a manner that strongly recalls that of the pre-revolutionary Treaty Ports.[2]

There is strong evidence that as China has increased the pace of 'reform and opening up' since the mid-1990s, the level of urban inequality has increased substantially. Official data show that the Gini coefficient of the urban distribution of income rose from 0.25 in 1992 to 0.34 in 2001 (SSB, *ZTN*, 1993 and 2002). They show also that the income of the richest 10 per cent of the urban population rose from 3.3 times that of the poorest 10 per cent in 1992 to 5.4 times in 2001. Over the same period the income of the poorest 10 per cent fell from 57 per cent of that of the 'medium income' to 44 per cent. However, the official data do not include most of the 150 million migrants who are not registered as part of the urban population. The data also greatly underestimate the income of the highest segments of the native Chinese urban population. Nor do they include the relatively (and absolutely) large incomes of the fast-growing population of foreign employees of the multinationals. If all these factors are taken into consideration, the distribution of China's urban incomes is likely to be close to those of the most unequal countries in the world. Progressive income tax accounts for a mere 6 per cent of government income compared with 30 per cent in many parts of Asia.

There has been much discussion about the growth of the Chinese urban 'middle class'. From one perspective this appears already to be quite large. Data for 2001 (SSB, *ZTN*, 2002) show that the top decile of the urban income distribution (around 48 million people) had an average per capita income of US$1,834, and the ninth decile (another 48 million people) had around US$1,258 per capita. In a sense, we may conclude that the Chinese 'middle class' is around 90–100 million. However, this is misleading. An average per capita income of US$1,258 is on a par with the GNP per capita of such lower-middle-income countries as Ecuador or Kazakstan (World Bank, *WDR*, 2001: 274–5), while an average per capita income of US$1,834 is on a par with the GNP per capita of such lower-middle-income countries as Iran or Namibia. The top two deciles, with around 90–5 million people, are comparable in size and level of income with a medium-sized lower-middle-income country such as Egypt, with a population of 62 million and an average per capita GNP of US$1,400. The number of people in the top two deciles of the urban income distribution is comparable with a developing country such as Mexico (with a population of 97 million). However, Mexico's average per capita GNP is around US$4,400, far beyond the average per capita income of the top 20 per cent of the Chinese urban income distribution. In other words, the proportion of the Chinese urban population that is a true 'global middle class' is still extremely small, certainly a lot less than 10 per cent of the total, and, in terms of total numbers, not yet significantly developed beyond that of a single lower-middle-income, middle-sized developing country.

The average per capita income of China's total of 480 million officially registered urban residents in 2001 was just US$830, on a par with the GNP per capita of low-income countries such as Albania, Uzbekistan, Sri Lanka or Côte d'Ivoire (World Bank, *WDR*, 2001: 274–5). If we were to include the unofficial urban population of around 150 million migrant workers, then the figure would be even lower.

One recent study estimates that among China's urban households, the income of only around 20 million has caught up with the average of the urban households in East Asia's Newly Industrializing Countries (Qu Hongbin, 2002). This amounts to only around 12 per cent of the total number of officially registered urban households, and a significantly smaller proportion of the total number of urban households. The study estimates that, if present growth rates continue, another 20 million 'global middle-class households' will emerge in China in the next decade. This is likely to still be less than one-fifth of the total number of urban households in ten years' time. In other words, China's emerging middle class, those who can afford, for example, to buy automobiles, will remain a 'besieged' minority among a sea of urban poor people, who vastly outnumber them: the twenty-first century meets the eighteenth century at the window of Starbucks. The vast majority of the urban population are excluded by their low incomes from Starbucks or Walmart and excluded by armed guards from the apartment blocks of the new middle class, except where they are employed for domestic service.

The privatization process in China to date has been characterized by widespread insider dealing and corruption. In the years ahead there is a prospect that as much as RMB10 trillion (around US$1.2 trillion) in government assets will be privatized (Qu Hongbin, 2002). The way in which the transfer of such a huge volume of assets takes place will have substantial implications for the distribution of wealth. One study that is optimistic as to the benefits of forthcoming privatization nevertheless warns: 'Privatization will benefit everyone, but the privileged classes are likely to find ways of further enriching themselves' (Qu Hongbin, 2002). Another recent study of mainland bank deposits estimates that just 0.16 per cent of the population controls 65 per cent of the nation's US$1.5 trillion liquid assets. Compared with the rest of Asia, China reportedly has the highest concentration of wealth in the fewest hands, with a very narrow group of just two to three million people able to 'get rich quickly' (*South China Morning Post*, 29 March 2003).

There is wide concern among Chinese policy-makers about the implications of these trends for social stability in the urban areas. Intense official research efforts have been devoted to analysing trends in social inequality and trying to understand their ramifications, as well as to creating policies to ameliorate the rising tide of inequality. Many analysts believe that the reform process has entered a tense period in which there is an increased danger of social instability compared with the previous twenty years. There has been extensive discussion among policy-makers about how to build a dynamic economy while 'laying the groundwork for a market that is moral and fair', thus sustaining China as a 'steady and harmonious society' and, in the vision of its leaders, an 'everlasting and peaceful nation'.

The global business revolution

A consistently stated goal of China's industrial policy has been to construct globally powerful companies that can compete on the global level playing field:

> In our world today economic competition between nations is in fact between each nation's large enterprises and enterprise groups. A nation's economic might is concentrated and manifested in the economic power and international competitiveness of its large enterprises and groups. International economic confrontations in reality show that if a country has several large enterprises or groups it will be able to maintain a certain market share and hold an assured position in the world economic order. . . . *In the same way now and in the next century our nation's position in the international economic order will be to a large extent determined by the position of our nation's large enterprises and groups.* (Wu Bangguo, Chinese State Council, quoted in *Jingji Ribao* [*Economic Daily*], 1 August 1998, emphasis added)

In pursuit of this objective, China's stated goal of industrial policy has been to construct a sizeable group of large-scale powerful industrial firms that can challenge the global leaders. The chosen corporations were supported through a sequence of industrial policies.[3] China's planners carefully studied the industrial policies used by the high-income economies in their early stages of development. From Britain during the Industrial Revolution, the US and Continental Europe in the nineteenth century, through to the East Asian 'Tiger' economies of the late twentieth century, almost without exception, late-industrializing countries used some form of industrial policy to nurture 'national champions'. Each of these late-industrializing countries was able through different methods to nurture a group of globally competitive large firms.

The most powerful influence on the thinking of China's policymakers was probably the Japanese experience. During a similar period in Japan's development, from the 1950s to the 1970s, Japan's industrial planners supported the growth of a series of giant companies that developed into globally powerful firms. In many sectors the state nurtured just two or three dominant firms that were in an oligopolistic position in the domestic market. After two decades of industrial policy, there was a whole corps of globally competitive Japanese companies. By the late 1980s, Japan had twenty of the largest one hundred corporations in the *Fortune* 500 list. These companies developed through extensive support from state industrial policies, very similar to those adopted by China forty years later.[4]

How capable are China's 'national champions' to compete on the 'global level playing field' within the WTO? In the course of the 'China Big Business Programme', we tried to answer this question, using detailed case studies from China's 'national team' in several different sectors (Nolan, 2001a, 2001b). These include aerospace, pharmaceuticals, oil and petrochemicals, power equipment, automobiles and components, steel and coal, consumer electronics, telecommunications, IT hardware and financial services. In each case we found evidence of progress, but with many problems remaining. Moreover, in each case the reform within China was taking place against a background of revolutionary global change. The micro-level evidence from our case studies suggests that in most key respects, China's industrial policies of the 1980s and 1990s did not succeed.

The aggregate data confirm this view. At the start of the twenty-first century, not one of China's leading enterprises had become a globally competitive giant corporation, with a global market, a global brand and a global procurement system. The Chinese companies included in the *Fortune* 500 all faced huge problems of downsizing. China had no less than six of the top ten companies in the *Fortune* 500 in terms of numbers of employees, a dubious achievement. Every one of China's *Fortune* 500 companies was predominantly or wholly a state-owned firm, operating with a high degree of state protection. China has just three companies in the *FT* 500, which ranks firms by market capitalization. These are CNOOC (China National Offshore Oil Company), China Mobile and China Unicom, each of which operates in a totally protected domestic environment. Moreover, the vast bulk of the IT hardware equipment for China's telecoms companies is purchased from the global giants.[5] China does not have a single company in the world's top 300 companies by R&D expenditure. Nor does it have any representatives in Morgan Stanley Dean Witter's list of the world's top 250 'competitive edge' companies, or a single company in *Business Week*'s list of the world's top 100 brands.

The blunt reality is that after two decades of reform China's large firms are still far from being able to compete with the global giants. The gap is especially marked in the high-technology sectors, such as aerospace, power equipment, IT hardware and pharmaceuticals. It is marked even in 'mid-technology' sectors such as oil and petrochemicals, auto assembly and auto components. Even in sectors with apparently less advanced technology, such as steel, coal and consumer electrical equipment, there is a significant gap compared to leading global companies in the high value-added segments of the market. The challenge is not confined to the manufacturing sector. China's four main banks lag far behind the global giants in almost all respects. They will face an intense battle to compete as the WTO rules come into effect. It is thought likely that at least two of the big four domestic banks will be split up into many smaller pieces.

By the simplest of measures of sales revenue, profits and R&D, China's vanguard of leading firms that are intended to 'compete on the global level playing field' are still far behind the global leaders. Indeed, if we look across the whole spectrum of industries, it may even be the case that China's leading firms are further behind the global leaders than they were when the industrial policies began almost two decades ago. In these fundamental senses, China's industrial policy of the past two decades must be judged a failure. The reasons are both internal and external.

On the internal front, China's industrial policy encountered a number of peculiar problems which substantially differentiate the Chinese policy environment from that which faced Japan and Korea during their comparable period of catch-up at the level of the large firm. Within the same industry, radically different policies have been pursued at different times.[6] In addition, completely different policies were pursued in different sectors.[7] The foundation of China's economic reform was to increase 'enterprise' autonomy. The core of most large 'enterprises' was a single large production unit. This had many benefits, including the development of a strong sense of corporate ambition at the enterprise level. However, it caused difficulties in the subsequent attempts to build multi-plant firms with unified central control over individual production units. China is still a poor country, with a relatively tiny middle class. A large fraction of domestic demand is for low-price, low value-added products. Large Chinese firms have to fight a battle on two fronts: on the one hand with global giants in high value-added products, and, on the other hand, with domestic small and medium-sized enterprises in low value-added products.

China has a tradition of relatively autonomous local government. There has been persistent local resistance to cross-regional mergers due to fears of downsizing and loss of control of a 'local asset'. Unlike the other 'late-comer' countries, China's large enterprises inherited huge manning levels, which are hard to reduce without causing social instability. This will remain a deep problem for many years. The inability of China's emerging large firms to compete on international markets, plus the fact that they each have a huge workforce, produced a high incentive for the individual enterprise to diversify. A single large enterprise could easily have hundreds of 'children' and 'grandchildren' subsidiaries and related companies. This gives the 'illusion of scale', but beneath an apparently large firm there are typically hundreds of uneconomically small firms and immense problems of corporate governance. The weaknesses of such East Asian diversified 'network' firms were starkly revealed by the Asian Financial Crisis, which dealt a comprehensive blow to the dream that they could compete on the 'global level playing field'.

China's bureaucracy, meanwhile, has lacked the powerful nationalist incentive to build large firms successfully that drove Japanese (and Korean) policy-makers, and its ability to implement industrial policy purposefully and successfully has been undermined by deep-rooted corruption. The country's leaders are engaged in an intensive drive to solve this problem, repeatedly emphasizing that this is crucial to the maintenance of system stability (see pp. 39–44 below). Many of the worst examples of corruption have been exposed in the financial services sector, which is at the heart of the Chinese economy and the whole reform process. For most of the reform period the commitment to state ownership remained a goal in its own right, rather than building powerful corporations by whatever means was suitable. It proved hard to achieve the essential separation of government and enterprise.

On the external front, the period in which China has attempted to build strong indigenous firms through industrial policy has been quite different from that of the East Asian Newly Industrializing Countries at a similar phase in their development. The global business system was much more stable during the period during which Japan, South

Korea and Taiwan were putting into place their industrial policy. Moreover, the high-income countries were willing to tolerate extensive state intervention in the NICs, because they were viewed as the front line in the fight against communism. By contrast, China's attempt to build large globally competitive firms coincided with the most revolutionary epoch in world business history, possibly even including the Industrial Revolution. Moreover, the country is regarded by the USA as a 'strategic competitor'.

There are a number of aspects to the global business revolution. The period since the late 1980s has witnessed for the first time the opening up of a truly global marketplace in goods, services, capital and highly skilled labour. The only market which still remains bound firmly by nationality is the vast sea of unskilled labour. There is no chance for the surging mass of China's hundreds of millions of rural underemployed workers to find employment outside China. The world's leading firms have massively increased their production capabilities in fast-growing parts of developing countries. Of course, large swathes of the developing world have been hardly touched by the forces of globalization. Nevertheless, the struggle among the world's oligopolistic firms has now deeply penetrated the most developed parts of the low- and middle-income countries. The total stock of FDI in developing countries rose from US$344 billion in 1985 to US$2,181 billion in 2001 (UNCTAD, 2002). China was the main single focus of attention, with the stock of FDI rising from US$25 billion in 1990 to US$395 billion in 2001.[8] This period was the world's most explosive period of mergers and acquisitions. The size of the merger boom of the 1990s eclipses that of any previous epoch, and will leave a long-lasting imprint on the global business structure. In almost every sector a small number of focused global producers dominate the world market. Competitive capitalism's in-built tendency to concentration and oligopoly, which is vigorously denied by both free market economists and the leaders of large corporations, has finally flowered on a global scale. There appears to be a near-universal rule that the top four to six companies (sometimes even fewer) control around 50 to 75 per cent of the entire global market, while large numbers of small and medium-sized firms fight for the 'niche' positions within local markets, typically confined to the low value-added parts of the market supplying the needs of poor people.

At the centre of each sector of the economy stand a small group of core firms which integrate the whole supply chain for their products. Not only have these core 'systems-integrator' firms experienced an explosive process of concentration, the deepening interaction between core companies and supplier companies has also created an explosive 'cascade' effect that is rapidly leading to concentration and focus among the first-tier suppliers and spilling over even into second- and third-tier suppliers. Concentration among leading aircraft assemblers, for example, has stimulated concentration among the main aerospace components suppliers: there are now just three makers of large aircraft engines across the world. Concentration among auto assemblers has stimulated concentration among auto components makers: the top three tyre makers account for almost two-thirds of global output. In sector after sector, the 'first-tier' suppliers are themselves multi-billion dollar companies with 'global reach'. Through the hugely increased planning function undertaken by systems-integrators, facilitated by recent developments in information technology, the boundaries of the large corporation have become blurred. In order to develop and maintain their competitive advantage, the systems-integrators deeply penetrate the value chain both upstream and downstream. They are closely involved in business activities that range from long-term planning to meticulous control of day-to-day production and delivery schedules. Competitive advantage for the systems-integrator requires that it must consider the interests of the whole value chain in order to minimize costs across the whole system. Far from becoming 'hollowed out' and much smaller in scope, the extent of control exercised by the large firm has enormously increased during the global business revolution.

Regions containing a small fraction of the world's population have massively dominated the global business revolution. The high-income economies contain just 16 per cent of the world's total population. They account for 91 per cent of the world's total stock market capitalization, 95 per cent of *Fortune* 500 companies, 97 per cent of the *FT* 500 companies, 99 per cent of the world's top 300 companies by value of R&D spending and 99 per cent of the world's top brands. North America is, by far, the world leader in this process. It has just over 5 per cent of the world's population, but accounts for 40 per cent of the *Fortune* 500 firms, 46 per cent of the world's top 300 firms by R&D expenditure (74 per cent of the top 300 IT hardware and software firms, ranked by R&D spending), 50 per cent of the *FT* 500 firms, 54 per cent of Morgan Stanley Dean Witter's list of the top 250 'global competitive edge' firms and 61 per cent of the world's top 100 brands.

Developing countries are massively disadvantaged in the race to compete on the 'global level playing field' of international big business. The starting points in the race to dominate global markets could not be more uneven. The whole of the developing world, containing 84 per cent of the world's population, contains just twenty-six *Fortune* 500 companies, sixteen *FT 500* companies, fifteen of Morgan Stanley Dean Witter's list of the 250 leading 'competitive edge' companies, one of the world's top 100 brands and none of the world's top 300 companies by R&D expenditure.

China's rapid move towards 'close' integration with the world economy is occurring at a time of revolutionary change in the global business system. Large Chinese firms are far from ready to compete on the 'global level playing field'. This presents an extreme challenge for China's industrial strategy. Privatization of China's large enterprises will not be sufficient to make them globally competitive. If China's firms cannot generally compete at the level of 'systems-integrator', it is hard to see either how in most industries they will be able to compete at the level of first-tier supplier. For a substantial period ahead, China will have to accept that, under the terms of the WTO Agreement, its best hope is to be a 'workshop' for the rest of the world,[9] housing the production facilities for the global giant firms and the leading parts of their supply chain, headquartered in the high-income countries. China's entry to the WTO greatly reduces the scope for industrial policy.

Conclusion

China is becoming increasingly 'dependent' in the classical sense used by the Latin American economists in the 1950s (Frank, 1967). In every case, successful late-comer industrializing countries, from the USA in the late nineteenth century to South Korea in the late twentieth century, have produced a group of globally competitive firms. China is the first successful late-comer not to have done so. It is remarkable that China has reached a position in which it is the world's sixth largest economy[10] without having a group of internationally competitive large firms. This is highly significant in the history of economic development. Already, over 30 per cent of industrial profits, and one-half of China's export earnings, are generated by foreign-invested firms.[11] If the 'bubble' of foreign direct investment in China were to burst, it would have serious consequences for the whole growth path and for China's stability. There is intense debate at all levels of Chinese society about the significance of this phenomenon. Many popular books and articles characterize China's development path as 'neo-colonial', drawing comparisons with the dependent nature of Chinese economic development from the mid-nineteenth century until 1949.

This situation presents a big challenge for China's policy-makers. We have noted the great difference between China's situation in terms of the international competitive challenge, and that of all previous 'late-comer' countries. It faces far greater global industrial concentration and competition than any previous late-comer country. In terms of military analogy, we may say that China's industrial policy has increasingly followed the dictum of Sun Zi's (Sun Wu) *Art of War*: 'If the enemy forces outnumber yours, retreat; if your forces are weaker in strength, avoid a decisive engagement' (Sun Wu, 1996: 33).

Given the drastic inequality in competitive power between its own firms and the global leaders, China has to find a different strategy from that adopted by other late-comer countries:

> New victories are not achieved by putting on old plays. The variations of the military tactics in accordance with the changing circumstances know no end. . . . There are no fixed forms or inflexible rules in military tactics. Only those who are able to vary their tactics according to the changing manoeuvre of the enemy and win victories have really miraculous skill. (Sun Wu, 1996: 61)

Even in large-scale 'retreat', even with important parts of the 'army' giving up the struggle and moving into the opposing camp, there are still strategies that a determined group of 'generals' can employ as long as they are clear where they are going.

The modern global corporation may be weaker than it appears. Despite their massive business capability, the global giants are encountering a period of high turbulence. They are mired in deep difficulties in terms of corporate governance and face huge cumulative difficulties arising from the collapse of the stock market. This drastically limits their ability to undertake mergers and acquisitions. It has placed enormous burdens upon their balance sheets due to the collapse in the value of their pension funds, and the massive increase in pension fund contributions that they are being forced to make. This eats deeply into their funds available for expansion. While the economists of the high-income countries ridiculed the 'cross-investments' among Japanese *keiretsu*, they had ignored the vast 'cross-investments' among themselves which arose as a consequence of the pension funds. The US economy is able to grow substantially mainly due to the support given to the US consumer through the massive flow of capital into the country, principally from East Asia. If this flow were to be reversed, and the dollar to collapse, the prospects for the US economy and US business would be even further impaired.

The economic impact of the USA's sharp turn towards a unilateral, aggressive foreign policy in the wake of 11 September is highly unpredictable, with massive potential consequence for the federal budget.

It is even possible that the high point of the US's economic and military power may already have passed; its 'prime' may already be over: 'Win the war, but do not boast; win the war, but do not show arrogance; whatever is in its prime is bound to decline, for, being in the prime goes against the *Dao*; whatever goes against the *Dao* will come to an early end' (from Lao Zi, 1995: 149–51).

The global corporation is in only the early days of its formation, whereas the nation state is far more robust and long-lived. The global corporation 'has no lasting social and political purpose': 'The only purpose of the average firm is to produce wealth for the shareholders; shareholders whose wealth is readily migrant and who can invest in infinite places' (Scott, 2001: 16). In terms of the strategies employed by Sun Zi, the rapid rise of FDI in China, dominating the local market in a wide range of products, can be viewed as ceding territory to the enemy: 'An experienced commander entices the enemy into going where he wishes them to be and prevents them from reaching their objective' (Sun Wu, 1996: 58). The rapid rise of Chinese people employed within the global corporation, gradually 'Sinifying' it, can be compared to the 'espionage agents' in Sun Zi:

> No-one in the army deserves a closer attention, higher rewards or deeper secrecy than the agents. . . . If all five kinds of agents are employed,[12] and the enemy cannot find out the patterns of their activities, then a magical power could be produced which is surely an incomparable treasure for the ruler. . . . Espionage is omnipresent; it stops at nothing; it is practically everywhere. (Sun Wu, 1996: 128)

The key for Sun Zi is strategy:

> Skillful military leaders conquer the enemy without fighting battles, capture cities without attacking them and overcome States without protracted warfare. They strive for supremacy without stationing their troops abroad, yet they win complete victory over their enemies. (Sun Wu, 1996: 33)

However, in the end it is the proficiency of the 'generals' that is the critical issue:

> Generals are guardians of the State. Their proficiency in warfare makes the State strong, their deficiency makes the State weak. (Sun Wu, 1996: 33)

To devise a strategy to deal with today's overwhelming imbalance in business power requires 'generals' of great skill and leadership ability.

The environment

China's environmental deterioration presents a further deep challenge for the state. This reflects the intense pressure of a huge and growing population upon the country's already fragile natural environment, with the impact hugely reinforced by high-speed industrial growth.

The area affected by serious soil erosion has increased to include around 38 per cent of the entire country (UNDP, 2000: 70). The area of desert is increasing at the rate of around 2,500 square kilometres per year, equivalent to the area of a medium-sized country. In the past four decades, almost one-half of China's forests have been destroyed, so that it now has one of the sparsest forest covers in the world. There is a serious and worsening shortage of fresh water, and 'rampant water pollution' is making the situation worse. The capacity to protect the environment has lagged seriously behind the speed of destruction: 'Thus, environmental quality continues to worsen and this has evolved into the most severe, large-scale and profound ecological destruction in Chinese history' (UNDP, 2000: 70).

China's explosive industrial growth has led to high-speed expansion of energy-intensive industries. By the late 1990s, these accounted for around 36 per cent of the country's manufacturing value-added, compared with just 23 per cent in Japan and 21 per cent in the USA (Nolan, 2001a: 700). China has a relatively limited amount of oil and gas, but has huge reserves of coal. By the mid-1990s, China had overtaken the USA as the world's biggest coal producer, accounting for almost 30 per cent of global output. Coal provides a low-cost way to meet a large fraction of China's booming demands for energy to meet the needs of the country's 'industrial revolution'. In the late 1990s, coal supplied the primary energy for around 70 per cent of the country's electricity supply (Nolan, 2001a: 699).

In the advanced economies, burning coal on open fires and in old-fashioned power stations was responsible for large amounts of atmospheric pollution through the generation of airborne particulates. Not until the 1950s did serious efforts get under way to improve the quality of the atmosphere consequent upon using coal as a main source of primary energy. Both government legislation and the demands of shareholders forced large changes in the way coal was mined, transported and used. Reclamation and rehabilitation work is now a central part of mine development. Coal is prepared, stockpiled and transported in a much more careful way: for example, it is washed, stockpiles are sprayed and it is covered in transport. The use of coal on open domestic fires and in primitive industrial boilers has been reduced drastically. The almost universal use of precipitators and filters means that power stations no longer emit large quantities of black smoke and dust, which were the primary cause of pollution. However, all these measures to ameliorate the environmental effects of coal use require appropriate legislation and enforcement, and involve high costs.

By contrast, in China, the ways in which coal is mined, transported and used as a fuel approximate those of the advanced economies before the 1950s. Large quantities of coal are mined and stored with little care for the environmental impact of mining operations. Coal is mostly transported unwashed and uncovered. Large quantities of high-sulphur coal are used. Huge amounts of coal are burned on open fires and in primitive boilers. This has caused a huge burden of air pollution, which is 'not surprising in a nation where combustion of one billion tons of coal, largely uncleaned and burned with minimal or no air pollution controls, supplies three-quarters of all primary energy' (Smil, 1993: 117). The recommended maximum daily mean total for suspended particulates is no more than 300 micrograms per cubic metre. In fact, in northern China in the early 1990s, the levels were commonly as high as 500–1,000 micrograms per cubic metre, and on the worst days reached as high as 2,000 (Smil, 1993: 117). Daily means of sulphur dioxide concentration in North America have now fallen to around 20–100 micrograms per cubic metre. In China in the 1990s, they were commonly between 100 and 400 micrograms per cubic metre, and regularly surpassed 600 micrograms in the heating season, sometimes reaching as high as 2,000 micrograms (Smil, 1993: 117).

Total discharges of particulate matter are officially reported to have reached 15 million tons by the 1990s, and are unofficially estimated to have reached 20 million tons (Smil, 1993: 117–18). Even the official figures show China as producing 15 per cent of the global total of 100 million tons, of which around two-thirds is generated by coal combustion (Smil, 1993: 118). China's share of global carbon dioxide emissions rose from 10.8 per cent in 1980 to 14.9 per cent in 1996, and in the not-too-distant future China should overtake the USA as the world's largest producer of carbon dioxide (the USA's share currently stands at 23.4 per cent) (World Bank, *WDR*, 2000: 248–9).

In addition to the production of particulates and carbon dioxide, coal-burning involves the production of sulphur dioxide, which produces acid rain. Despite very high levels of sulphur dioxide in the atmosphere, North China has only low levels of acid rain. This is due to the large amounts of calcium, potassium and magnesium compounds in the atmosphere. These neutralize the emitted sulphur dioxide. However, South China has serious problems of acid rain, caused mainly by burning coal with high sulphur content. Much of the sulphur could be eliminated through washing, but only around 10 per cent of China's high-sulphur coal is washed (Smil, 1993: 118). Sulphur dioxide is especially expensive to control: 'Until very recently even many rich countries avoided this costly commitment' (Smil, 1993: 121). Indeed, Smil estimates that the capital cost of installing de-sulphurization facilities increases the cost of electricity by 25–30 per cent, and operating costs 'add a similar mark-up to the electricity generation cost' (Smil, 1993: 235).

China's leaders are fully aware of the damage that large-scale consumption of coal does to the country's environment and to public health. At the 1999 annual session of the Chinese National People's Congress, Premier Zhu Rongji recognized that 'the deterioration of the ecological environment remains a glaring problem', and pledged to 'improve the air quality in the capital and punish polluting enterprises' (quoted in the *FT*, 6 March 1999). However, there are powerful economic pressures for continued increases in the consumption of coal.[13]

The implications of China's mode of industrialization are of the greatest importance for the physical sustainability of life on this planet. Already, in addition to high and rising levels of particulates in the air, China is now the world's second largest producer of 'greenhouse gases' after the USA. Its commercial energy use (1,113 million metric tons of oil equivalent) is already over one-half that of the USA (2,162 million) (World Bank, *WDR*, 2001: 292–3). If China follows the US free market approach to industrialization, allowing, for example, complete dominance to the automobile, then the prospects for the world are terrifying. If China's 1.4 billion people were to sustain their current growth path and at some point catch up with today's US level of per capita income, and were to use similar technologies, the country's use of commercial energy and emission of carbon dioxide would be one-fifth greater than those of the entire world today.

One of the deepest threats to the Chinese environment has come from the combination of forces (population growth, industrial growth, agricultural intensification and climate change) that has reduced the flow of the Yellow River to a mere trickle for long periods of the year (see Wang Xiaoqiang et al., 1999). In an attempt to deal with the crisis the central government has initiated a massive scheme to transfer water from the south to the north along two or three separate routes to feed into the Yellow River. This is estimated to require investment much in excess of the US$24 billion that was needed to build the Three Gorges Dam. It will rival the great ancient long-distance waterways constructed in Chinese history, notably the Grand Canal. Like other large-scale water conservancy projects, the finance is to be raised through a combination of central and local budgets, bank loans, international funds and user fees. It is expected that the unit price of water used as a result of the scheme will be considerably higher than current water charges.[14]

Whatever combination of measures is adopted, involving more or less use of the price mechanism to achieve the hoped-for results, the Chinese state will be central to the country's ability to achieve environmentally sustainable development.

The capability and role of the state

The reform period in China has been accompanied by great changes in the function of the state, including a drastic reduction in direct state instructions. However, as we have seen, China is a vast, poor country with urgent development needs, many of which can only be met by state action of one sort or another. During the reform period, the state's fiscal capacity has sharply declined. The share of budget revenue in GDP fell from over 31 per cent in 1979 to a low of just 10.7 per cent in 1995 (SSB, *ZTN*, 2001: 256). This was far below that for most high-income countries. In 1997, tax revenue as a proportion of GDP stood at over 30 per cent in all Western European countries, and as high as 43 per cent in Belgium and the Netherlands (World Bank, *WDR*, 2001: 256–7). The USA stands out strikingly against this pattern, with tax revenues in 1997 accounting for just 20 per cent of GDP, but still substantially above those for China. By the late 1990s, the share of government revenue in GDP was not only below that of many developing countries, such as Indonesia and Malaysia, but was also below that of Russia, which is widely perceived as having experienced 'state desertion' during the reform period. In these terms, one can say that China's level of 'state desertion' during the 'transition' period outstripped even that of Russia, leading the UNDP to comment: 'The decline of the state's fiscal role and position has gravely undermined the [Chinese] government's capacity to promote economic development' (UNDP, 2000: 41).

In the critically important health and education sectors, the state's reduced fiscal strength has forced it to look for drastically increased contributions from fees paid by people when they use the services (see below). However, its weakened fiscal capability has had other more immediate dangers for social stability. In order to dampen the impact of large-scale lay-offs, the Chinese government has been trying for many years to develop a comprehensive social security system. However, this programme had made very limited progress by the end of the 1990s. The transitional needs of these programmes are large. While they are being established, they require a large infusion of government funds, but the state's fiscal weakness has made this impossible (UNDP, 2000: 76).

The government is well aware of the need to increase its fiscal strength in order to undertake the wide range of activities necessary to meet the numerous areas of market failure. Recognizing the key function of the state in supporting public goods provision, the Chinese state attempted to increase its fiscal strength after the mid-1990s, with a series of important reforms. However, even in 1999 the proportion of government revenue in GDP still stood at only 14 per cent, which greatly inhibited its ability to provide public goods on the scale required by China's urgent development needs.

An unusually high proportion of state expenditure takes place at the local level. The share of the localities in total state budgetary outlays was already high in the late 1970s, but has increased still further during the reform period. By the late 1990s, the localities accounted for 64 per cent of total budgetary expenditure (World Bank, 2002: 31). The responsibilities of the localities are especially high in relation to social welfare spending. In the late 1990s, the localities accounted for 89 per cent of total budgetary expenditure on culture, education and health (World Bank, 2002: 31). The lowest level of public administration, the counties and townships, account for fully 70 per cent of the country's total budgetary outlays on education and 55–60 per cent on health (World Bank, 2002: ii). However, after the reform of the public finance system in 1994, the local governments' share of total revenue fell to less than one-half of the country's total (World Bank, 2002: 16). The transfers from the central government to the local governments were conducted through a 'complex and befuddling system' (World Bank, 2002: 17). The net result was that the local governments were increasingly left to their own devices to fund their expenditure, and faced a serious 'fiscal squeeze' (World Bank, 2002: 36).

The 'pushing down' of a large fraction of expenditure responsibility to the township level has 'forced the rural sector to "tax" itself through fees or community contributions to cover the cost of provision' (World Bank, 2002: 42). By the end of the 1990s, budgetary allocations covered just 46 per cent of actual expenditures on education (World Bank, 2002: 85). A wide variety of other sources of funding have been mobilized to finance education, including surcharges, fees collected from students, revenues from school-run enterprises, work study programmes, donations and gifts.

The outcome of the increasing use of the market to provide educational services has been 'growing disparities in per capita [education] expenditure across regions, both inter-provincial and intra-provincial': 'What is of particular worry is that . . . the low end is not improving despite the efforts [made] to raise the minimum provision of education in poor regions' (World Bank, 2002: 101). There appear to be 'significant gaps between the stated national goals and the actual provision of education and health services in poor regions' (World Bank, 2002: 42). A large-scale rural household survey found that between the late 1980s and mid-1990s, there was 'a substantial deterioration in the educational status of the poor' (World Bank, 2002: 42). The survey showed that among 'poor' people, between 1988 and 1995 the proportion who had completed five years of schooling fell from 68 per cent to 53 per cent in non-poor regions and from 54 per cent to 42 per cent in poor regions (World Bank, 2002: 43).

Over the past five decades, China has built an impressive rural health system, and overall health achievements are impressive, with a life expectancy of seventy and an infant mortality rate of 31 per 1,000 live births. At the peak of the rural people's communes before 1976, around 85 per cent of villages had a co-operative medical system, albeit often rudimentary (World Bank, 2002: 116). The economic reforms led to a large increase in average personal income. This facilitated substantial increases in household expenditure on health, and much improved diet and nutritional status for the average Chinese person.

When the agricultural collectives were disbanded in the early 1980s, the financial basis for risk-sharing was largely eliminated, except in the coastal areas, where prosperous township and village enterprises continued to generate substantial resources belonging to the collective. However, poor areas lacked such collective resources, and in rich areas, there has been widespread *de facto* or *de jure* privatization of collective enterprises. The World Bank estimates that at the end of the 1990s, more than 90 per cent of the rural population, or 700 million people, were without any coverage from collective risk-pooling schemes (World Bank, 2002: 116).

Each level of government largely finances its own health facilities. This means that the quality of health services in each locality is highly dependent on the financial health of the local budget (World Bank, 2002: 118). The World Bank estimates that in 1999, the government budget funded just 11 per cent of total health expenditure, while 59 per cent came from out-of-pocket payments. Among poor people, the shift in the nature of health service provision has resulted in large real increases in private payments for health care. One study estimates that the share of poor households' income allocated to medical expenses rose from less than 1.5 per cent in 1988, to 5.6 per cent in 1995 (World Bank, 2002: 43).

These changes have resulted in a system that provides highly unequal access to health services. The *World Health Report*, 2000, ranked China 61st out of 191 countries in overall quality of health, but 188th in terms of fairness in financial contribution (quoted in World Bank, 2002: iv).

The crisis in the rural health system caused deep concern among China's leaders about the decline in preventive medicine, and, especially, the ability to halt the spread of infectious diseases. In October 2002, the central government announced an ambitious plan to create a new rural collective medical system. However, no sooner had this initiative been announced than the country was plunged into the SARS crisis. In the event, SARS was largely contained in the urban areas and the rural areas were not heavily challenged by it.

International relations

By the end of the 1990s, there were several threats to China's socio-political stability. In key respects they greatly exceeded the difficulties facing other developing countries. Like India and Indonesia, China faced a special challenge in attempting to prevent the separatist tendencies inherent in a large country with wide racial, cultural and religious differences. Unlike those giant countries, China is still ruled by the Communist Party, whose ideology is hostile in principle to free market capitalism. China's highly successful development policies since the late 1970s have produced a powerful economy that is viewed as becoming a serious potential rival for the dominant world power, the USA, within a relatively short period of time. Those who wish to emphasize the size of the Chinese 'challenge' point to the fact that, measured in 'purchasing power parity' (PPP) dollars (essentially using the prices of the USA), China is already the world's second largest economy, 36 per cent larger than Japan, and over one-half the size of the USA (World Bank, *WDR*, 2001: 230–1). Even if one disregards the PPP figures, it is indisputable that, if China maintains its high growth rate, at some point in the not-too-distant future it will, indeed, become a serious challenger to the USA's dominant position. Therefore, unlike the other large developing countries, China's must face the reality that it is regarded by many in the US foreign policy establishment as a 'strategic competitor'.

The USA is massively dominant in terms of its military capability, accounting for 36 per cent of the world's total military spending, and a much larger fraction of the production of the world's most advanced weapons. In 1999, the USA spent US$35 billion on R&D in the military sector, compared with just US$9 billion in NATO Europe countries. By 1999, the USA's military budget stood at US$253 billion, compared with just US$135 billion for NATO Europe (IISS, 1999: 37). However, since then, the USA has announced that the military budget will rise to US$379 billion by 2006, while there are no plans to increase real military expenditure by NATO Europe countries (*FT*, 18 February 2002).

The possibility of military collaboration between the US and Europe is being undermined by the growing technological gap between leading European and leading US companies. The 1990–1 Gulf War shocked military thinkers around the world. It provided a vivid demonstration of the way in which warfare had changed since the end of the Cold War, with the application of the principles of what is termed the 'revolution in military affairs' (*International Herald Tribune*, 14 June 1999). It showed clearly that the US stood at the centre of this revolution, in terms both of the production of the relevant technologies and of the assembly of arms to deliver these technologies in battle, and it emphasized the growing gap between the US and Europe.

The war in former Yugoslavia revealed that the gap was growing: 'European leaders lamented their countries' yawning technological gap with the US, revealed by the Kosovo war. Europe contributed only a fifth of the warplanes and very little intelligence to the bombing campaign, while mustering even a peacekeeping force showed up deficiencies in logistics' (*FT*, Editorial, 20 July 1999). The allied governments were supportive of the war effort, but were unable to conduct high-level bombing raids at night due to their inferior technology.

Precision-guided munitions were almost monopolized by US warplanes. Only France and Britain had laser-guided bombs. Even these comparatively advanced European allies remain ill equipped for the revolution in military affairs. Europe fears a situation in which 'the US provides the high-technology aerial surveillance and smart weapons and it provides the footsoldiers' (*FT*, 1 July 1999).

The Afghanistan conflict of 2001 showed that the gap was getting even wider: 'The larger lesson from [the Afghanistan conflict] – and one that is stupefying to the Russian and Chinese military, worrying to the Indians, and disturbing to the proponents of a common European defence policy – is that in military terms there is only player on the field that counts' (Paul Kennedy, *FT*, 2 February 2002). European forces had almost no contribution to make beyond providing the footsoldiers to attempt to control the country after US bombing had destroyed the initial Taliban resistance. Although they were ready to support the US militarily, the NATO allies were simply not needed to fight the war in Afghanistan: 'There has always been a gap in miltary capabilities between the US and most of its other allies. . . . But we are on the verge of a very dramatic disparity precisely because of the way technology is now starting to affect war-fighting doctrine' (*FT*, 18 February 2002).

The attack on Iraq in spring 2003 demonstrated that the gap is growing still wider, and will continue to do so as the US military budget rises while that in Europe shrinks.

The USA has made clear its nervousness about China's growing military capability. Section 1202 of the USA's National Defense Authorization Act for Fiscal Year 2000 provided that each year the Secretary of Defense should provide a report on the 'current and future strategies of the People's Republic of China'. The 2002 Report pronounced that China's defense spending 'may be some four times larger than its public announcement in March 2002 of a defense budget of only about US$20 billion' (*Annual Report*, 2002). It argues that by 2010 'the PLA will have all the elements of a modern air force and should have developed the operational concepts and the training needed to fight as an integrated force' (*Annual Report*, 2002: 18). The Report estimates that China has around twenty intercontinental ballistic missiles capable of targeting the USA, and that this number 'may reach 60 by 2010' (*Annual Report*, 2002: 27). The Report believes that China 'looks upon Russia as its primary source of modern military technologies', with estimates of agreed sales from the former USSR reportedly ranging between US$10 and US$20 billion: 'Since at least 1993, China reportedly has acquired advanced

Russian weapon system technologies for the development of PLA [People's Liberation Army] air, ground, and naval weapon systems, as well as advanced materials and manufacturing technologies associated with missiles, lasers, and space systems' (*Annual Report*, 2002: 43–4).

President Bush's policy statement 'America's Security Strategy' (*FT*, 21 September 2002) warns China:

> [A] quarter century after beginning the process of shedding the worst features of the Communist legacy, China's leaders have not yet made the next series of fundamental choices about the character of their state. In pursuing advanced military capabilities that can threaten its neighbors in the Asia Pacific region, China is following an outdated path that, in the end, will hamper its own pursuit of greatness. It is time to reaffirm the essential role of American military strength. We must build and maintain our defenses beyond challenge. . . . Our forces will be strong enough to dissuade potential adversaries from pursuing a military build-up in hopes of surpassing, or equaling, the power of the US.

As the 2003 war against Iraq demonstrated, today's friends in international relations can be tomorrow's enemies. The current international situation is one of the most unstable for a long time. However unlikely it may appear, China's strategists cannot rule out the possibility that at some point the object of 'regime change' may even include China. It has to shape its foreign policy with this as one possible scenario.[15]

In the year 2000, the US Congress also established the Congressional–Executive Commission on China (CECC) to 'monitor China's compliance with international human rights standards, encourage the development of the rule of law, establish and maintain a list of victims of human rights abuses, and promote bilateral co-operation' (CECC, 2002). The CECC's first Annual Report was produced in September 2002. The Report was extremely critical of many aspects of alleged human rights abuses in China. It also made numerous policy recommendations. It recommended, for example, that Congress and the US Administration 'expand US Government efforts to disseminate human rights, workers' rights, and rule of law-related information in China through radio, television, and the Internet'. It recommended that Congress should 'appropriate funds to an American university, NGO, or other organization to train individuals from US faith-based or other organizations with links to religious groups in China to assist Chinese religious leaders in asserting their existing right of freedom to practice religion under the Chinese Constitution and international human rights'.

The Report points out that 'Chinese leaders are keenly aware of the role that labor unions played in undermining Communist Party rule in Eastern Europe and are determined to prevent similar challenges in China.' It details allegations of Chinese government mechanisms to control the trade union movement, including government actions to break up worker demonstrations, and prevent strikes. It alleges that 'regulations on workplace health and safety, as well as on work hours and overtime pay, are often ignored'. The Commission recommends that the US Administration 'facilitates meetings of US, Chinese and third-country companies doing business in China to identify systemic worker rights abuses, develop recommendations for appropriate Chinese government entities, and discuss these recommendations with Chinese officials'.

The Report argues that the 'massive migration from rural to urban areas and the increased unemployment from shrinking and closing state-owned enterprises have seriously exacerbated worker unrest'. It recommends that the Congress and the Administration 'provide assistance to legal clinics to expand the availability of legal representation in cases involving worker rights, and that special assistance be provided to legal aid centres in communities with large numbers of migrant workers, and migrant women in particular, to build expertise and capacity in resolving the issues of concern to this vulnerable group'. It recommends that Congress 'authorize the development of programming in popular legal education for groups in China, such as farmers in remote areas, and migrant workers, who are unaware of their rights under existing law'.

China faces a fundamentally different position in its international relations than did Japan, South Korea or Taiwan at comparable stages in their development. Japan, Korea and Taiwan each achieved their modern 'take-off' as close allies of the USA in the international struggle against communism, especially the People's Republic of China. Consequently, the USA was willing to tolerate a 'developmental state' in each case, which heavily protected the economy, kept global financial institutions at arm's length, and strongly controlled international financial flows. But after the collapse of the USSR and China's opening-up, the USA exerted strong pressure on each to follow the US model.

As well as intense and mounting military and diplomatic pressure from the USA upon China, there is, as we have seen, an explicit commitment from the US Congress to promote activities within China that would contribute to increased social and political instability in the country at a critical stage in its system evolution. The final shape of the USA's view of how best to 'engage' with China is still unclear. However, there is a powerful set of interests that believes that serious conflict with China is unavoidable. Joseph Cirincione of the Carnegie Endowment warns: 'There are many people in this [Bush junior] administration who think that a war with China is likely, perhaps even inevitable in the next 20 or 30 years. [They think] China will challenge us [and] we'd better be ready for it.' Henry Kissinger, meanwhile, cautions that the hawks see China 'as a morally flawed inevitable adversary' and believe that the US should act 'not as a strategic partner, but as it treated the Soviet Union during the cold war, as a rival and a challenge'. General Brent Scowcroft, former security adviser to two Republican administrations (Gerald Ford and George Bush senior), comments: 'If there is a real division within this [Bush junior] administration, it is probably on China. There is a division between those who see China as inexorably developing into the primary security threat to the US, and those who feel China is transforming rapidly but . . . that it's been overwhelmingly positive' (all quoted in *FT*, 20 August 2001).

Even before 11 September, there had emerged a powerful shift towards unilateralism in US foreign policy under the combined influence of traditional 'realist', but more inward-looking, conservatives and the so-called 'neoconservatives'.[16] In the first year of the Bush administration, the US pulled out of the Kyoto Protocol on climate change and torpedoed the talks to add verification procedures to the Biological Weapons Convention. However, 11 September tipped the balance of influence towards the neocons. The consensus among the inner core of the Bush administration shifted to the view that 'in the long term the US would only find security in a world in which US values were widely held and spread' (*FT*, 6 March 2003).

The 'neocon' version of US 'primacy' is 'revolutionary in the sense of transforming the world in America's image' (*FT*, 6 March 2003). The central assertion of Bush's National Security Strategy 'all but expunges the instinctive internationalism of Roosevelt or Truman': 'America's global power must not be challenged or chained. The US reserves the right to decide who might be its enemies and how they are to be dealt with. No other nation can be permitted to challenge its primacy. Ever.' The powerful shift in US foreign policy towards the neocons' position has been described as one in which 'confidence and insecurity somehow manage to sit side by side': 'At one level, the present administration delights in America's unique power. At another, it lives in terror of the nation's unique vulnerability' (both *FT*, 7 March 2003).

By casting itself adrift from the moderating influence of international institutions, including the cautious voices of 'Old Europe', the US constitutes a dangerous and unpredictable force at the heart of international relations. It remains to be seen whether the shift is a temporary 'blip', marking the final apogee of conservative influence on US foreign policy, or constitutes a seismic shift following 11 September. The increased unpredictability in the foreign policy of the world's hegemonic power constitutes a formidable challenge for China's own foreign policy.

The challenges within the Chinese Communist Party

The Chinese Communist Party, with 64 million members, faces immense ideological and organizational challenges. Leadership by the Party is the foundation of the Chinese modernization drive. In his speech of 1 July 2001 to celebrate the eightieth anniversary of the founding of the CCP, Party General Secretary Jiang Zemin stated that the Party must 'address the two major historic subjects of enhancing the Party's ability of exercising state power and art of leadership and resisting corruption and warding off risks'.

In the late 1980s and early 1990s, Deng Xiaoping had repeatedly warned of the dangers of China collapsing into chaos if the wrong decisions were taken. In the early twenty-first century, in the face of the numerous internal and external challenges outlined above, such dangers are still taken extremely seriously by the leadership. In his speech of July 2001, Jiang Zemin pointed out:

> To rally the 1.2 billion and more people behind the socialist modernization drive in a large and multi-ethnic developing country like China, it is a must to have the strong leadership of the Communist Party of China. Otherwise, the country will . . . not only fail to realize its modernization but also sink into a chaotic abyss. This is a conclusion drawn by reviewing the modern history of China's development and after analysing the experiences and lessons of many countries in their development course.

It is also recognized at the highest levels of the Party leadership that within the Party itself there is a rising tide of corruption. The leadership is acutely aware of the rising social tensions that threaten the continued rule of the Chinese Communist Party. In his above-cited speech, Jiang cautioned: '[W]e must be strict in Party discipline. We should have a deeper understanding of the loss of political power by some Communist Parties in the world that had long been ruling parties and learn a lesson from them.' As the Chinese economy has advanced, and the impact of market forces and integration with the global economy has increased, so the challenges for the Party have intensified, not diminished. Jiang's speech drew attention to the challenges arising for the Party from increasing opening-up and marketization: 'With the progress of reform, opening-up and development of a socialist market economy, the social fabrics, economic composition, forms of organization, means of employment, interests of different sectors, and modalities of income distribution have increasingly diversified. We should be sober-minded about this and pay attention to the trend. Otherwise our country would be deprived of cohesiveness.' Despite immense success in economic reform, Jiang warned that the challenges facing the Party were intensifying: 'The longer the Party is in power, the more necessary it is for the Party to strengthen self-improvement, and the stricter it should be with its members and cadres.'

In his speech Jiang made numerous references to the critical importance of dealing with the rising tide of corruption within the Party as the country moved further down the road of marketization of economic life. He urged Party cadres to 'support and help others first instead of only thinking about how to get rich themselves'. He acknowledged that combating corruption and building clean government was 'vital for the survival of our Party'. In other words, elimination of corruption was vital to the very continuation of Communist Party rule in China. He emphasized that in order to solve the problem of corruption in the Party it was necessary to 'remove the soil and conditions breeding corruption through creative institutional measures', and to 'work harder to prevent and address corruption at its root'. He laid great stress on the importance of solving the problem of corruption among Party leaders at each level, and was blunt about the extent of abuse of power by Party members: 'All the Party members, leading cadres in particular, must always be clean and honest and have a strong integrity. . . . They will by no means be allowed to abuse power for personal gains, take bribes or bend the law. Party organizations and leading cadres at all levels must take a clear stand to oppose corruption.'

In their determined efforts to purge the Party of corruption, the level at which Party members were investigated and brought to trial for corruption rose to include many in high positions. A succession of high-level government officials were forced out of office, and, in several cases, were even sentenced to death, for corruption.

In autumn 2000, a former deputy governor and former mayor of Shijiazhuang, Hebei's largest city, were arrested, charged with 'economic crimes' (*FT*, 22 January 2001).

In December 2000, it was reported that Mu Suixin, the mayor of one of China's largest cities, Shenyang, in Liaoning province in Northeast China, had resigned after being linked with a gambling scandal which had already forced out three other senior city officials, including the deputy mayor (*FT*, 27 December 2000). Mu had become nationally famous for his successful campaign to transform the city's old state-owned enterprises. Chinese state television reported that 'mafia power' had become 'rampant' in Shenyang's politics and economy, which had placed great pressure on Mr Mu. It was later revealed that over 100 officials from the city had been detained. These included some sixty officials from the city's tax bureau, 'from the highest-ranking to the most menial', who were said to be under investigation (*FT*, 2 June 2001). Mr Mu was accused of accepting 'huge bribes' from local 'mafia' groups. These included one run by Liu Yong. Liu was accused of having 'attacked or murdered some 42 people', according to *Xinhua News*. He was formerly the head of the Jia Yang Group, 'a business conglomerate', a representative in the Shenyang People's Congress and a member of the Communist Party. Official sources said that he had bribed 'dozens of city administrators or their wives, including Ma Xiangdong, the former deputy mayor'. Ma was arrested for gambling away US$4.8 million in public funds during seventeen trips to casinos in Macau.

In September 2000, it was reported by the Supreme People's Procurate that a former Vice-Minister of Public Security, Li Jizhou, had been arrested at the end of the previous year.

In December 2000, the former Chief of Military Intelligence, General Ji Shengde, was reported by the international press to have been sentenced to fifteen years in prison for embezzlement and bribery (*New York Times*, 23 December 2000). The main focus of the case against General Ji was his links with Lai Changxin in Xiamen (see below). He was reportedly accused of accepting 'huge bribes' from Lai. General Ji was also reported to have used his position to embezzle millions of dollars from military-run corporations, using the money to invest in the stock market and in real estate. The case of General Ji is of special significance because he is the son of a revolutionary hero and former Foreign Minister of China. General Ji reportedly escaped the death penalty only due to the intervention of his mother.

In March 2000, Chen Kejie, one of nineteen deputy chairmen of
the National People's Congress, was sentenced to death for corruption. Chen was the former Deputy Governor of Jiangxi province. He
was accused of amassing US$4.7 million in kickbacks from land deals
and in return for granting development contracts (*International Herald
Tribune*, 1 August 2000).

At the same time, the ongoing campaign revealed important cases
of local corruption that raised fundamental issues about the relationship of Party to society at the local level. One of the most notorious
concerned the case of Xiamen, the port city in South China's Fujian
province. It was to be the largest corruption case in China's recent
history up until that point, and atttracted great attention at all levels
of society and government.

At the centre of the Xiamen case was a peasant's son, Lai Changxin.
His family was too poor to educate him beyond primary school. He
began as a clerk with a trading company in Xiamen. Lai 'showed a
knack for business and building contacts with police and military
officials' (*Asia Week*, 22 December 2000). He set up the Yuanhua
Group in the 1980s and in the early 1990s expanded its business to
Hong Kong: 'Using his links with the PLA and Hong Kong's position
as a regional business hub, Lai built a multi-billion dollar empire in
just a few years.' He then began rapidly to develop smuggling operations: 'He started illegally to import everything from cars and gasoline
to electronics on behalf of his highly placed friends.' According to
official accounts in the Chinese media in late 2000, from 1996 on,
Lai and his operatives brought in goods worth RMB53 billion (US$6.4
billion), evading RMB30 billion in taxes. Unofficial reports say that
at one point, as much as one-sixth of national crude oil supplies were
being smuggled onto the Chinese market by Yuanhua through Xiamen,
distorting national oil prices and influencing national energy policy.

In the first round of court cases, eighty-four of Lai Changxin's
associates and employees were arrested and convicted. Lai was tipped
off and was able to elude arrest. He fled to Canada with his family.
Eleven of the eighty-four convicted were sentenced to death. Another
three had suspended death sentences, twelve had life sentences and
fifty-eight received fixed-term sentences. A second batch of over 200
offenders were eventually tried in connection with the case.

Lai Changxin reportedly bought off 'representatives of almost every
arm of the state, including the local Communist Party committee, the
customs administration, the police and even the local Bureau of the
Ministry of State Security and the People's Armed Police' (*Asia Week*,
22 December 2000). According to the official news reports, Lai bribed

the head of the Xiamen customs adminstration, Yang Qianxian, with RMB1.4 million and maintained a mistress for him. Lai had at least three other top Xiamen customs officials on his payroll. He gave the Deputy Director of the Fujian Provincial Police Department, Zhuang Runshun, RMB555,000 in bribes, and Xiamen Vice-Mayor Lan Pu, RMB5.1 million. Others in the pay of Lai included at least one of Xiamen's deputy Communist Party leaders, Liu Feng, the head of the Xiamen Police External Liaison Department, Wang Kexiang, and a top official in the Provincial Police Border Defence Force, Zhang Yongding. Many other top local officials were also later brought to trial, including another deputy Xiamen deputy Communist Pary chief, and a second vice-mayor. The manager of the Fujian branch of the Bank of China (BOC) and the manager of the Xiamen branch of Industrial and Commercial Bank of China (ICBC) were also bought off by Lai. According to the China News Service, the trials included cases against the heads of several of Xiamen's largest state-owned enterprises. The Xiamen Dongfang Group, for example, illegally rented out its export licence and official stamps to Lai's Yuanhua Group for an annual fee of RMB20 million, which was shared by the leaders of the former group.

Lai reportedly 'wined and dined and bribed local police and customs officers into turning a blind eye'. He built a luxurious six-storey entertainment compound, nicknamed the 'Little Red Mansion', 'where official visitors would be treated to karaoke and sex with hostesses'. Sometimes the guests were 'secretly filmed and reportedly blackmailed into co-operating with him' (*Asia Week*, 22 December 2000). According to the Vice-Minister of China's Ministry of Supervision, speaking on CCTV, other types of bribes used by Lai included study abroad for officials' children, apartments, cars and travel permits to visit Hong Kong (procured from Lai's police contacts).

It is striking that the city was able for many years to circumvent the many channels of control that are supposed to prevent such activities. These channels include the Communist Party discipline inspection committees, procurates, courts, the police and the auditing adminstration: 'The completeness with which that system was circumvented in a large, wealthy community that isn't so poor its officials needed to be corrupt, is striking' (*Asia Week*, 22 December 2000).

So deep was the control exercised by Lai Changxin that it proved necessary to send a massive team of investigators from the Central Inspection Commission in Beijing to penetrate the city's ruling apparatus. The team had several hundred members. Naturally, those involved had the strongest possible interests in trying to thwart the inquiry.

The very reason that so many cases of corruption have come to light, and been written about in the Chinese press, is precisely the fact that the Chinese leadership is fully aware of the deep threat that it poses, and is trying hard to do something about it. Official reports to the National People's Congress in early 2003 declared that in the previous five years the war against graft had been substantially stepped up, with a total of almost 13,000 prosecutions of government officials (*South China Morning Post*, 11 March 2003). Chief Justice Xiao Yang reported that a total of 2,622 officials at the county level or higher had been convicted of embezzlement, taking bribes or other forms of graft, representing a 65 per cent increase over the previous five-year period, ending in 1998. It was reported in early 2003 that in Guangdong alone, in the previous five years the government had investigated 1,388 cases of corruption involving 1,470 people, 61 of which had been at the rank of director or higher (*South China Morning Post*, 26 March 2003).

The psychological challenge

Every society depends for its cohesion, for the happiness of its people and for the provision of meaning to life, upon codes of moral conduct conveyed through the family, school, religion or quasi-religious beliefs. Sociologists have devoted much attention to the psychological challenge that faces all fast-modernizing societies as old values are eroded. China confronts unprecedented challenges in this regard. Few countries have undergone such sustained high-speed modernization. However, as we have emphasized, the process of modernization is taking place alongside a sustained role for a massive rural population that will continue to exist for many decades ahead. As we have also emphasized, there is effectively a collision of the eighteenth century with the twenty-first century.

China is integrating with a global economy that has never witnessed such a concentration of business power in the hands of such a small group of giant firms. It is integrating at a time of unprecedented individualism and materialism in global culture. It is integrating at a time of comprehensive influence of one particular culture, that of the USA. It is naïve to imagine that this culture simply repels. It also provides immense attraction to huge numbers of people across the world, especially to young people who are searching for a new frame of reference to provide order and meaning to their lives. This attraction is hugely reinforced by the influence of US-dominated global mass media, which already have deeply penetrated daily life.

China's psychological challenge is greatly increased by the transition from traditional communist values. The values of the Maoist period have been deeply undermined by the rise of the market economy. The struggle to find a new moral content to Chinese communism is a massive, ongoing endeavour that absorbs a great deal of energy of the Chinese leadership. The transition from Maoism has also created powerful generational differences. These are more profound in China today than in most other societies. The older generation was brought up in a radically different moral environment from today's young people. One generation was continually imbued with the values of self-sacrifice, and the model of revolutionary heroes such as Lei Feng. The successor generation is confronted everywhere by the values of a selfish, materialistic market economy.

The whole of Chinese society has been dramatically affected by the unprecedented impact of the one-child policy. No society in human history has implemented such a drastic policy to control population growth. The result has been a uniquely rapid transition in family structure. The proportion of people under the age of fifteen fell from 33.4 per cent in 1982, to just 22.9 per cent in 2000 (Banister, 1987: 34; SSB, *ZTN*, 2002: 96). There has been intense debate among professional analysts and ordinary people about the consequences of this for the psychology of China's young people. In all previous modernizing experiences, siblings have provided a source of mutual support during the stresses of modernization. This psychological 'umbrella' has been removed during China's modernization process since the late 1970s. The widespread view is that the one-child family policy has produced a generation that is unusually aggressive and isolated. Moreover, the drastic decline in family size has heavily influenced the rationale for developing socially cohesive patterns of relationships that may reward dense patterns of family-based inter-dependencies.

China's diverse social groups confront numerous sharply different psychological challenges. At the apex is the small, but immensely powerful, new global middle class, which is fast absorbing the values of the globalized affluent society. Below them are the upward of 40 million people who have been cast out of the secure world of employment in the state sector, and had new, immensely threatening insecurities thrust upon them. Below them are the 150 million or so migrants who have moved from secure poverty in a rural setting to a harsh world of subsistence income with little social protection, feeling the full force of the market economy at its most brutal point. China's farmers also are feeling great insecurity from the impact of environmental deterioration, which is beyond the scope of any individual or group of people to resolve, as well as the threat produced by China's entry to the WTO, and the disruption of rural society caused by the departure for lumpen work in the cities of a large fraction of the most able young people.

Finance

The process of China participating in the international financial system has been compared by many analysts to a boat setting out to sea. There are two key questions to consider. First, what are the prospects for the 'weather'? Second, how well constructed is the 'boat'?

What are the prospects for the weather?

The concept of free movements of capital is fundamentally different from that of free trade in goods. Capital flows are particularly subject to asymmetric information, agency problems, adverse selection and moral hazard. Although such problems may occur also in trade in goods and services, they are intrinsic to financial flows and are far more important in this sphere. Keynes (1936: ch. 12) provides the foundation of the modern critiques of the potentially de-stabilizing effects of uncontrolled financial markets. He strongly attacks the idea that stock markets and currency markets are efficient, and based on rational expectations. He emphasizes the powerful influence of speculation in determining prices in financial markets. He distinguishes 'speculation', meaning 'the activity of forecasting the psychology of the market', from 'enterprise', meaning 'the activity of forecasting the prospective yield of assets over their whole life' (Keynes, 1936: 158). He famously warned of the negative impact of speculation, which he likens to gambling: 'Speculators may do no harm as bubbles on a steady stream of enterprise. But the position is serious when enterprise becomes the bubble on a whirlpool of speculation. When the capital development of a country becomes a by-product of the activities of a casino, the job is likely to be ill-done' (Keynes, 1936: 159).

More recently, Robert Shiller has pointed out the shortcoming in 'many of the major finance textbooks today', which 'promote a view of markets working rationally and efficiently', and 'do not provide arguments as to why feedback loops supporting speculative bubbles cannot occur': 'In fact, they do not even mention bubbles or Ponzi schemes. . . . These books convey a sense of orderly progression in financial markets, of markets that work with mathematical precision' (Shiller, 2001: 67). Shiller has shown that bubbles in financial markets are 'so natural that one must conclude that if there is to be debate about . . . speculative bubbles, the burden of proof is on the sceptics to provide evidence as to why [they] cannot occur' (Shiller, 2001: 67). The initiating factor is often the optimism generated by a feeling that the economy has entered a 'new era', such as the 'internet revolution', the 'Asian Miracle' or the 'new paradigm for the US economy'. Once the speculation process gets under way, powerful positive feedback loops drive markets ever higher. News media 'are fundamental propagators of speculative price movements through their efforts to make news more interesting to their readers' (Shiller, 2001: 95). Once the market starts to climb, 'public speakers, writers, and other prominent people suddenly appear armed with explanations for the apparent optimism seen in the market' (Shiller, 2001: 98). Eventually, the bubble bursts.

The orthodox view is that as markets become more transparent and availability of information increases, the possibility of crises will decline. On the contrary, Keynes believes that speculation is 'a scarcely avoidable outcome of our having successfully organised "liquid" investment markets' (Keynes, 1936: 159). Indeed, he believed that as the organization of investment markets improves, 'the risk of the predominance of speculation increases' (Keynes, 1936: 158). He made much of the fact that Wall Street was 'one of the greatest investment markets in the world', but there 'the influence of speculation was enormous' (Keynes, 1936: 159). Doubtless, the rise of modern technologies to facilitate instantaneous transfers of vast sums of capital would have only reinforced his concerns on this score.

Liberalization of controls on capital movements since the 1980s has precipitated a turbulent period in the history of developing countries. The period has seen a vast amount of capital surge into different parts of the world in search of maximum short-term profit, with powerful 'herd' instincts influencing the behaviour of the investing institutions. Developing countries are especially susceptible to such bubbles, because the size of the financial flows are massive in relation to the size of the economies concerned. The total funds under management of a single asset management company, Fidelity, are around US$1 trillion, several times larger than the value of the entire Chinese stock market, and around the same size as the entire Chinese national product. Directing these giant funds towards developing countries' financial markets is like 'putting an elephant in a bath of water'. These bubbles have been a form of 'Ponzi' scheme, with capital attracted by the prospect of super-normal profits nurtured by a 'growth story', such as the 'East Asian Miracle', inflating asset prices, thus giving further stimulus to capital inflows. Flows of short-term capital for equity investment and private lending have proved far more volatile than long-term FDI. In each case the resulting 'bubble' burst, with disastrous consequences for the real economy and ordinary people, as asset prices collapsed and capital flows were reversed.

The period has seen an unprecedented number and intensity of financial crises: the largest of these were the Mexican 'Tequila crisis' of 1994/5; the Asian Financial Crisis of 1997/8; the Russian crisis of 1998; and the Argentinian crisis of 2001/2. The bubble has burst in hugely different types of economy: these ranged from 'small, well-regulated and open' Hong Kong at one end, to huge, state-interventionist Indonesia at the other. The common factor of the countries caught up in the Asian Financial Crisis was financial liberalization and asset bubbles. The bursting of the bubble has in each case had massive social and economic consequences. In the case of Indonesia, this resulted in 'regime change'. One of the most successful 'developmental states' in the Third World was overthrown in a matter of months from the onset of the Asian Financial Crisis.

Immediately prior to the eruption of the Asian Financial Crisis, at its meeting in Hong Kong in April 1997, the IMF proposed changing the Articles of Agreement to extend the Fund's jurisdiction to include capital movements. It was striking to all international observers that only China and India escaped the worst effects of the crisis, and that they both had strict controls over international capital flows, with only limited convertibility of the national currency. Today, the Chinese economy is growing fast, but the lesson from the past, especially the Asian Financial Crisis, is that perceptions can change overnight. China is today the last remaining large 'growth story' in the world; it already has a huge 'bubble' of FDI, with the largest FDI inflows of any economy in the world.

If controls on financial flows were substantially liberalized, it is highly likely that short-term funds would flood into the country, fuelling asset inflation. China already has extremely high savings rates, and high rates of fixed investment, but with low returns; a large fraction of the massive potential inflow would be highly likely to fuel asset inflation, especially in the property market. It is easy to imagine how the bubble might burst, and the flow of capital be reversed, with huge potential de-stabilizing consequences for the economy and society. There would then be a full-blown 'Chinese Financial Crisis'. A central goal of policy must be to avoid such an outcome.

China has been fortunate in its reform path of 'groping for stones to cross the river'. At the end of the 1980s and in the early 1990s, when there was intense pressure in China for high-speed political reform to precede deepening of economic reform, the former USSR collapsed. This provided an important object lesson for China: it showed that there were huge dangers in pursuing extensive political reform prior to economic system reform; this reality was quickly understood by everyone in China, and people across the world, who could see the dramatic contrast in the outcomes of system change in China and the USSR (Nolan, 1995). The Asian Financial Crisis provided another deep lesson to China's policy-makers: financial system reform is the most sensitive and difficult part of the whole process of system change; if mistakes are made in this area, with its deep roots in the everyday lives of the whole population, they threaten the whole socio-political fabric. The Asian Financial Crisis reinforced the need for China's policy-makers to be incredibly cautious in liberalizing capital flows and moving towards full convertibility.

How strong is the boat?

The Asian Financial Crisis provided China's leaders with a shocking insight into the fragility of the country's financial institutions. China appeared to escape any effects of the crisis, due to the fact that the *renminbi* was not fully convertible. In fact, the crisis had a deep impact through the medium of Hong Kong and Guangdong province.

Guangdong province had two large non-bank financial firms established by the provincial government during the reform period. One was GITIC (Guangdong Trust and Investment Company), based in Guangdong, but with extensive interests in Hong Kong. The other was GDE (Guangdong Enterprises), whose main activities were in Hong Kong, including five floated 'red chip' companies. During the Asian Financial Crisis, GITIC went into bankruptcy and GDE was insolvent, and faced massive restructuring to meet the demands of its creditors. The bankruptcy of GITIC and the restructuring of GDE allowed the outside world to look closely inside Chinese financial institutions for the first time.

Immediately prior to the crisis, they each had been regarded as outstanding institutions by international lenders. In May 1994, Huang Yantian, head of GITIC, had appeared on the cover of *Business Week* magazine, which described GITIC as 'a financial powerhouse that is helping to remake China'. Just before it was restructured, the Hong Kong government awarded GDE the Territory's annual 'Best Management' award. Morgan Stanley selected Guangnan, one of GDE's red chip companies floated in Hong Kong, as one of the world's 'top fifty small and medium-sized companies'.

However, the investigations of both companies in the full glare of international scrutiny showed that they each had huge failures in corporate governance. Both were shown to have followed disastrous lending policies: a large fraction of their loans and investments were made to firms and institutions that were unable or unwilling to repay their debts to GITIC or GDE. A substantial part of their 'investments' were highly speculative, including heavy participation in the property boom in Guangdong and Hong Kong. Even worse, investigations into Guangnan, one of GDE's 'red chip' companies, revealed that it was basically a 'criminal company': a total of thirty-five people from Guangnan were either arrested or had warrants for their arrest issued by the Independent Commission Against Corruption in Hong Kong. Guangnan was a Hong Kong-listed company, a 'red chip', operating in Hong Kong's environment of high-quality rules on corporate governance; over 40 per cent of its shares were owned by public investors; its accounts were audited by a famous international accountancy firm; it had two independent directors, both prominent businessmen from Hong Kong.

The crisis in Guangdong was closely related to a much wider crisis in China's financial system. As well as GDE, there were innumerable other red chip companies operating in Hong Kong; these were able to borrow huge amounts from international financial institutions, frequently acting as guarantors for each other's borrowing. As well as GITIC, there were, literally, hundreds of other 'trust and investment companies' (TICs). The TICs were able to borrow huge amounts from international financial institutions, who believed that the booming local economies from which they originated would ensure high returns. During the crisis it became clear that the total international borrowings by the TICs and red chips totalled as much as US$60–80 billion, amounting to around one-half of China's total foreign exchange reserves. This huge build-up of borrowings had strong 'Ponzi'-style characteristics. International lenders were intoxicated by the 'China growth story', especially that of the 'miracle' economy of

Guangdong province. In true 'Ponzi' fashion, the borrowers systematically borrowed new funds to repay old debts.

As the Asian Financial Crisis exposed the shortcomings of the borrowers ('the rocks appear as the tide goes out'), the international creditors insisted that GITIC and GDE's debts were the equivalent of 'sovereign debt', and that the Chinese government had a duty to repay them. If the Chinese government had accepted this argument, it could have been a disaster for the country's financial system, as the same argument could then have been applied to the entire TIC and red chip system.

Alongside the massive international borrowings by its non-bank financial institutions, a much less noticed form of massive domestic 'Ponzi' scheme was unfolding, most noticeably in Guangdong province. In the 1990s, a mass of newly established, government-backed local financial institutions sprung up. They attracted tens of billions of *renminbi* from across the whole country through the illegal offer of interest rates far in excess of the official rate of interest. This was termed '*gaoxi lanchu*', or 'pulling in deposits through high interest'. The greedy depositors hoped to participate in the 'Guangdong growth miracle'. The collapse of the region's property bubble, followed by the severe impact of the Asian Financial Crisis, led to widespread insolvency in the local financial institutions, and huge anger among small depositors when accounts were frozen, as frequently happened.

The combination of the local *renminbi* 'Ponzi' schemes with the international 'Ponzi' schemes that lured foreign capital to Guangdong presented a huge challenge to the Chinese government. This was a fast-moving 'fire' that threatened the whole Chinese financial system. The critical action that warded off the crisis was the bold and extremely difficult decision taken by the Chinese government to let GITIC become bankrupt. This prevented the 'domino' effect operating from GITIC through GDE and into the entire TIC and red chip system, which was widely insolvent and unable to repay its international debts. This bold action, which incurred deep opposition, can be termed 'cutting the trees to save the forest' (*kanshu jiulin*). It erected a 'fire-break' around the Chinese financial system and gave the government a breathing-space in which to attempt a thoroughgoing 'clean-up' of the country's non-bank financial institutions. Guangdong was in the front line of this critical process, and the government mobilized large numbers of cadres to close around 1000 rural financial institutions and urban credit co-operatives, as well as many trust and investment companies. The episode served as a deep warning of the dangers in China's close involvement with the global financial system.

China's four main banks are in the process of comprehensive restructuring. They have faced deep difficulties over their corporate governance. The cases of GITIC and GDE demonstrate how long and complex will be the process of changing China's financial institutions into well-governed, modern financial institutions. They demonstrate that 'privatization' and stock market flotation, operating according to global rules and regulations on corporate governance, and with close scrutiny from investigative financial journalists, are not sufficient to ensure that China's financial institutions operate in a way that eliminates risk for the country's financial system. They show that for Chinese financial firms to go out into the 'high seas' of global finance before their corporate governance structures have been fully transformed would be incredibly dangerous.

In the big four commercial banks, despite the removal of large tranches of non-performing loans (NPLs) in the late 1990s, the NPLs still stand at an estimated US$500 billion. If the government's exposure to welfare and pension payments is included, then the central government's foreign and domestic liabilities are estimated to be well in excess of China's total GDP. International experts have become more vocal in pointing to the serious risk of financial sector collapse. In late 2002, one senior official at the Bank of International Settlement said: 'This situation can't last for too long if the underlying problem is not dealt with' (quoted in *Far East Economic Review* [*FEER*], 14 November 2002). International commentaries on the Chinese economy have increasingly begun to consider the possibility of a 'sudden loss of confidence that sparks a run on the state-owned banks' (*FEER*, 14 November 2002). Nicholas Lardy, of the Brookings Institution, has argued that the conditions are 'ripe for a financial crisis' (*FEER*, 14 November 2002).

In the late 1990s, especially after the shocking revelations during the Asian Financial Crisis about Guangdong province's financial institutions, and in the light of the central role that finance played in that crisis, the central government began a massive attempt to 'clean up' the country's main financial institutions, as well as local small-scale institutions. These revealed shocking evidence about the state of corporate governance in China's main banks. In the course of the clean-up of the country's financial institutions, huge problems were found from the bottom to the top of the country's financial system.

In early 2002, it was revealed that the five bank officials at the Bank of China (BOC) branch in Kaiping city (Guangdong) had stolen the equivalent of 'nearly US$500 million'.[17] This was the biggest embezzlement case since the founding of the PRC. Xu Chaofan was the branch manager at Kaiping in the early 1990s, until he was promoted to the BOC's offices in Guangzhou. His successors were Yu Zhendong and then Xu Guojun. According to Hong Kong government officials, the three were 'already well-prepared' as their families had already been sent abroad using false passports (*FEER*, 30 May 2002). It is alleged that on 25 October 2001 the three fled to Hong Kong, also using fake documents. From there, they were reported to have fled to the USA and Canada. Some of the money was laundered through Macao as well as in Las Vegas. (*FT*, 16 March 2002). Hong Kong police said that they had arrested two solicitors and a barrister in connection with the laundering of money from the Kaiping branch. The three former managers and their three accomplices were said to have been 'doing this for nine or ten years': 'These guys were massive high rollers. They were gambling and travelling overseas with their families' (investigator, quoted in *FEER*, 30 May 2002).

Relative to the size of Kaiping city, this was a huge theft. Kaiping has a population of only around 680,000 people (SSBG, *GTN*, 2001: 629). In other words, the theft was the equivalent of around US$740 for every citizen of Kaiping. In 2000, Kaiping's GDP totalled US$1,080 million, and its total residents' savings totalled US$1,130 million (SSBG, *GTN*, 2001: 631 and 655). In other words, the theft was the equivalent of around one-half of Kaiping's GDP and one-half of its total savings. Immediately after the managers fled, rumours began to circulate about the alleged theft. On 17 October depositors started to queue at the branch, and the authorities were forced to send in truck-loads of cash to meet demands for withdrawals. The *Far East Economic Review* commented: 'Calm was restored within days, but the incident shows how wary the government is of any loss of public confidence in the banks. Some analysts warn that a run on China's debt-laden banks might spark a nationwide financial crisis' (*FEER*, 30 May 2002).

The publicly available information made it impossible to identify exactly how the three managers had exploited loopholes in the BOC's internal accounting systems and escape detection for so long. BOC (HK)'s listing prospectus simply said that the theft had taken various forms, including 'foreign exchange trading activity in violation of regulations, off-balance sheet loans, and the diversion of bank funds to third parties'. Chinese and Hong Kong investigators said that the three men had 'established a pipeline into the Bank of China's foreign currency reserves in Beijing' (*FEER*, 30 May 2002). One method that investigators say was used by Xu Chaofan to shift money offshore was through issuing bogus loans to local township and village enterprises, which then transferred the funds as payment for orders of raw materials to companies controlled by Xu in Hong Kong (*FEER*, 30 May 2002). Veteran police investigators in Hong Kong said that it was 'highly unlikely that the three managers had acted alone'. Other managers were replaced in a 'sweeping clear-out of local branches' (*FEER*, 30 May 2002). By May 2002, the Hong Kong police had arrested four people in connection with money laundering associated with the case, and further arrests were expected. The Royal Canadian mounted police were reported to be investigating a number of people in Canada in connection with the case (*FEER*, 30 May 2002). Part of the embezzled funds were used to build a luxury hotel in Kaiping and a twenty-two-storey office block that housed the BOC office. The hotel manager was a former BOC employee. After the scandal erupted, he committed suicide by jumping from one of the hotel windows (*FEER*, 30 May 2002).

Although senior officials at the BOC, such as its President, Liu Minkang, emphasize that the bank is determined to stamp out graft and improve management, the 'Kaiping affair shows that it has a long way to go' (*FEER*, 30 May 2002). In its report on the Kaiping scandal, *Caijing* (5 May 2002) concluded that it illuminated the 'terrifying complexity and scale of the challenge facing China': 'Only by drawing a lesson from this bitter experience and facing reality bravely will the Chinese banking industry be able to make up for lost time.'

When the National Audit Office (NAO) completed an audit of BOC from the period 1992 through to the year 2000, covering the head office and seven provincial branches, it identified twenty-two possible incidents of fraud or misconduct with respect to transactions totalling RMB2.7 billion (BOCI, 2002: 169). BOC (HK)'s listing prospectus acknowledged that 'incidents involving embezzlement, misappropriation and bribery by BOC officers and employees, as well as parties outside BOC, have also occurred at other BOC branches' (BOCI, 2002: 169).

The deep problems in Chinese financial institutions do not simply apply to the lower levels. At the very apex of the country's banking system, three high-profile senior banking officials encountered serious difficulties, namely Zhu Xiaohua, Li Fuxiang and Wang Xuebing: 'All three were close associates. All spoke excellent English and had cultivated relationships with many of the world's top bankers, to whom they seemed to embody the market-savvy face of a new China. The illusion is now shattered' (*FT*, 16 January 2002). Even more deeply troubling is the fact that Zhu Xiaohua, Li Fuxiang and Wang Xuebing were part of Premier Zhu Rongji's team of 'can-do-commanders'. They attacked issues of critical importance in China's vital financial reforms.

From 1993 to 1996, Zhu Xiaohua held the positions of deputy governor of the BOC and head of the management of China's foreign exchange reserves. In 1996 he was appointed head of China Everbright Bank (CEB). It was one of the group of innovative state-owned banks that was allowed to operate 'free from the mountains of non-performing loans that characterize the traditional big four state banks' (FT, 11 October 2002). In 1999, Zhu Xiaohua vanished from public view. It was later revealed that he had been placed under house arrest and required to confess to his mistakes. In December 2000, Zhu's wife, Ren Peizhen, committed suicide by jumping from a building in Chicago. Zhu's daughter, Zhu Yun, suffered a mental collapse. In May 2001, Zhu Xiaohua was formally arrested. On 10 October 2002, the official Chinese news media broadcast that Zhu had been sentenced to fifteen years' imprisonment for crimes committed while Chairman of CEB, including taking a bribe of RMB4 million (FT, 11 October 2002). China Everbright Bank had planned to launch an initial public offering (IPO) in 2003, but in early 2002 it was announced that this had been 'postponed indefinitely' (FT, 13 August 2002). It was reported that the bank had been subjected to a sweeping government investigation, involving a team of up to 500 officials, who had uncovered 'many improprieties' (FT, 13 August 2002).

Li Fuxiang was formerly the head of the Bank of China's foreign exchange dealings in New York, and subsequently became the official in charge of the whole country's foreign exchange reserves, following Zhu Xiaohua. In May 2000 he committed suicide by jumping out of the seventh-floor window of a hospital in Beijing as investigators moved in. The official reason given for Mr Li's death was depression. At the time of his death he was being questioned about his conduct while at the Bank of China and the State Administration of Foreign Exchange, the body which handles Chinese foreign exchange reserves: 'Questions over what happened to the billions of "missing" reserves remain unanswered to this day' (FT, 16 January 2002). It was estimated that over the course of the whole year of 1998, the combined total of foreign investment and the trade surplus was US$89 billion. However, the foreign exchange reserves grew by only US$5.1 billion. In 1999, the foreign exchange reserves grew by US$9.72 billion, compared with a trade and investment surplus of US$76 billion (FT, 16 January 2002). Most observers believe that a substantial part of the discrepancy can be attributed to capital flight, propelled by widespread concern over the possibility that China might devalue the *renminbi*. However, estimates of capital flight account for only around US$35–40 billion a year, according to some analysts, leaving unexplained the remainder of the discrepancy (*FT*, 16 January 2002).

In early 2002 it was revealed that Wang Xuebing, who had formerly been the head of both the Construction Bank and the Bank of China, two of the 'big four' Chinese commercial banks, was 'being invest-igated for "credit problems" while at the Bank of China branches, while he was president from 1993 to February 2000' (*FT*, 16 January 2002). In July 2002 it was reported that Wang Xuebing 'and other senior managers' might face prosecution for their role in the alleged fraudulent transactions involving the BOC's New York branch.

There has been much speculation about the circumstances that might spark a full-blown 'Chinese Financial Crisis'. One potential catalyst would be a further significant downturn in the growth rate. The Chinese government is already 'straining its finances to the limit' in order to stimulate growth. Much hinges on the economy's ability to find markets for its surging exports. Another danger is that which would arise 'if the government mistimed its plan to make the *renminbi* fully convertible at a later stage, so that it crashes when savers panic and seek refuge in the dollar' (*FEER*, 16 November 2002). Another potential catalyst would be if the international banks were able to make more rapid progress than is currently predicted in competing within the Chinese market, provoking a run on state banks to transfer deposits to the international banks.

In late 2002, Moodys rated the prospects for Chinese banks as 'stable', but it headlined its report, 'China's banks walk on a tightrope'. The *FEER* commented: 'While it is clearly possible to be stable on a tightrope, the image hardly inspires much confidence' (16 November 2002). It is now widely recognized that a financial meltdown would 'almost certainly be a catalyst for political and social upheaval' (*FEER*, 16 November 2002).

It was only through the bold action of 'cutting the trees to save the forest' (i.e. to make GITIC go through bankruptcy proceedings in order to save the rest of the financial system) that China was able to remain insulated from the worst effects of the Asian Financial Crisis. This action provided a breathing space for the central govern-ment to attempt to undertake deep structural reform in the financial system after 1998. However, the depth of the crisis in GITIC and GDE revealed just how deep was the task that faced the Chinese policy-makers.

Under the terms of the WTO Agreement, China's financial firms will face steadily escalating competition from global financial institutions. Structural reform of the country's financial institutions is, therefore, being carried out in extremely challenging circumstances. The period since the 1980s has seen a revolution in global business systems. This includes financial institutions just as much as manufacturing and other service sector firms. Leading financial services firms, all from the high-income economies, have been through a period of unprecedented merger and acquisition, to take advantage of global markets, benefiting from economies of scale and scope in respect to research and development, branding, human resource acquisition, and central procurement (e.g. IT systems). The period has seen the emergence of super-giant financial services firms, such as Citigroup, J.P. Morgan Chase, Deutsche Bank and Mizuho Group. Citigroup alone has annual revenues of US$112 billion and profits of around US$14 billion, many times greater than the entire group of China's 'four big banks'. The explicit objective of the global giants is to penetrate the financial markets of developing countries. They have at high speed acquired dominant positions in the financial markets of most of Latin America and Eastern Europe. When Citigroup acquired Banamex, Mexico's 'national champion' in financial services, the *Financial Times* commented: 'The acquisition of Banamex underscored the rapacious appetite of Citigroup for assets in the developing world.' Citigroup itself said: 'China is top of our radar screen.'

The challenge for China's large financial firms is likely to intensify rapidly within the country as the global giants gain increasing access to the China market. The less able are China's indigenous large financial firms to achieve their own self-reform, the stronger will be the argument made by the global giants to allow them to 'take command of the boat', as experienced sailors who can run the country's financial institutions well. Citigroup argues that the big four banks in China should be 'torn apart into small units in order to avoid a financial crisis'. Undoubtedly this would make it far easier for the global giants to 'rout the enemy one by one' (*gege jipo*).

Conclusion

There is a high probability of 'bad weather'. Policies should not be shaped on the assumption that the 'fine weather' currently being experienced will persist. At sea, storms can develop with frightening speed and devastating results, especially for fragile craft. The 'boat' of the Chinese financial system still faces enormous challenges in getting itself into condition to set out safely upon the high seas of 'close' integration with global financial markets. The fact that so many deep problems in Chinese financial institutions have come to light is precisely because the government has tried to do something to clean up the sector from the highest to the lowest level.

Conclusion

As China enters the twenty-first century, it faces a wide-ranging series of deep challenges that threaten the entire social, economic and political system. The country is in a period of high-speed economic and social change. It has long been pointed out by political analysts that the potential for political instability is especially acute during such periods. The Chinese government is working extremely hard to try to increase its risk management capabilities to meet this challenge.

For each of the enormous challenges that the Chinese government confronts, painful, hard work is required by the country's leaders and by the local Party apparatus. Reforming the Party itself is a massive task. Huge efforts have been expended on raising the capability of the Chinese bureaucracy. The massive effort to try to clean up the country's financial institutions after the Asian Financial Crisis demonstrated vividly the continued and improved effectiveness of this mighty apparatus. In Guangdong province alone, a vast clean-up operation involved thousands of Party cadres at every level. They closed hundreds of local financial institutions, and ensured that their massive obligations were dealt with in a way that preserved social stability. Such tasks are vital for the Chinese development effort in the period ahead. In respect to each of the challenges it faces, important successes have been achieved, but in each there are still huge problems ahead. Because the task is difficult, however, does not mean that it should be abandoned. 'Regime improvement' rather than 'regime change' is the only logical way to proceed in order to meet the needs of China's vast population.

Huge challenges face the leadership in dealing with the deep problems in the agricultural sector, in fast-rising inequality, in the fast-deteriorating environment, and in the challenge of the global business revolution. In each of these areas, intense work by government policy-makers has gone on for many years. Finding a way to minimize the difficulties within severe constraints will require great skill by China's policy-makers.

However, owing to the number and intensity of the challenges that China faces, there is a high possibility that at some point a 'fire' will break out. It cannot be predicted where, when or how. It is highly likely that it will be connected with the financial system. China faces a massive challenge in the financial sector. Deep problems remain within the non-bank financial institutions. China's leading financial firms still have huge unresolved problems of non-performing loans. They will face intense competition within the WTO from global giant financial service firms. Even more dangerous is the prospect of full integration with global financial markets. All economies, but especially developing countries, face huge challenges to their financial and economic system from unregulated flows of international capital.

During the Asian Financial Crisis, China came close to a major financial and, by implications, a social and political crisis. Only by bold and effective policy measures was the country able to survive. With full convertibility of the national currency it would be far harder to survive a collapse of confidence by global financial markets of the kind that has regularly occurred in other developing countries under financial liberalization. If the 'fire' does not begin with the financial system, then it is likely that it will quickly spread into the financial system. If China were to face a financial crisis of the dimensions of those that have regularly attacked developing countries during the epoch of globalization and liberalization since the 1980s, it would be immensely difficult to maintain system stability. The relationship of political instability with financial crisis is long-standing. As Karl Marx pointed out in 1853: 'Since the commencement of the eighteenth century there has been no serious revolution in Europe which has not been preceded by a commercial and financial crisis' (Marx, 1853a: 9).

2

China at the Crossroads
Which Direction?

China's political economy has reached a crossroads. There is intense debate among the country's policy-makers and advisers about the development path that might be followed in response to the challenges outlined in chapter 1. The actual path taken will be the result of a complex set of social, economic and political forces within and outside the country. A variety of models have been suggested as suitable for the Chinese reform process in the period ahead. Three stand out in this intense debate. The first, 'realist' approach advocates a tough authoritarian state as the only way to control Chinese society in the face of fast-growing socio-economic inequality. The second, 'human rights' approach believes that only through comprehensive political change can China survive this turbulent period. The third approach argues that the China must return to the 'mass line' of the Maoist period in order to develop in an independent and socially cohesive fashion. We may term this the attempt to 'turn back' at the crossroads and try to return home.

Harsh 'primitive capitalist accumulation'?

Some observers both inside and outside China believe that the country has no choice but to follow the harsh logic of 'primitive' capitalist accumulation. Many observers consider that China is already becoming a more and more explicitly capitalist country. The *Financial Times* recently commented: 'During the past two decades China's neighbours have watched in awe as the most populous nation has re-emerged as the "factory of the world" and the most dynamic economy in the region. . . . A spectre is haunting Asia, the spectre of capitalist China' (3 December 2002). Those who support the 'primitive capitalist accumulation' approach argue that China's rulers must accept, initially *de facto*, and subsequently *de jure*, that China is destined to become a 'standard' capitalist economy. They argue that it is already well advanced on this path. They note that the state-owned sector now occupies far less than one-half of national output, maybe a third or less. They consider that much of the *de jure* 'collective' sector is in fact *de facto* privately organized.[1]

Those adopting a 'realist' approach to China's current situation often employ historical analogies, drawing comparisons with the experience of countries during the phase of early industrialization. They compare China's current development phase with that of 'primitive capitalist accumulation' in Marx's *Capital*, Vol. 1. Marx argues that from the last third of the fifteenth century through to the end of the eighteenth century there took place a long-drawn-out process of 'primitive accumulation', as rural labour was pushed out of the countryside into the cities. The so-called 'primitive accumulation' is 'nothing else than the historical process of divorcing the producer from the means of production' (Marx, 1887: 714):

> The spoliation of the church's property, the fraudulent alienation of the State domains, the robbery of the common lands, the usurpation of feudal and clan property, and its transformation into modern private property under circumstances of reckless terrorism, were just so many idyllic methods of primitive accumulation. They conquered the field for capitalistic agriculture, made the soil part and parcel of capital, and created for town industries the necessary supply of a 'free' and outlawed proletariat. (Marx, 1887: 733)

The 'realists' argue that stable capitalist accumulation requires a strong pro-capitalist state to cope with the stresses and strains of early industrialization. This school of thought argues that there is no alternative to the path first trodden by the UK. They draw comfort from the wider lessons of the history of early capitalist industrialization.[2] Democratic institutions were introduced in all cases only after the harsh phase of early capitalist accumulation had been accomplished:

> Bourgeois democracy, in the same way as its Athenian predecessor, first arose as a democracy for male members of the ruling class alone. Only after a protracted period of struggle were these rights extended to the ruled and exploited classes as well. Sometimes the ruling class of

these early regimes was extremely narrow. . . . Sometimes it was fairly
broad. . . . But in every case the propertyless were excluded. (Therborn,
1977: 33–4)

They note approvingly the experience of authoritarian dictatorships
that have achieved rapid growth, especially in East and Southeast
Asia. They note the apparent paradox that China is already one of
the developing countries ranked lowest in terms of 'corruption indicators' compiled by organizations such as 'Transparency International',[3] yet it is the largest single developing-country recipient of FDI
by far, and by 2002 it had overtaken the USA as the largest recipient
in the world. Guangdong, arguably the most corrupt province in the
country, has received the lion's share of FDI in China. Clearly, international corporations are interested primarily in political stability, not
political transparency. It is argued that both the rigours of the domestic
capital accumulation process and the logic of attracting international
flows of FDI necessitate the construction of a pro-capitalist authoritarian regime in China.

Commentators who adopt this approach have typically drawn
intellectual support from analysis of the British case and from examples of late industrialization in East Asia. In each case, the city-
states apart, there was an initial phase of harsh political rule, with
rapid absorption of rural surplus labour into the urban workforce at
a constant real wage. Once the supply of rural surplus labour dried
up, real wages for ordinary workers started to grow in the urban
areas. It was at this point that demands for political democratization
began to develop.[4] In fact, China's development is different from that
of the surrounding region. In terms of structural change in employment, as we saw in chapter 1, China is still at a relatively early stage
in the industrialization process. Even after two decades of high-speed
industrialization, it still has over 320 million people employed in the
farm sector, amounting to 45 per cent of the total workforce (SSB,
ZTN, 2002: 122). This places a powerful constraint on the rate of
growth of real wages for unskilled or low-skilled workers in the non-
farm sector.

China has nothing to learn in this respect from the 'development'
experience of either of the city-states, Hong Kong or Singapore. Neither of them had a farm sector of any size at the start of the modern
take-off process. Indeed, the case of Hong Kong is a highly significant
hybrid. Hong Kong itself has become a modern financial centre, 'the
shop at the front', but it benefits hugely from investment in the 'workshop behind', namely the Pearl River Delta. In the Delta, the political

economy is firmly that of the 'Lewis model', with vibrant capital accumulation for Hong Kong capitalists made possible by an unlimited supply of labour to their factories in the Pearl River Delta at a constant, or possibly even a declining, real wage for unskilled labour. Taken as a whole, the 'Greater Pearl River Delta' (i.e. including Hong Kong) resembles a giant 'Lewis-type' accumulation machine, siphoning vast amounts of 'surplus value' for Hong Kong capital out of the Delta, for the benefit of consumers in high-income countries. Hong Kong supplies the capital, while China educates, feeds and polices the workforce.

In the cases of take-off in Taiwan and South Korea, under Japanese colonization in the first half of the twentieth century, each had already made considerable progress through the 'Lewis phase' of development. At the initial point at which they began their modern take-off, the share of agriculture in total employment had already fallen to around the level in China today. Thereafter, they were able to achieve a rapid fall in agriculture's share of total employment. In Taiwan, the share of the primary sector in total employment fell from 47 per cent in 1965 to under 20 per cent in 1980 (Council for Economic Planning and Development, 1989: 16). In South Korea, the share of agriculture in total employment fell from 55 per cent in 1965 to 16 per cent in 1989 (UNDP, *HDR*, 1993: 168). During the 'Lewis phase' of modern economic growth, post-colonial Taiwan and South Korea were both undemocratic, authoritarian states. In one sense, in Taiwan and South Korea the period of authoritarian modernization during the 'Lewis phase' of development was short. However, if we include the period of development under Japanese colonial control, fifty years in the case of Taiwan and thirty-five years in the case of South Korea, it was quite long.

Some commentators believe that more relevant historical analogies for the Chinese industrialization and accumulation process today are Britain from 1750 until the mid-nineteenth century and the Meiji Period in Japan.

In Britain, the Industrial Revolution was preceded by a long period of 'primitive capitalist accumulation', from the Elizabethan period through to the late eighteenth century (see Dobb, 1963; Hilton, 1976; Hoskins, 1976). During this period, politics remained undemocratic, save for increased involvement of the rising bourgeois class (Hill, 1961). A powerful lever for capitalist accumulation was the dissolution of the monasteries in the sixteenth century and the distribution of their vast assets to the rising gentry class. This process has been likened to the process of privatization of state assets in the former

USSR and Eastern Europe, namely an 'Age of Plunder' (Hoskins, 1976).

In Britain during the take-off into capitalist industrialization, it took many decades before the large rural reserve army of labour was absorbed into the modern sector. This provided strong downward pressure on urban real wage rates. There was no significant trend improvement in urban real wages in the British Industrial Revolution between 1750 and the 1820s at the earliest: '[T]here was no worthwhile improvement in real consumption of goods and services per head during the first six decades of industrialization. It was not until the 1820s that the average level of consumption rose appreciably above the level of the 1760s, and so far as the mass of the population was concerned the benefits of industrialization were delayed for a very long time' (Feinstein, 1981: 136; see also Lindert, 1994). Other authors estimate that there was no trend improvement in real wages even between 1816 and 1840 (O'Brien and Engerman, 1981: 169).[5] Non-material aspects of urban working-class conditions were appalling, and were meticulously chronicled by Engels (1845). It is hard to imagine how a system with such horrific conditions could survive. Marx and Engels (1848) were confident that such conditions would produce a communist revolution. Nevertheless, despite these long-lasting barbaric conditions of early capitalist accumulation, this never materialized.

By the mid-nineteenth century, Britain had finally passed through the 'Lewis phase' of development. Data for 1861 show that employment in farming had fallen to just 19 per cent of the total (Floud, 1981: 12). Thereafter, real wages began to rise significantly, but this was not until after almost 100 years of 'Industrial Revolution', and well before the development of mass trade unionism. It occurred mainly through the working of supply and demand in the labour market; in other words, owing to the tightness of the labour market due to the drying up of the rural reserve army of labour.[6]

For the capitalists and for the educated middle classes there were large rises in real income during the first phase of the British Industrial Revolution. By the mid-nineteenth century there were wide income differences among the urban classes. Data for 1851 estimate that the average annual earnings of solicitors and barristers were £1,837; for engineers and surveyors, the figure was £479, compared with £45 for 'common non-farm labourers' and £29 for farm labourers (Lindert and Williamson, 1985; 180–1). This meant that there was a prolonged phase of early capitalist accumulation during which there was a sharp widening of income disparities, and no diminution of absolute poverty.

The widening social divisions meant that the capitalist class found the idea of democratic politics deeply threatening, since the 'interests' of the mass of the population were so divorced from their own. It meant that the process of capitalist accumulation required harsh measures of social control to maintain political order. These considerations were reflected in the ideas of the dominant British political theorists in the late eighteenth and early nineteenth century. The predominant political philosophy in Britain considered that the wide divergence of interests between socio-economic groups made it impossible to obtain a democratically achieved compromise consistent with advancement of the national economy (Hirschman, 1977).

Supporters of the 'realist' view argue that the brutal nature of the accumulation process during the 'Lewis phase' of industrialization, with its foundation in 'economic development with unlimited supplies of labour' at a constant real, subsistence wage, demanded an authoritarian political structure, with voting rights confined to the narrow ruling class. Oppressed workers were unlikely to vote for the continuation of their own exploitation. Britain had to wait until the late nineteenth century, more than one hundred years after the Industrial Revolution began, for progressive factory legislation, the beginnings of social welfare and expansion of voting rights to a wider group of the population. Indeed, universal male suffrage did not come about until 1918. Polanyi has identified the nature of the political structure necessary to sustain capital accumulation in Britain during the Industrial Revolution: 'In England it became the unwritten law of the constitution that the working class must be denied the vote. . . . The Chartists [in 1848] had fought for the right to stop the mill of the market which ground the lives of the people. But the people were only granted rights when the awful adjustment had been made' (Polanyi, 1957: 266).

Turning now to the second historical analogy, Meiji Japan, here the industrialization process is especially relevant to China's current political economy. During the Meiji Period (1868–1912), the intense pressure of rural surplus labour meant that real wages in Japan rose by only 0.6 per cent per annum between 1882 and 1902, during the phase of intensive industrialization, and by only 0.9 per cent per annum over the whole period from 1882 to 1912: 'In considering the pattern of financing Japanese economic development in the Meiji era, the class bias, the spur to growing inequality in the distribution of income and wealth, and the detrimental effects on the welfare of the people become evident' (Lippitt, 1978: 71). The structure and ideology of the Japanese state during this period was critical to maintaining social order in the face of intense social and class conflict. In the early years of the Meiji Restoration, the key political decisions were taken by a tiny group, 'without any kind of formal consultation with any segment of the population' (Halliday, 1975: 29). The political situation in these years was volatile. Even the position of the Emperor was 'fragile' (Halliday, 1975: 36). Towards the end of the 1870s, 'the government felt itself beset by dangerous new ideas' and was faced with political opposition which it was 'not confident of crushing' (Halliday, 1975: 35).

The leaders responded by powerfully emphasizing the importance of traditional Confucian ideas in schools. They reorganized Tokyo University as a school for government bureaucrats, with strong emphasis on Confucian morals. It was placed under tight government control. Many contemporaries were shocked. One leading contemporary Japanese critic wrote: 'The government began to advocate the queer policy of Confucianism. . . . It also brought together old-fashioned Confucianists to compile readers, and otherwise staged the farce of trying to restore past customs in a civilized world' (quoted in Halliday, 1975: 36).

In the following years, the Japanese leaders devoted intense efforts to creating a constitution that could provide political stability in a time of great social tension. Alongside the huge re-emphasis on the role of traditional Confucian ideas, with 'heavy Confucian moral indoctrination', the government turned to European experience to help construct a political structure that they hoped would enable them to establish a stable socio-political environment for economic modernization. The Japanese leaders chose as the model for their new constitution 'the most advanced and repressive model available elsewhere in the world'. Their principal inspiration was Prussia: 'This determination to construct a certain kind of state took priority over all other ventures. The Meiji oligarchs put politics firmly in command' (Halliday, 1975: 3). The objective was to 'make sure all the key areas of power would be out of reach of any democratic organizations which might emerge as the result of the introduction of the new Constitution', which introduced a 'parliament' with functioning political parties (Halliday, 1975: 31). In 1887, prior to introducing the new Constitution, the government introduced a basic civil service and entrance examination system based on the Prussian model: 'The main purpose of these changes was to strengthen the power of the state by concentrating all stages of the formation of government cadres under state control' (Halliday, 1975: 38).

For the ruling samurai oligarchy, the object of the Constitution was not to introduce a parliamentary system, but to establish imperial rule through a centralized organization, with strong executive powers and weak public representation, with the emphasis on a powerful bureaucracy (Moberg, 2002: 45). The new Constitution provided the basis for stable political rule for more than half a century thereafter. The first elected Japanese parliament (the Diet) was installed in 1890. The franchise for the lower house (House of Representatives) was limited to men over 25 years of age who paid more than a minimum amount in tax. The effect was to restrict the franchise to only 1.2 per cent of the total population. Universal manhood suffrage was not introduced until 1925. In 1888, a Council, consisting of fourteen members, directly responsible to the Emperor, was established. The members of the Council were the self-selected founding fathers of the Meiji Restoration. The Meiji leaders 'formed a powerful oligarchy that created a strong centralized authority' (Moberg, 2002: 42). Under the 1889 Constitution, the power to create legislation was in the hands of the Emperor, advised by the Cabinet. The Cabinet was responsible to the Emperor, not to the Diet.

Under the new Constitution, the bureaucracy was regulated by ordinance, not law: '[I]ts members, like the Cabinet, were "servants of the Emperor", beyond the control of either the political parties or the Diet – not to mention the people' (Halliday, 1975: 39). The bureaucracy 'first stifled the Diet and then the parties, which it virtually absorbed' (Halliday, 1975: 39). In 1937, 74 per cent of the civil officials and 50 per cent of the judicial officials came from government-controlled Tokyo University. Only five of the thirty-five heads of government in the twentieth century up until 1972 had not had a bureaucratic background. The bureaucracy, along with the economy, 'has been the greatest achievement of Japanese capitalism' (Halliday, 1975: 39).

The men who crafted the Constitution included both Japanese and Germans. The key person in this process was the German scholar Carl Roesler. He headed the body charged with designing the Constitution. The body was attached directly to the Imperial Household Department, so that it 'became sacrosanct and completely removed from any outside influence' (Halliday, 1975: 37). Roesler's commentaries on the Constitution 'show that he grasped with ex-ceptional lucidity the entire range of problems involved: the social and class contradictions which economic change was bringing about and how these contradictions could be mobilized' (Halliday, 1975: 39). Roesler 'argued brilliantly for the installation of a bourgeois-capitalist state which could handle the problem of class-consciousness, deal with the contradictions of property, involve the state in banking and industry, and strengthen the bureaucracy' (Halliday, 1975: 39).

Under this highly repressive political system, Japanese capital was able to able to operate a harsh system of labour organization and accumulation. During the Meiji Period and afterwards, workers were typically housed in 'dormitories' (usually slum huts) on the factory grounds, and 'were not allowed off the grounds until several months after arrival' (Halliday, 1975: 62). The state assumed almost no responsibilities at all in relation to the factory workers. Much of the early industrial proletariat consisted of women. Unions were stigmatized as being 'un-Japanese'. Where they were formed, 'employers frequently smashed them with physical violence and dismissed the workers involved' (Halliday, 1975: 66). When the first Factory Act was finally introduced in 1911, it allowed the employers fifteen years to carry out the requirements of the act. The mining companies, 'which enforced the most horrible conditions, were allowed until 1933 to let boys under sixteen and women have two days' rest a month' (Halliday, 1975: 68). Although the 'ferocious repression' detonated numerous working-class reactions, organization of large-scale working-class actions was rendered extremely difficult by the effectiveness of the ideological and political control. Censorship was severe, with translations banned not only of Marx and Engels, but also of Zola, Tolstoy and Kropotkin, until 1914.

Eventually, in 1918, a massive social explosion occurred (Halliday, 1975: 70–1). During the First World War, Japanese industry forged ahead at high speed. However, real wages fell 'drastically'. Between 1917 and 1918 there was a sudden large jump in the price of rice, which precipitated a nationwide uprising, lasting for two months and involving around 10 million people. There were 107 interventions by the army across the country. The government fell. However, the overall system of Emperor and bureaucracy ruling an authoritarian state which provided the framework for high-speed capitalist accumulation survived intact.

Conclusion

There are significant differences between the current Chinese situation and that of the countries analysed above. China's modernization is taking place in the midst of explosive globalization and technical change. This provides unprecedented opportunities for access to global technology and capital, the classic 'late-comer' advantages. However, the 'realistic' school argues that underlying these difference there is a fundamental similarity with the early phase of capital accumulation in a labour-surplus economy. We have seen that in terms of structural change in employment, China is at a relatively early stage in the industrialization process, with 45 per cent of the total workforce still employed in the farm sector.

It will be many decades before China's rural surplus-labour supply is exhausted. In this regard, the experience of Britain in the Industrial Revolution and Meiji Japan are more relevant than Taiwan or South Korea (unless one includes the period under Japanese colonization) and far more relevant than Hong Kong or Singapore. In the case of both Britain and Japan, the early industrialization process of drawing labour out of the countryside into the cities was prolonged, and accompanied by harsh political rule. If the main rationale for political authoritarianism is the existence of a 'Lewis-type' process of capital accumulation, then China would face the prospect of an exceptionally long period under such a structure. It is highly questionable whether this structure would be stable over such a long period as would be in prospect, given the prospects for growing inequality in the midst of accelerated integration of China into the global economy, and the prospect of relatively small total amounts of high-quality employment within the Chinese subsidiaries of multinational firms and their immediate supply chain. In the unlikely event that such a structure were, indeed, able to survive, it would constitute a uniquely lengthy and oppressive form of late industrialization.

Some 'optimists' believe that, following the example of Brazil, the need for strong political control will recede as China develops further. Brazil has managed to combine the shift to multi-party democracy alongside persistent mass poverty and grotesque inequality. Despite the fact that Brazil is an upper-middle-income country, with an average per capita income of over US$4,400 (in PPP terms it is US$7,600), no less than 27 per cent of the population lives on less than US$2 per day (UNDP, *HDR*, 2002: 151).[7] The top 20 per cent of Brazil's income earners account for 64 per cent of the country's personal income, while the bottom 20 per cent account for just 2.2 per cent (UNDP, *HDR*, 2002: 195). A large fraction of the urban population lives in a *Blade Runner*-style nightmare of squalid *favelas*, run by armed drug gangs, while the middle class live adjacent to them in heavily policed wooded oases of peace and civilization. Despite the long-term persistence of such huge inequality, mass squalor and injustice, Brazil's political system has been relatively stable for many years. There is no significant revolutionary movement. Does this example provide hope for China?

Regime change?

Large-scale state system transformation in Chinese history

No theme has been more important in Chinese history than that of the possibility, and terrible consequences, of system disintegration.

There is a strong school of thought among Chinese business people, especially in the private sector, among intellectuals, especially economists, and among international advisers to China which believes that the fundamental condition for continued successful Chinese development is a drastic downgrading of the role for the Chinese state. Indeed, a major reason for advocating that China joined the WTO on the terms agreed with the USA in late 1999 was precisely, they argue, in order that the role of the Chinese state would be radically reduced. Even some of the most sympathetic and understanding analysts of Chinese political economy have argued that enforcing the disciplines of the WTO will be the most effective solution to the problem of corruption in the Chinese state.[8]

There is also, both within China, but especially among the international community of politicians and intellectuals, a strongly expressed view that is explicitly committed to ending rule by the Chinese Communist Party. During the occupation of Tiananmen Square in 1989, a significant proportion of the protesters called for the Chinese Communist Party to 'step down'. Their enduring symbol was the erection of the 'Goddess of Liberty', explicitly modelled on the USA's Statue of Liberty. Dissident Chinese inside and outside the country still call for the overthrow of the Chinese Communist Party, given a firm basis of support by international human rights organizations.

As was noted in the previous chapter, the hawks in the US foreign policy establishment regard China as a 'morally flawed inevitable adversary' and believe that the US should treat Communist China 'as it treated the Soviet Union during the cold war, as a rival and a challenge'. At international meetings and in their writings, leading US government advisers on China policy under George W. Bush, who remain implacably opposed to allowing a 'communist country' to exist, have strongly promoted the desirability of 'regime change' in China, which they feel it is their duty to work towards. We have seen that as well as intense and mounting military and diplomatic pressure from the USA upon China, there is an explicit commitment from the US Congress to promote activities within the county that would contribute to its increased social and political instability at a critical stage in its system evolution. The 'good work' accomplished in helping to topple communism in the former USSR should be completed in China. It is in the strong interest of those in the US government who fear the rise of China to argue that the existing Chinese regime should be overturned because it is basically an unreformed 'communist' state. In this respect, there is a 'happy alliance' of hawks and human rights activists.

Many scholars and policy advisers talk of the need for 'pain' in China today in language that is strongly reminiscent of that directed towards the former USSR in the late 1980s and early 1990s.[9] No idea was more pervasive in the early years of 'transition' in the former USSR and Eastern Europe than that which argued that the state should first be destroyed before it could be reconstructed. A representative such view is that of Steinherr, espoused in 1991: 'Big leaps can only occur in the aftermath of destruction of an ossified and non-performing system. . . . In history, major dynamic rebirths have only occurred in the aftermath of catastrophic destructions' (quoted in Nolan, 1995: 56). In China at the end of the 1980s, before and during the occupation of Tiananmen Square, a consensus among international opinion developed which believed that the overthrow of the Chinese Communist Party would lead to a great improvement in welfare for the Chinese people. It was given added impetus by the development of *perestroika* and *glasnost* in the former USSR, which quickly led to the downfall of the Communist Party of the Soviet Union. This was lauded in the West as 'Gorbachev's finest achievement' (Miller, 1993: 205). János Kornai, the doyen of reformers in Eastern Europe, believes that 'historians will view Gorbachev and all others who initiated and supported the process of reforming the socialist system as people who earn undying merit' (Kornai, 1992: 574).

Such attitudes that applauded the 'revolutionary' overthrow of the Communist Party in the USSR, and call for a similar overthrow of the Chinese Communist Party, provide a modern parallel to the widely held view of pre-1840s China as an 'Oriental despotism' for which forcible integration into the world economy would allegedly bring great benefits.[10] From Montesquieu onwards into the nineteenth century, the predominant 'scholarly' view of China in the West was of an Oriental despotism without the self-propelling political and economic dynamism of Europe (Anderson, 1974: Note B, 'The Asiatic mode of Production'). This view of China as a country 'without a history' reached its apogee in Karl Marx's writings. In Marx's view, Asiatic despotisms (including China) were characterized by an absence of private property in land; large-scale, state-run irrigation systems in agriculture; autarchic village communities combining craft with

tillage and communal ownership of the soil; passively rentier or bureaucratic cities; and a despotic state machine which obtained the
bulk of the economic surplus. Unlike European political economy,
which Marx viewed as progressing from slavery to serfdom, feudalism,
capitalism and, ultimately, communism, the Asiatic mode had merely
cycles of the rise and fall of dynasties, but not an evolutionary history
(Anderson, 1974: 483).

This led Marx to view the violent intrusion of Western colonialism
in a positive light, liberating Asian peoples from 'Oriental despotism',
which 'restrained the human mind within the smallest possible com-
pass, making it the unresisting tool of superstition, enslaving it beneath
traditional rules, depriving it of all grandeur and historical energies'
(Marx, 1853b: 94). In the *Communist Manifesto* Marx and Engels
waxed lyrical about the progressive role of free trade for the destruction of the 'despotic' Chinese state, which they saw as the fundamental
force holding back Chinese progress: 'The bourgeoisie, by the rapid
development of all instruments of production, by the immensely facilitated means of communication, draws all, even the most barbarian,
nations into civilization. The cheap prices of its commodities are the
heavy artillery with which it batters down all Chinese walls, with
which it forces the barbarians' intensely obstinate hatred of foreigners
to capitulate' (Marx and Engels, 1848: 39–40).

The blunt reality is that the overthrow of the Chinese Communist
Party would plunge the country into social and political chaos.

In 1979, Deng Xiaoping delivered a crucial speech outlining the
government's approach to system reform. At the core of this approach
was an acute awareness of the possibility of system disintegration,
and the awful consequences that would follow for the Chinese economy and society:

> At present, when we are confronted with manifold difficulties in our
> economic life which can be overcome only by a series of readjustments
> and by consolidation and reorganization, it is particularly necessary to
> stress publicly the importance of subordinating personal interests to
> collective ones, interests of the part to those of the whole, and immediate
> to long-term interests. . . . [T]alk about democracy in the abstract will
> inevitably lead to the unchecked spread of ultra-democracy and anarch-
> ism, to the complete disruption of political stability and unity, and to
> the total failure of our modernization programme. If this happens
> then the decade of struggle against Lin Biao and the Gang of Four will
> have been in vain, China will once again be plunged into chaos, division,
> retrogression and darkness, and the Chinese people will be deprived of
> all hope. (Deng Xiaoping, 1979: 55)

This solemn warning is as relevant today as it was in 1979, notwithstanding China's US$400 billion in accumulated FDI or its 150 million mobile phones. When Deng Xiaoping issued his warning, he had at the centre of his thinking the age-old preoccupation of Chinese political thought: system stability. China has experienced long periods of system disintegration. The 'dynastic cycle' was a regular phenomenon, with high levels of bureaucratic efficiency at the start of each dynasty, followed by a gradual disintegration of the morality and effectiveness of the central government. One such decline was chronicled in Ray Huang's book *1587, A Year of No Significance*:

> During the greater part of [Wan Li's] reign of 48 years, when the top of the hierarchy, in despair, found that central leadership did not exist, cynicism and slack discipline spread through all the ranks. The diligent had less reason to maintain their diligence; the corrupt, on the other hand, had a better chance to indulge their corruption. . . . If the dynasty did not collapse at this point it was largely because no alternative to it existed. The decline of the bureaucracy was steady and gradual. . . . [W]hen the bureaucracy began to disintegrate, the empire became ungovernable. . . . [U]nder such conditions the state could not long remain in peace and order. (Huang, 1981: 78–9)

The dynastic cycle was so regular and so devastating when it entered a downward path at the end of each dynasty that the theme of avoidance of 'great turmoil' (*da luan*) has been the focus of all Chinese political thought from the earliest times right through to the present day. At the core of the Chinese reform programme after the death of Chairman Mao was a resolute belief in the need to prevent China's political economy from disintegrating and the country descending into 'big turbulence', which would 'deprive the Chinese people of all hope'.

The consequences of political disintegration in China have been horrific. The end of the Song dynasty (960–1279) saw a protracted war fought by the Mongols to conquer the country, 'one of the bitterest and most prolonged wars of conquest in world history' (McEvedy and Jones, 1978: 172). The country as a whole lost 'perhaps a third or more' of its population by the time the war was over: 'The loss – around 35 million on this estimate – is a staggering one for the era' (McEvedy and Jones, 1978: 172). Not only were large numbers of people put to the sword, but crops and grain stores were systematically destroyed so that vast numbers starved to death (Perkins, 1968: 24). During the long years of military struggle, regular government activities of water control and famine relief were substantially in abeyance, further aggravating the terrible direct effects of the war. The conflict produced huge disruption to the transport system, undermining the beneficial effects of trade and division of labour. As is common in such circumstances, the disastrous decline in food production weakened both people and animals, reducing the productive capability of the rural economy. Moreover, a malnourished population was highly susceptible to infectious diseases.

The end of the Ming dynasty (1368–1644) was accompanied by severe decline in the administrative capabilities of the rulers. There were widespread rebellions in the second quarter of the seventeenth century. These are said to have 'drastically reduced the population of many localities in north China and nearly exterminated the population of the Red Basin in Sichuan' (Ho Pingti, 1959: 236). The impact of the civil disturbance was widely felt. For example, the officially estimated arable area for the whole country is estimated to have fallen from 700 million *mu* to just 400 million in 1645 (Ho Pingti, 1959: 236). This was a complex result of decline in population through warfare and disease, and decline in the state's ability to maintain water conservancy facilities. The turmoil was made even worse by the Manchu invasion and conquest of China Proper. This took the form of a prolonged struggle between the Ming armies and the Manchu invaders. Moreover, it took the new rulers many years to pacify the main part of the country. It is estimated that the Manchu conquest 'cost China about one-sixth of her population, say 25 million people' (McEvedy and Jones, 1978: 172).

The weakening of the Qing dynasty (1644–1911) in its final phase was accompanied by intense civil disturbance. Following the usual pattern of the decline of dynasties, the increased corruption and fiscal weakening of the central government undermined its capability to organize efficiently the military and public works. Beginning with outbreak of the insurrection of the White Lotus sect in 1796, China entered an epoch of great civil disturbances, which culminated in the Taiping Rebellion of 1851–64. Overlapping with the Taiping Rebellion was the prolonged warfare associated with the Nien Rebellion. These wars were marked by 'slaughter of both military and civilian populations on a scale difficult to imagine by modern war ethics' (Ho Pingti, 1959: 237). Altogether 'these mid-century conditions probably accounted for a decline in population of over 50 million' (Perkins, 1968: 28). So severe was the disaster that in four of the five provinces worst affected (Anhui, Hubei, Zhejiang and Jiangxi), population totals had still not recovered by the mid-1950s, and the same would have been true for the fifth (Jiangsu) if it had not been for the rise of Shanghai. As in all previous epochs of 'great turmoil', the devastating demographic impact was due not mainly to direct loss of life in battle, but rather to the complex set of inter-related socio-economic effects that typically accompanied such episodes in China's history.

The collapse of the Qing dynasty was not followed by the establishment of another dynasty which was able to establish a peaceful environment within which the economy could recover, people could begin to live a more secure and prosperous life, and the population could again start to grow. Instead, it was followed by decades of disunity and turmoil. This was interrupted only briefly in the late 1920s and early 1930s by a degree of stability over a significant part of the country. For most of the first half of the twentieth century, China lacked any kind of central political organization. It was wracked with internal political and military struggles. For a whole decade, from 1917 to 1927, when the Nationalist regime was established in Nanjing, there were 'incessant civil wars' in various parts of the country. Even after 1927, there were still civil wars in certain provinces. In Sichuan province, there were over 400 large and small civil wars fought after the founding of the Republic in 1911 (Ho Pingti, 1958: 248–9). Between 1932 and 1934, the population of fifteen northern Sichuan counties was estimated to have been reduced by no less than 1.1 million people (Ho Pingti, 1958: 249). After 1928, the Communists were repeatedly at war with the Nationalists. In its gravely weakened political state, China was unable to resist the Japanese invasion in 1936. This was followed by war with Japan until 1945. As soon as Japan surrendered to the allied forces, full-scale civil war once again broke out between the Nationalists and the Communists. Under these conditions, population growth was only around 0.8 per cent per annum over the period 1912–49.

The Western powers forced the Chinese government to allow the establishment of almost fifty 'Treaty Ports'. Within these, the foreign powers were able to establish islands of stability within the wider sea of social turbulence. It was only in these areas that any kind of sustained modernization was able to proceed in the first decades of the twentieth century. They provided a safe haven within which both Chinese and foreign capital could advance: 'These city-ports, or mini-Hong Kongs, with their free markets and enlightened city governments, provided the freedom, security, and monetary incentives for the Chinese to develop modern industry. The modern sector really only emerged in these cities and their environ communities within a radius of fifty miles or so' (Myers, 1980: 139–40). However, despite the progress within the Treaty Port economy, the impact of the devastating turmoil over the first half of the twentieth century prevented any significant economic growth outside the Treaty Port areas, in which a modern sector did begin to develop, especially during the 'Nanjing decade' from 1927 to 1936. However, the overall pace of economic growth was extremely slow. One careful estimate concludes: 'A cautious weighting of what is definitely known suggests that aggregate output grew only slowly during 1912–1949, and that there was no increase in per capita income' (Feuerwerker, 1977: 1).

From the mid-nineteenth century through to the middle of the twentieth century, the central state was far too weak to lead economic modernization. At the end of the nineteenth century, government revenues came to less than 1–2 per cent of China's GNP: '[This was] an extraordinarily low figure. Under the circumstances the government could not begin to spend much money on modernization of any kind' (Perkins, 1967: 487). From 1911 to 1927, the economy proceeded without any central direction at all: '[F]or all practical purposes a central state had disappeared . . . warlord rule became the norm rather than the exception', and 'the state became powerless to use the budget for promoting modern economic growth' (Myers, 1980: 138). Even during the so-called 'Nanjing decade', the revenues of the central government were extremely weak, amounting to a maximum of 5 per cent of GNP, reflecting, 'on the one hand, the failure of the national government to mobilize the resources of the rural sector, and, on the other, its inability or unwillingness to levy income taxes on society in general' (Feuerwerker, 1977: 76). Moreover, throughout the hundred years of turmoil, a large share of the central government's budget was typically allocated to military outlays. For example, even during the decade of relative peace and stability, from 1927 to 1936, close to one-half of total government expenditure was on the military: 'Expenditures for public works were small, and welfare expenditure was almost non-existent' (Feuerwerker, 1968: 58).

The contrast between the inability of the central government to lead the modernization process and that of Japan over the same period is dramatic. D.H. Perkins has drawn attention to the striking disparity between the capability of the state in China and Japan in the late nineteenth and early twentieth century: '[O]ne can only wonder what would have happened in China if central government revenues had been five per cent of GNP or even ten per cent' (Perkins, 1967: 487). Even the establishment of peace and political stability is unlikely to have been sufficient to have enabled modernization of the vast, agrarian-based economy. India under British rule was able to achieve such stability, but it remained an economy forced to remain open to free trade, and in which the role of the state was kept to an irreducible minimum. Subramanian Swamy has commented on the weakness of both the Chinese and the Indian state under British colonial rule as the key factor explaining the failure of these two countries to modernize in the Japanese fashion: 'It is the absence of good leadership in the areas where it would have been most effective that appears to explain the backwardness of these two countries' (Swamy, 1979: 43).

China's new generation of leaders under Party General Secretary Hu Jintao face enormous challenges on several fronts simultaneously. Some Chinese authors have tried to anticipate the way in which system collapse might occur (e.g. Wang Lixiong's futuristic 'novel' *Yellow Peril*). The consequences of this would be devastating for China, and would have serious implications for the global political economy. Under this scenario, the outcome in China would be far worse than that in the former USSR in the 1990s. The threat of Chinese system disintegration needs to be taken very seriously indeed.

It is perfectly possible that the entire Chinese system of political economy could disintegrate. In the late 1980s, few people could imagine that the USSR would disintegrate, yet this hugely sophisticated country, with massive human and technological resources, which had huge potential for high-speed advance in economic performance and living standards, has been sent spinning backwards (Nolan, 1995). It has been 'de-developed' in a way never witnessed before in peacetime. China is still a poor country. Comparable 'de-development' for China would cause immense suffering. It was unimaginable beforehand to most people that there could be system meltdown in the USSR, in the sophisticated European state formerly known as Yugoslavia, in the IMF's favourite pupil in Latin America, Argentina, or in the exemplar of the East Asian model, Indonesia. Yet there was just such a comprehensive meltdown, with disastrous consequences for the people of those countries. The reasons were easy to understand in hindsight. The central task of Chinese political economy is to learn from those experiences and avoid such an outcome in China.

The 'freedom' of free market capitalism?

A widespread view among those who wish for 'regime change' in China is the belief that China, like the Hong Kong Special Administrative Region, can 'follow the American path'. The 'Goddess of Liberty' in 1989 symbolized this dream, which exerts a strong pull on the imagination, especially for highly educated young Chinese people. American foreign policy is based on the premise that the whole world, including China, should, and will, follow this 'natural' path of development. Intense external pressure is exerted already through innumerable channels upon Chinese internal ideology to promote this view of the desirable future political economic structure for China. The same populist illusion was fostered among the population of the former USSR in the late 1980s and early 1990s. Such views will become ever more influential as the US-dominated global mass media increasingly penetrate the Mainland following the 'opening-up' of the mass media in accordance with the WTO Agreement.

The historical context of the US mission to spread 'freedom' to the whole world

President Bush's national security strategy document of September 2002, 'America's Security Strategy', states: 'Freedom is the non-negotiable demand of human dignity; the birthright of every person – in every civilization. . . . Today, humanity holds in its hands the opportunity to further freedom's triumph over all [its] foes. The US welcomes our responsibility to lead in this great mission' (FT, 21 September 2002). It commits the USA to 'defend liberty and justice because these principles are right and true for all people everywhere'. It also commits the USA to 'stand firmly for the non-negotiable demands of human dignity: the rule of law; limits on the absolute power of the state; free speech; freedom of worship; equal justice; respect for women; religious and ethnic tolerance; and respect for private property'. The 'equation of [America's] national interests with the liberation of mankind and of its antagonists with hostility to freedom' is not something new. From the earliest days of American territorial expansion, it has 'infused the rhetoric of American statecraft to the present day, often to the bemusement and annoyance of other nations' (Foner, 1998: 78).[11]

In fact, the interpretation of the word 'freedom' has been the object of intense debate within the history of the USA: 'Freedom has always been a terrain of conflict, subject to multiple and competing interpretations, its meaning constantly created and re-created' (Foner, 1998: xv). At the heart of the struggle for the meaning of 'freedom' in the USA was the battle over the role of the state, and its function in the achievement of 'negative' and 'positive' freedoms. Was the US state to serve purely as the guardian of individual liberties or 'negative freedoms', or was it to serve the as the instrument for the achievement of positive freedoms of all citizens to enable them to be fulfilled human beings? These struggles over the interpretation of 'freedom' have existed in America since the eighteenth century.

In his farewell address to the nation in 1837, Andrew Jackson declared: 'Never has any population enjoyed so much freedom and happiness as the people of the United States' (quoted in Foner, 1998: 48). By 1860, nearly 4 million black Afro-Americans were slaves. Well beyond the middle of the century, in America's West there were indentured Indian workers, Mexican-American peons and Chinese immigrants working under long-term contracts. Freed blacks were barred from taking advantage of the opening of the West to improve their economic status through land acquisition. White male immigrants were able to vote almost from the day of their arrival, while blacks, whose ancestors had lived in the country for centuries (and Indians who had been there even longer), were barred from so doing. For eighty years after the Naturalization Act of 1790, only white immigrants could become naturalized citizens. Blacks were added only in 1870. Incredibly, not until the 1940s did immigrants of Asian origin become eligible to become US citizens.

After emancipation in 1865, during the Reconstruction period, black Americans were finally admitted to the political community and given the vote. However, from 1890 onwards they were progressively disenfranchised in the South. Woodrow Wilson, then a professor at Columbia University, said that black people were 'unpractised in liberty' and 'excited by a freedom they did not understand' (quoted in Foner, 1998: 132). The *Plessy* decision of 1896 affirmed the right of the state of Louisiana to segregate black from white people on the railroads. It was quickly followed by state laws which required racial segregation in every aspect of life, from schools to hospitals, waiting rooms to toilets, pay windows to cemeteries. Beginning in 1882, Congress excluded immigrants from China from entering the country altogether: 'Exclusion profoundly shaped the experience of Chinese Americans, long stigmatizing them as unwanted and unassimilable, and justifying their isolation from mainstream society' (Foner, 1998: 133).[12] The focus on race in the interpretation of the boundaries of political democracy 'drew ever more tightly the lines of exclusion of America's imagined community' and 'helped to solidify a sense of national identity among the diverse groups of British and European origin that made up the free population' (Foner, 1998: 79).

From the middle of the nineteenth century, the USA achieved explosive industrialization behind protectionist barriers. By the beginning of the twentieth century, the top 100 firms accounted for 22 per cent of total manufacturing output (Schmitz, 1993: 35). Nearly two-thirds of the top 100 firms were in the heavy industries, characterized by especially strong economies of scale and in which technical progress through R&D expenditure was crucial to their competitive capability (Schmitz, 1993: 36). Giant corporations dominated large swathes of the economy, such as US Steel, which accounted for 60–70 per cent of US output of all major steel products, and Standard Oil, which totally controlled the oil market.

Already, the giant corporations powerfully influenced the activities of both major parties and political decision-making at the national, state and local levels. The 'Gilded Age' witnessed a tremendous concentration of wealth and income. By 1890, the richest 1 per cent of the population received the same total income as the bottom 50 per cent, and owned more wealth than the bottom 99 per cent: 'The emergence of a wealthy and powerful industrial class and a proletariat living on the edge of poverty, coupled with the closing of the frontier, posed a sharp challenge to inherited definitions of freedom' (Foner, 1998: 117). The period saw bitter and often violent confrontations between capital and labour.

The idea that 'freedom' essentially meant freedom of contract became the bedrock of 'liberal' thinking at the end of the nineteenth century: 'As long as economic processes and labour relations were governed by contracts freely arrived at by autonomous individuals, Americans had no grounds to complain about loss of freedom' (Foner, 1998: 120). In this view, the true realm of freedom was 'the liberty to buy and sell, and mend and make, where and how we please, without interference from the state' (Foner, 1998: 120). The period saw the rise of Social Darwinism, which strongly opposed any form of state interference with the 'natural' workings of society. Laws regulating labour conditions were seen as a form of slavery, since they interfered in the rights of free agents to dispose of their property as they saw fit.

The leading exponent of Social Darwinism was Yale professor William Graham Sumner. For Sumner, freedom properly understood meant the 'abnegation of state power and a frank acceptance of inequality'. In his view, society faced only two possible alternatives: 'liberty, inequality and the survival of the fittest; not-liberty, equality, survival of the unfittest' (quoted in Foner, 1998: 122). The task of social sciences, wrote iron manufacturer Abram Hewitt, was to devise ways of making 'men who are equal in liberty' content with the 'inequality in distribution' inevitable in modern society (quoted in Foner, 1998: 119).

Alongside the rise of Social Darwinism, between 1880 and 1893, nearly two thousand injunctions were issued prohibiting strikes and labour boycotts (Foner, 1998: 123).

The 1890s saw deep class struggle in the USA, including the massive 1892 strike at the giant Homestead Steel Mill, Pennsylvania, in which strikers fought pitched battles with the Carnegie Corporation's private police force. Powerful critiques of free market fundamentalism emerged, deeply opposed to the idea that meaningful 'freedom' could exist in circumstances of extreme inequality, both economic and racial, such as those of the USA. Public discourse at this time was fractured along class lines.

In the academic sphere, the American Economics Association was founded in 1885 with the express purpose to combat both Social Darwinism and 'laissez-faire orthodoxy'. The founder of the AEA, Richard T. Ely, wrote: 'We regard the state as an educational and ethical agency whose positive assistance is one of the indispensable conditions of human progress' (quoted in Foner, 1998: 130).[13] Many younger economists believed that private property had become a 'means of depriving others of their freedom', and that 'poverty posed a far graver danger to the republic than an activist state' (Foner, 1998: 130).

Intense debate surrounded US foreign policy at the turn of the twentieth century: 'America's triumphant entry into the Spanish–American War tied nationalism and American freedom ever more closely to notions of Anglo-Saxon supremacy. . . . Without any sense of contradiction, proponents of an imperial foreign policy . . . adopted the language of freedom' (Foner, 1998: 134). The USA 'pacified' the Philippines through a long and brutal war, crushing the indigenous independence movement. This was justified as the only alternative to the existing situation of 'anarchy and barbarism'. In the same way as the North had done after the conclusion of the Civil War, under the first US Governor of the Philippines, American policies left intact the land-based power of the local oligarchy. They bequeathed a legacy of enduring poverty to the mass of the rural population.

During the Progressive Era leading up to the First World War, a broad coalition of forces emerged to nourish the idea of an activist national state to enable the realization of 'freedom' for the mass of people. Laissez-faire became 'anathema among the lovers of liberty'. It was thought that only 'energetic government' was able to 'create the social conditions for freedom'. The Progressives were wedded to the idea that freedom required conscious creation of the social conditions for full human development. T.H. Green, the British philosopher, made a profound impact with his lecture in the USA in which he argued that freedom was a 'positive concept'.[14] Leading Progressive thinker John Dewey argued: 'Effective freedom [is] far different from the highly formal and limited concept of autonomous individuals that need to be protected from outside restraint' (quoted in Foner, 1998: 153). For Dewey, freedom meant 'effective power to do specific things', and it was therefore 'a function of the distribution of powers that exists at a given time'. William F. Willoughby argued that Progressivism 'looks to state action as the only practicable means now in sight, of giving to the individual, all individuals, not merely a small economically strong class, real freedom' (quoted in Foner, 1998: 153).

The influence of the Progressive movement reached its high point in the 1912 election, a four-way contest between incumbent Republican president William Howard Taft, former president Theodore Roosevelt, now running as a candidate for the Progressive Party, Democrat Woodrow Wilson and Eugene V. Debs, representing the Socialist Party, now at the height of its influence. The central theme of the campaign was the relationship between political and economic freedom in the age of the large corporation. Debs' Socialist Party campaigned with the ultimate goal of abolishing the capitalist system altogether, propelling the country 'from wage slavery to free co-operation, from capitalist oligarchy to industrial democracy'. Although his party was thoroughly permeated with laissez-faire ideology, under the influence of the widespread Progressive thinking, Wilson maintained: '[F]reedom today is something more than being left alone. The program of a government of freedom must in these days be positive, not negative merely.' However, in the end, Wilson argued that 'the history of liberty is a history of the limitation of government power, not the increase of it' (quoted in Foner, 1998: 159).

Roosevelt excoriated Wilson, arguing that he failed completely to understand the nature of big business and its impact on American economics and politics. He argued that Wilson's vision of limited government action was 'a recipe for the enslavement of the people by the great corporations who can only be held in check by the extension of governmental power; [only the] regulatory, the controlling, and directing power of the government [can represent] the liberty of the oppressed' (quoted in Foner, 1998: 160). Roosevelt lost the election, but his campaign helped to give freedom a modern social and economic content. It established an agenda that would continue to define political liberalism for much of the rest of the century.

The Great Depression had a major impact on the struggle over the interpretation of 'freedom' in the USA. By 1932, the US's GNP had fallen by one-third, prices by nearly one-half, and over 15 million Americans were out of work. For those able to find jobs, real wages fell precipitously:

> Hungry men and women lined the streets of major cities; thousands more inhabited the ramshackle shanty towns called Hoovervilles that sprang up in parks and on abandoned land. . . . No part of America was untouched by the crisis. When he assumed the Presidency in 1933, Franklin D. Roosevelt proclaimed: 'For too many Americans, life is no longer free; liberty no longer real; men can no longer follow the pursuit of happiness.' (quoted in Foner, 1998: 196)

Under Roosevelt's guidance, the Democratic Party led the country towards large-scale state intervention to reconstruct the economy and provide citizens with social security. The Depression discredited the idea that social progress rested on the unrestrained pursuit of wealth and transformed expectations of government. It reinvigorated the Progressive conviction that the national state must protect Americans from the vicissitudes of the marketplace. It placed 'social citizenship', with a broad public guarantee of economic security, at the forefront of American discussions of freedom.

These ideas remained as the mainstream of US political thought for long into the post-war world, reinforced by the massive task of economic and social reconstruction in war-ravaged Europe. For example, in 1975, Arthur Okun, Chairman of the President's Council for Economic Advisors, and, of course, a 'child of the Depression', said: 'The market needs a place and the market should be kept in its place. . . . Given the chance, it would sweep away all other values and establish a vending-machine society. I would not give it more than two cheers' (quoted in Yergin and Stanislaw, 2000: 375).

In the 1950s, a group of conservative thinkers set out to 'reclaim the idea of freedom'. For them, freedom meant de-centralized political power, limited government and a free market economy. The immediate intellectual origins of the movement can be traced back to the publication in 1944 of Friedrich Hayek's book *The Road to Serfdom*. The theme of the book was simple: 'planning for freedom' was an oxymoron, since 'planning leads to dictatorship' (Foner, 1998: 235). Hayek argued that all planning restricted individual liberty, and without 'freedom in economic affairs', political and personal freedom were impossible. Hayek's ideas had a massive influence: 'In effectively equating fascism, and the New Deal, and identifying economic planning with a loss of freedom, he helped lay the foundation for the

rise of modern conservatism, offering a powerful weapon with which
to attack liberalism and the left and inspiring a revival of classic
economic thought' (Foner, 1998: 236). Hayek's ideas were a 'clarion
call for conservatives to reclaim the word "freedom", which, he
charged, had been usurped and distorted by socialists' (Foner, 1998:
236).[15] Milton Friedman became the most famous and influential
intellectual leader of the conservative resurgence. He argued that the
free market was the 'truest expression of freedom' since competition
'gives people what they want', rather than what government planners
think they ought to have (quoted in Foner, 1998: 309).

By the 1980s, and even more forcefully in the 1990s, the dominant
view of 'freedom' in the USA came to be the equation of 'freedom'
with individual choice in the marketplace with minimal interference
from the state. As the US business system became increasingly powerful
globally, the idea gained force that the US should lead the world
towards a single universal free market. One of the earliest expres-
sions of this vision of a 'New World Order' led by the USA was
provided by Barry Goldwater, during the 1964 election campaign.
In his acceptance speech for the Republican Party's nomination for
presidential candidate, he said that God had intended ' "this mighty
republic to be . . . the land of the free", and invoked a vision of a
world united, under American leadership, in "a mighty system" of
freedom, prosperity and interdependence' (quoted in Foner, 1998:
313).

The collapse of the USSR deeply reinforced Americans' confidence
in the free market, and in the country's duty to lead the world towards
this as a universal form of socio-economic organization. By the 1990s,
in the USA there was no serious intellectual challenge to the economic
philosophy of the free market: 'Market utopianism has succeeded
in appropriating the American faith that it is a unique country,
the model for a universal civilization which all societies are fated to
emulate' (Gray, 1998: 104). Free markets have come to be seen not as
'merely one local way of organising a market economy'. Instead, they
have become to be understood to be 'a dictate of human freedom
everywhere' (Gray, 1998: 105). This produced a coincidence of 'the
interests of corporate America and the demands of human freedom'
(Gray, 1998: 109). The explosion of mergers and acquisitions in the
USA in the 1990s helped to increase greatly the political influence
of US big business, with the deep inter-locking power system of
corporate directorships. This influence was reinforced by large changes
in the nature of electoral campaigns that increased the role of big
business in shaping party agendas (see below). This reached new

heights under George W. Bush, with his relationships with the US energy giants (see also below).

The idea that the free market is a moral concept stands at the centre of political discourse in the USA at the start of the twenty-first century. President Bush's security strategy declaration of September 2002 states:

> The concept of 'free trade' arose as a moral principle even before it became a pillar of economics. If you can make something that others value, you should be able to sell it to them. If others make something that you value you should be able to buy it. This is real freedom, the freedom for a person – or nation – to make a living. (Bush, in *FT*, 21 September 2002)

In his speech to West Point Military Academy in 2002, President Bush said: 'Moral truth is the same in every culture, in every time, in every place' (quoted in *FT*, 7 February 2003). In his State of the Union Address to Congress in 2003, he said: 'The liberty we prize is not America's gift to the world, it is God's gift to humanity' (quoted in *FT*, 7 February 2003).[16] The *Financial Times* commented: 'Put another way, America's unparalleled might is to be deployed on the side of indisputable right. You have to go back a while to find such a stark assertion of moral certitude and strategic power' (7 February 2003).

In the wake of 11 September, the US government is even more firmly convinced of its historic function to spread the moral principle of the free market across the whole world:

> The great struggles of the twentieth century between liberty and total-itarianism ended with a decisive victory for the forces of freedom – and a single sustainable model for national success: freedom, democracy and free enterprise. Today, the US enjoys a position of unparalleled military strength, and great economic and political influence. . . . We seek to create a balance of power that favors human freedom. . . . The US will use this opportunity to spread the benefits of freedom across the globe. . . . We will make freedom and the development of democratic institutions key themes in our bilateral relations. (Bush, in *FT*, 21 September 2002)

Bush goes on to say that the US will 'use this moment of opportunity to extend the benefits of freedom across the globe'. In other words, 11 September is viewed as an 'opportunity' to push forward, under the guise of a 'War on Terrorism', US conceptions of a new world order based on the US model.

The idea that the free market is an inherently moral concept, and that the rich, powerful nations are justified in waging war on poorer countries to assert the moral right to extend the sway of the free market, is an old one. In his comments on the British government's violent intrusion into China during the Opium Wars, in order to promote 'free trade', Karl Marx commented: '[T]he artificial obstacles foreign commerce was supposed to encounter on the part of the Chinese authorities, formed, in fact, the great pretext which, in the eyes of the mercantile world, justified every possible outrage against the Celestial Empire' (Marx, 1859: 88).[17]

Through its massive influence within the IMF, and through numerous other channels, the US government has worked tirelessly to promote the free movement of capital around the globe. It presents this as the key to development in poor countries:

> International flows of investment capital are needed to expand the productive potential of [emerging market] economies. These flows allow emerging markets and developing countries to make the investments that raise living standards and reduce poverty. Our long-term objective should be a world in which all countries have investment-grade credit ratings that allow them access to international capital markets and to invest in their future. (Bush, in *FT*, 21 September 2002)

There are still immensely powerful roles in the US economy for the American state, including massive and rising military spending, huge funding of R&D for key sectors in national development, and support for international institutions that advance its ideas. However, among large, developed countries, the USA is now closest to the free market model. It has levels of taxation that are far below those in other high-income countries: under 20 per cent of GDP is taken in taxation, compared with over 30 per cent in the UK, Denmark, France and Sweden, and over 40 per cent in the Netherlands and Belgium (World Bank, *WDR*, 2001: 256–7). Despite this low rate of taxation, the Bush administration is still committed to further tax cuts.

When China tries to 'learn from the USA', which tradition should it turn to: that which argues for a powerful role for the state to ensure positive freedoms for all citizens, or 'free market fundamentalism', whose current intellectual and political ascendancy may turn out to be a relatively brief intermission in the long sweep of US history? The 'United States of America' is not the New Right. As this brief summary has shown, the concept of 'freedom' has been the subject of as much intense debate in the USA as in any other part of the world. The fact is that the pinnacle of influence of the USA's New Right coincides with the period of unprecedented US international business and military power and ideological influence. This is the reality that China has to confront.

The shortcomings of US 'free market fundamentalism' as a model for China

We have seen that in the late twentieth century, as in the late nineteenth century, 'free market fundamentalism' has come to dominate the upper reaches of US political and corporate life. What kind of society has free market fundamentalism produced in the USA since the rise of the New Right? Is this a model that all other societies should wish to emulate? Is it able to solve the complex challenges that China faces?

Inequality   Among the high-income countries, the USA is uniquely unequal. The top 10 per cent of US income earners account for 29 per cent of total income, while the bottom 20 per cent account for less than 5 per cent (World Bank, *WDR*, 2001: 238–9).[18] The Gini coefficient for the inequality of income distribution in the USA stands at 0.40, which places it among a group of developing countries with very unequal income distributions, such as Indonesia (0.37), Nigeria (0.45) and Thailand (0.46). The Gini coefficient for income distribution in the USA is well above that for countries such as the UK (0.33), the Netherlands (0.32) and France (0.33), and far below that of countries such as Finland (0.26), Germany (0.28), Denmark (0.25) and Sweden (0.25). The USA has 19.1 per cent of the population living in poverty, higher than in any other Western industrialized country, and the bottom 10 per cent of the income distribution are absolutely poorer than their counterparts in Europe, Canada and Japan (Hutton, 2002: 149). At the apex of American society stands a group of stupendously rich and powerful people: the top 1 per cent of the population owns 38 per cent of the country's private wealth, a concentration more marked than in any other comparable country (Hutton, 2002: 149). Moreover, there is an abundance of evidence to indicate that levels of inequality in the US have become greater in recent years. Average wages fell steadily in real terms for the twenty years before 1995 for all but the top 20 per cent of the workforce (Hutton, 2002: 164). Only in the late 1990s was there a brief period of growth in average real wages.

The USA has historically been highly unequal, but recent trends have led to polarization between the top and bottom of the distribution of income, wealth and life chances. The scale of inequality is 'almost medieval in scope':

> This inequality is the brutest fact of American life, a standing offence to the American expectation that everyone shall have the opportunity for life, liberty and happiness. It discredits the entire conservative belief system: in the face of this reality, a just society cannot be conceived as an aggregation of morally pure individuals pursuing their own liberty with minimal taxation, minimal government and minimal welfare. (Hutton, 2002: 150)

It is impossible to imagine a justification for the dimensions of inequality in the US in terms of any rational conception of a just society. Numerous political philosophers, from Adam Smith to John Rawls, have argued that the critical criterion of a just society is the way in which it treats it poorest members:

> Servants, labourers, and workmen of different kinds, make up by far the greater part of every great political society. But, what improves the circumstances of the greater part can never be regarded as an inconvenience to the whole. No society can surely be great and flourishing of which the far greater part of the members are poor and miserable. It is but equity besides that they who feed, clothe, and lodge the whole body of the people, should have such a share of the produce of their own labour as to be themselves tolerably well fed, clothed and lodged. (Smith, 1776, Vol. 1: 88)

It is hard to imagine an acceptable theory of justice that could justify such differences even if there were very high degrees of mobility. However, it is precisely the alleged high levels of mobility that the free market provides which have provided the 'moral cement' to justify such extremes of inequality. Milton Friedman, in his book *Capitalism and Freedom*, made the following defence of the US's high degree of inequality:

> Consider two societies that have the same distribution of annual income. In one there is great mobility and change so that the position of particular families in the income hierarchy varies widely from year to year. In the other, there is great rigidity so that each family stays in the same position. Clearly, in any meaningful sense, the second would

be the more unequal society. The one kind of inequality is a sign of dynamic change, social mobility, equality of opportunity; the other of a status society. The confusion behind the two kinds of inequality is particularly important, precisely because competitive free-enterprise capitalism tends to substitute the one for the other. (quoted in Hutton, 2002: 151–2)

In fact, in the USA the degree of social mobility out of the lower part of the class structure is low. Fifty-four per cent of those who were in the bottom 20 per cent of the US income distribution in the 1960s were still there in the 1990s. Only 1 per cent had migrated to the top 20 per cent (Hutton, 2002: 164). An international comparative study of the US, France, Germany, the UK, Norway, Sweden and Denmark found that the USA had the lowest percentage of workers moving from the bottom fifth into the second fifth, and the lowest percentage moving from the bottom fifth into the top 60 per cent (Hutton, 2002: 166). Despite the abundance of evidence, the myth of high mobility persists. Will Hutton comments: 'America is developing an aristocracy of the rich and a concomitant serfdom of the poor. . . . Not only is it deluding itself, it is deluding the entire globe before which it holds itself up as the economic and social model to emulate' (Hutton, 2002: 167).

The high levels of stratification and low levels of social mobility have produced a large underclass with only limited links to the rest of society. This helps to explain why the level of violent crime in the US is far above that in most other high-income countries: the male homicide rate is 12.4 per thousand, compared with only 1.6 per thousand in the EU, and less than one per thousand in Japan (Gray, 1998: 118). In 1997, one out of every fifty adult American males was in jail, and one in twenty was on parole, which is around ten times the rate in Europe (Gray, 1998: 116).

The wide and growing inequality in the distribution of income is reflected in wide and growing inequalities in access to education. In 1979, a student aged 18 to 24 from the top income quartile was four times more likely to obtain a degree by the age of 24 than a student from the bottom quartile. By 1994, he or she was ten times more likely to do so (Hutton, 2002: 155). Behind these figures lies the powerful role for private school and university education. In the battle for success in such a system, income is the crucial determinant of life chances. Studies in the US over many years have consistently shown that around two-thirds of educational achievement is explained by family income (Hutton, 2002: 154).

Social cohesion Numerous writers have analysed the wider human costs of the free market in the United States. A critical weakness is its failure to sustain forms of social cohesion that meet people's fundamental need for security and stability.

The US has a notoriously 'flexible' labour market, with very limited protection from dismissal. The Tennessee Supreme Court in 1884 made the precedent-setting judgement that employers were 'free to discharge or retain employees at will for good cause or for no good cause, or even for bad cause without thereby being guilty of an unlawful act' (quoted in Hutton, 2002: 162). Despite long battles against the employers' freedom to pursue 'employment at will', the trend in recent years has been for rising impermanence of employment. Around 30 per cent of American employees work in 'non-standard' jobs, including part-time, temping, on-call or day-labour (Hutton, 2002: 163). By the end of the twentieth century, 'a young American with at least two years of college [could] expect to change jobs at least eleven times in the course of working, and change his or her skills base at least three times during those forty years of labour' (Sennett, 1998: 23).

US workers are 'free' to work far longer hours than in other high-income countries, and their hours of work are getting longer, with little protection from trade unions. On average, Americans work around fifty hours per week, up from forty in 1973. Moreover, American workers have less paid holiday than other high-income countries. A major reason for the US's recent 'success' in creating jobs has been the necessity of both husbands and wives in the lower income groups to work in order to survive. The fastest-growing category of work has been in female employment in low-paid service sector jobs. Taken in conjunction with long and rising hours of work, this has placed intense pressure on family life. It makes it even harder for parents to raise their own educational level or to provide the necessary support for their children to learn effectively and to be effectively socialized.

In a path-breaking, and much-debated, study, Robert Putnam (2000) has subjected Americans' pattern of living to a meticulous dissection. He has analysed the degree to which social capital has changed, insofar as this can be measured. He believes that social capital develops because people develop patterns of reciprocal behaviour in which mutual support by one party can enable that party to benefit at some future point in their own life (and/or can allow other family members, or future generations of that party's family, to benefit from such support). He believes that the most valuable form of reciprocity is 'generalized reciprocity':

I'll do this for you without expecting anything specific back from you,
in the confident expectation that someone else will do something for
me down the road. . . . A society characterized by generalized reciprocity
is more efficient than a distrustful society, for the same reason that
money is more efficient than barter. If we don't have to balance every
exchange instantly, we can get a lot more accomplished. (Putnam,
2000: 21)

This views social capital as a form of enlightened self-interest based
around inter-temporal 'transactions'. There is an alternative view,
which views support for others as being of intrinsic worth because
the supporting party simply can appreciate what it would feel like to
be assisted in a situation of disadvantage. This is what Confucius and
Adam Smith termed 'benevolence' and Chairman Mao termed 'serve
the people' (see chapter 3).

Putnam found that Americans were 'ceasing to be a nation of par-
ticipators'. Instead, they were turning into 'individualist, suspicious
litigators'. Putnam found that 'America's stock of social capital – the
social networks and norms of reciprocity and trust that make a country
more productive and effective – has been declining' (Nye, 2002: 123).
His conclusion is striking:

For the first two-thirds of the twentieth century a powerful tide bore
Americans into ever deeper engagement in the life of their communities,
but a few decades ago – silently and without warning – that tide
reversed and we were overtaken by a treacherous rip-current. Without
at first noticing, we have been pulled apart from one another and from
our communities over the last third of the century. (Putnam, 2000: 27)

Television occupies a central place in analyses of the role of the
market and consumer choice in the USA. Putnam's study of the decline
of social capital in the USA identifies a powerful potential role for
TV: 'Americans at the end of the twentieth century were watching
more TV, watching it more habitually, more pervasively, and more
often alone, and watching more programs that were associated speci-
fically with civic disengagement (entertainment as distinct from news)'
(Putnam, 2000: 246). Putnam found that those programme types
that are most closely associated with civic isolation 'constitute a massive and growing share of television programming' (Putnam, 2000:
244). The key to this pervasive trend is the impact of the 'free market'
upon the nature of what is offered on US television; moreover, this
trend is gaining strength: ' "Target marketing" and the advent of five-
hundred channel cable TV portend further fragmentation of audiences

along lines of social, economic and personal interest' (Putnam, 2000: 244). Putnam also believes that the drastic increase in the role of TV in daily lives has been associated with a pronounced increase in individualistic, materialistic values conveyed through formal advertising, but, also, increasingly, through advertising embedded within programmes, so that 'fast-forwarding' does not allow an escape from advertising. He found that 'materialism among college students has risen noticeably during the era of maximum television exposure' (Putnam, 2000: 245).

The research for Putnam's study pre-dated the revolution in information technology in the late 1990s. Already, around one-fifth of US homes have a 'home entertainment centre', consisting of a big-screen television and 'surround-sound'. One cultural analyst has commented:

> We are in a period in our culture where we're looking in our leisure time for things that will anaesthetize us: It's no surprise – if you are reasonably fortunate, the American home is a seductive place, with incredibly comfortable armchairs, TVs with an unimaginable choice of channels, a refrigerator with plenty of high-cholesterol snacks and a microwave to prepare them in. (Robert Thomson, quoted in *FT*, 25 January 2003)

Already, millions of Americans use digital links to shop, learn, work and play, 'liberated from the messiness of physical contact with others': 'The ability to construct a domestic lifestyle adorned with pleasures, services and adventures once attainable only by venturing out of the home has been brought to millions by willing carriers – from the pizza delivery boy to broadband cable' (*FT*, 25 January 2003). This is already uncomfortably close to Aldous Huxley's *Brave New World*, with 'soma', 'feelies' and 'pneumatic sex'.

The extreme emphasis on individual rights rather than social duties has produced the world's most litigious society: after the 1970s, the ratio of lawyers to the rest of the population 'suddenly exploded, more than doubling in the next quarter century. . . . We rely increasingly on formal institutions, and above all on the law, to accomplish what we used to accomplish through informal networks reinforced by generalized reciprocity – that is, through social capital' (Putnam, 2000: 146). The USA has 300 lawyers per 100,000 citizens, compared with 12 per 100,000 in Japan, and around 100 per 100,000 in the UK and Germany (Gray, 1998: 118). The law has become one of the US's fastest-growing professions: 'Co-operation is giving way to a pervasive adversarialism in which confrontation and litigation, rather than community endeavour or political action, are seen as the principal means of achieving one's goals.' As the individualization and competitiveness of society has penetrated ever more deeply into the moral fabric, the appeal to litigation has permeated large areas of private life, 'where norms, traditions and expectations of reciprocal behaviour used to define accepted practices' (Hutton, 2002: 160) such as bringing up children, responses to death, and relationships between the sexes.

A consequence of the breakdown in social cohesion and rise in insecurity has been the rapid rise of high-income people living in privately guarded buildings or housing developments, with around 28 million Americans (10 per cent of the total) living in this fashion (Gray, 1998: 116): 'The private, gated communities whose high walls and electronic security devices protect their inmates from the dangers of the society they have deserted are a mirror image of America's prisons. They stand as a symbol of the hollowing-out of other social institutions – the family, the neighbourhood, even the business corporation – that in the past supported a functioning society' (Gray, 1998: 119). The phenomenon of the gated community achieves its most extreme form in the fully independent incorporated cities where residents 'declare their political independence'. Exempt from state (but not federal) taxes, they collect their own taxes and provide their own benefits: 'Formally called "home-owners associations", they are the most complete expression of opting out and detachment; their members need never come near public institutions or participate in wider civic life' (Hutton, 2002: 159). The terms of admission to the communities can include 'a minimum age for children and weight for dogs'. Intruders can be shot.

In the wake of 11 September, the whole of the United States adopted a siege mentality that eerily parallels the efforts of rich Americans to protect themselves from the poor within their own society. By 2007, the US government will be spending US$31 billion on the newly created Department of Homeland Security. It will ultimately house 170,000 employees and parts of twenty-two different government agencies. Despite the 'extraordinary efforts' taken in the wake of 11 September, there are 'few in Washington who believe the country is safer than it was before September 11' (FT, 19 November 2002). A 'blistering' study from the Council on Foreign Relations released in October 2002 concluded: 'America remains dangerously unprepared to prevent and respond to a catastrophic terrorist attack on US soil. In all likelihood, the next attack will result in even greater casualties and widespread disruption to American lives and the economy' (quoted in FT, 19 November 2002). The worries were greatly accentuated by the war against Iraq: 'The more we move to tighten up on external threats, the higher the risk becomes at home' (Gary Hart, chair of the panel that produced the report).

Consumption choices   US businesses have more 'freedom' to produce freely in the pursuit of profit than in any other high-income country. This has produced perverse results. That 'freedom' is reflected in the comprehensive dominance of the whole structure of transport by the auto industry for private consumption. The auto industry has a massive network of related businesses, including auto components, highway construction, auto finance, advertising, auto and personal insurance, oil, steel, glass, electronics, aluminium and plastics. No less than eight of the top ten *Fortune* 500 companies are in the auto and oil sectors. US consumers have the 'right' freely to consume autos, but the country has a hopelessly inadequate system of public transport. Largely due to the dominance of 'individual choice' in respect to the consumption of autos, the US accounts for over 22 per cent of total world CO_2 emissions. It consumes 60 per cent more commercial energy per capita than the average for high-income countries, and the country has 70 per cent more injuries and deaths from road accidents per 100,000 people than the average for high-income countries (UNDP, *HDR*, 1999).

The dominance of 'individual choice' in the food industry has contributed to an alarming rise in obesity. The US Surgeon-General estimates that 61 per cent of Americans are overweight and warns that there are now 300,000 obesity-related deaths per year (*FT*, 23 November 2002). It is estimated that around 9 million Americans are 'morbidly overweight', and 10 million more are 'almost there, teetering on the edge' (*Guardian*, 11 January 2003). The associated public-health costs are estimated at US$117 billion a year (*Fortune*, 3 February 2003). Around US$33 billion per year spent is spent on weight-loss products and schemes (*Guardian*, 11 January 2003). The US food industry spends around US$4.5 billion each year to advertise its products (*Fortune*, 3 February 2003). Children are the prime target for advertising. The average American child watches over 20,000 TV advertisements for food products each year: 'the more television children watch, the more they eat' (*Guardian*, 11 January 2003). In the USA, it is children who increasingly dictate family food choices: 'Entire households are immersed in a miasma of one-dimensional sweet taste that reinforces juvenile preferences' (*Guardian*, 11 January 2003). Moreover, the food industry has a powerful incentive to persuade children to eat more: 'Fat is money. By creating heavier individuals who need more calories to feel satisfied and maintain their weight, the food industry is literally growing a bigger market for itself' (*FT*, 23 November 2002).

Political choice   The ever-greater impact of the 'free market' has been felt strongly in the political process. The growth in importance of the mass media in winning elections has contributed to escalating costs of running campaigns. The large and growing inequality of income and wealth has given free market conservatives a steadily increasing voice in US politics. The power of corporate lobbyists to influence the political agenda has long been recognized. Of those who made individual contributions, in 1997, 81 per cent earned over US$100,000, giving a powerful bias towards the voice of the upper income earners.[19] The influence of powerful financial interests, both corporate and individual, was centrally important in the liberalization of financial services in the US in the 1990s, as well as in the US-led drive to liberalize financial services across the world (see below). Within both the Democrats and the Republicans, the fundraisers have become the key figures in selecting which politicians will be chosen to represent the party: 'If they feel they cannot sell a politician to their donors, then effectively they have the right of veto. Thus, both the face of the politician and the policies they espouse are effectively dictated by money' (Hutton, 2002: 171). Hutton considers that this 'ever onward encroachment of the market and its values' has 'invaded and polluted the heart of the [US] political process' (Hutton, 2002: 170).

The driving force of the conservative lobby has been to maintain low taxes and a small state: 'The watchwords for a successful capitalism are liberty, flexibility, self-interest, welfare and enterprise. Its enemies are the "burdens" of regulation, taxation, welfare and any form of social obligation' (Hutton, 2002: 178). A small group of super-rich have become so appalled at the prospect for American society of current trends that are destroying social cohesion that they have opposed the policies to reduce taxation still further, and in 1997 established a 'Campaign for Responsible Taxation'. The group of billionaires, led by Warren Buffet, promised to use their tax savings from recent legislation (which planned to reduce, and eventually eliminate, capital gains and inheritance tax) to fund a campaign to establish a system of fairer taxation. Buffet argues that the US is in danger of 'developing an aristocracy of the wealthy', in which 'the society's likely leaders of tomorrow are the children of the wealthy today' (quoted in Hutton, 2002: 153). The pleas of this eccentric group fell on deaf ears. In 2003 George W. Bush introduced legislation that proposed massive tax cuts that were widely acknowledged to deliver heavily disproportionate benefits to the rich.[20]

The mainstream of US political opinion maintains a contemptuous attitude towards the attempts in Europe to retain a sense of social cohesiveness through state action. For example, Zbigniew Brzezinski observes: 'The crisis of political legitimacy and economic vitality that Western Europe increasingly confronts . . . is deeply rooted in the pervasive expansion of the state-sponsored social structure that favors protectionism and parochialism. The result is a cultural condition that combines escapist hedonism with spiritual emptiness' (Brzezinski, 1997: 73).

Financial de-regulation   After the 1970s, the US moved remorselessly towards removing regulation of financial markets. This process was powerfully driven by the self-interest of Wall Street banks and their ability to influence US politicians. The pursuit of 'market fundamentalism' in the financial industry to the immense benefit of private financial interests produced disastrous results.

De-regulation in the early 1980s lay behind the Savings and Loans (S&Ls) disaster. The move to de-regulate the industry was 'spearheaded in large part by members of Congress with ties to the thrift industry' (Calavita et al., 1997: 11). The original objective of the S&Ls had been to provide home mortgages on a tightly regulated basis. In the early 1980s, de-regulation included lifting the controls on interest rates; removal of constraints on the categories of investment that the S&Ls could make; removal of controls over brokering of deposits; and removal of requirements that each S&L should have a minimum number of stockholders (Calavita et al., 1997: 12–13). On signing the 'fateful' Garn–St Germain Depository Institutions Bill of 1982, which provided the final seal on most important aspects of de-regulation in the S&L industry, President Reagan said: 'I think we've hit a home run here.' He called the law the 'Emancipation Proclamation for America's Savings Institutions' (quoted in Calavita et al., 1997: 12). At the same time, federal insurance for the industry was strengthened, 'laying the foundations for risk-free fraud' (Calavita et al., 1997: 11). De-regulating interest rates stimulated an escalating 'competition for deposits, as brokered deposits sought ever higher returns' (Calavita et al., 1997: 14). De-regulation led to intense competition among the thrifts for 'hot' brokered deposits, and opened up the door to 'pervasive and systematic fraud': 'With federally insured deposits flowing in, virtually all restrictions on thrift investment powers removed, and new owners flocking to the industry, deregulators had combined in one package the opportunity for lucrative fraud and the irresistible force of temptation' (Calavita et al., 1997: 14).

The 1990s saw an unprecedented wave of de-regulation in the US financial services industry. This culminated in the Gramm–Leach–Bliley Act, passed in 1999, which demolished the 1930s-era walls which had prevented brokerage firms from moving into other financial services, such as insurance. Part of the reason that Wall Street is able to 'keep regulators and legislators at bay' through de-regulation is the 'immense amount of money the firms spend on political donations and lobbying' (FT, 24 July 2002). It is estimated that Wall Street banks and securities firms donated more than US$30 million to politicians and their parties in 1999 while de-regulation was being debated. Citigroup, 'which has been perhaps the most active of the Wall Street firms in Washington', spent US$25 million in lobbying in the three years leading up to the Gramm–Leach–Blilely Act, 'one of the largest expenditures on influence-peddling by any US company over the period (FT, 24 July 2002). The commercial banks have 'not let up'. They donated US$1.3 million to George W. Bush's presidential campaign, four times their donation to his opponent Al Gore. Citigroup gave US$2.8 million to political campaigns in 2000 (FT, 24 July 2002).

Enron's driving goal for much of the 1990s was to achieve de-regulation of the energy industry. This opened the door for it to become a multi-channel financial firm under the guise of an 'energy trader'. A key to Enron's growth was the de-regulation of the credit derivatives industry: 'On Friday night 15 December 2000, Congress passed complex and highly technical legislation which essentially ensured that much of the US$94,000 billion (94 trillion) over-the-counter derivatives industry would operate outside the nation's commodity laws' (FT, 7 January 2002). The legislation specifically excluded energy swaps from government oversight. Enron's e-commerce site, EnronOnline, was technically trading in energy derivatives, but it rapidly expanded into almost every single field of derivatives, basically free of government regulation. It swiftly became one of the world's most active players in the de-regulated credit derivatives market (FT, 7 January 2002).

Wendy Gramm was a former chairman of the Commodities Futures Trading Commission. Her husband is Texas Senator Phil Gramm, who was instrumental in passing the Gramm–Leach–Blilely Act. Both were strong proponents of de-regulation. In 1992, Wendy Gramm began the process of legislation that was to lead to the eventual de-regulation of energy swaps. Shortly after leaving the Commission she joined the board of Enron. Between 1993 and 2001, she earned over US$500,000 in fees as an Enron board member. She also received stocks and dividends worth between US$915,000 and US$1.85 million over the same period. Her tax return for 2001 listed her as owning assets of US$250,000–$500,000 in an Enron Deferred Compensation Fidelity Balanced Fund (*FT*, 7 January 2002). Phil Gramm 'played a key role in getting the Commodities Futures Modernization Act passed in December 2000', which 'deregulated all financial derivatives and relaxed oversight of commodity exchanges' (*FT*, 7 January 2002).

In the last presidential cycle, many of the leading US corporations each donated multi-millions of dollars to the US political parties. For example, Microsoft gave US$4.6 million, Citigroup, US$3.9 million and Enron, US$2.5 million (*FT*, 16 January 2002). Enron spent US$10.2 million 'influencing Washington politicians during the previous two election cycles' (*FT*, 9 February 2002).[21] President George W. Bush alone received US$623,000 in Enron campaign contributions over the course of his political career (*FT*, 12 January 2002).

It was revealed also that Mr Bush made US$12 million as a result of 'two remarkable windfalls' connected with his involvement with the Texas Rangers baseball team. These were a big tax increase levied on local residents in order to fund a new stadium for the Rangers, and the decision by his partners to reward him for his efforts by handing him a large part of their share of the partnership. Some of these partners 'did very well in their dealings with the state of Texas after Mr Bush became governor' (*FT*, 19 July 2002). Mr Bush's Vice-President, Dick Cheney, was revealed to have cashed out his shares in energy services provider Halliburton, the company of which he was the CEO, close to the top of the market in the summer of 2000. Thereafter, the share crashed by 75 per cent in two years. Halliburton was under investigation by the Securities and Exchange Commission (SEC) for alleged misreporting of revenues and profits (*FT*, 19 July 2002). Mr Bush's Army Secretary, Thomas White, was formerly Vice-Chairman of Enron Energy Services. In the summer of 2002, it was alleged that Mr White knew about trading practices at the company that inflated electricity prices in California, and that he sold US$12 million in Enron stock during a five-month period as the company was collapsing (*FT*, 19 July 2002).

When Mr Bush lamented that the 'economic binge' of the 1990s had resulted in 'hangover' that needed to be cured through 'a new era of responsibility', the *Financial Times* commented:

Here was a man who grew rich in the 1990s beyond the wildest dreams of any 401(K) investor, lecturing us on the perils of exuberance and importance of the hairshirt. Here was a man who made his money through a combination of impresssive connections and a huge subsidy from taxpayers bemoaning the morals of those who tried to make a quick buck. Here was a man who spent much of his time in office richly rewarding the wealthy friends who helped put him there, wagging his finger at the lowering of standards among those in public life. Here was a man whose loyal lieutenant, Dick Cheney, vice-president, made tens of millions of dollars as boss of a classic go-go company of the late 1990s. (19 July 2002)

The 'free market' in financial services produced a string of gigantic financial scandals. The first great scandal was the aforementioned Savings and Loans débâcle in the 1980s, facilitated by de-regulation of the industry. The Resolution Trust Corporation (RTC), established by the US government to direct the gigantic 'clean-up' of the sector, concluded that criminal activity was suspected in two-thirds of all RTC-controlled institutions (Calavita et al., 1997: 28). The scale of criminal activity was enormous. In 1987 and 1988 alone, the Federal Home Loan Bank Board referred more than 11,000 S&L cases to the Justice Department for investigation and possible criminal prosecution (Calavita et al., 1997: 28). A study of the S&Ls by Akerlof and Romer concluded: 'evidence of looting abounds'. They estimated the cost to the US taxpayer of criminal wrongdoing in the S&L crisis at no less than US$54 billion (quoted in Calavita et al., 1997: 29).

In the wake of the bursting of the US equity market bubble, another set of incredible financial scandals erupted, calling into question the consequences of de-regulation in financial markets. Among other effects, de-regulation of financial services allowed non-financial firms to enter the financial sector on a widespread basis. Using the proliferation of techniques made available by modern information technology, closely advised by Wall Street's leading banks and by the leading accountants, it became almost impossible to control these entities, which were able to speculate on a vast scale.

Enron was the most dramatic, but by no means the only, example. The incredible complexity of Enron's business structure made regulation a nightmare. The complexity was greatly increased by the de-regulation of US financial services, which allowed financial firms to enter almost any area: 'Enron turned itself from a power company into a trader in everything from energy to bandwidth' (*FT*, 18 January 2002). At its height it offered 'more than 1,200 products, including bandwidth derivatives, weather derivatives, emission credits, pipeline capacity and credit derivatives' (*FT*, 7 January 2002). It would have required armies of highly skilled experts to monitor the company's behaviour.

Accounts are at the heart of the capitalist system. Without agreed methods of constructing company accounts, and without honest and accurate public accounts, the capital allocation process cannot function effectively. By the late 1990s, a spate of mergers and acquisitions had resulted in the situation that only five giant accountancy firms were left across the world. The 'Big Five' (PwC; Andersen; Deloitte, Touche and Tohmatsu; Ernst and Young; and KPMG) accounted for almost all the auditing work in global corporations. Alongside their auditing work, the giant accountancy firms had developed lucrative business as financial consultants. The auditing side of the firm typically was then required to evaluate the various accounting artifices introduced by the consulting side of the firm.

The collapse of Enron in late 2001 brought the problems of the accountancy profession sharply into the public light. When Enron began its transformation from 'a boring pipeline company' into an energy trading business in the mid-1980s, it began a long partnership with Andersen. Andersen both audited the company and closely advised on financial issues: 'This gave them an almost incestuous relationship' (*FT*, 12 January 2002). The Enron scandal erupted when the company was forced to re-state its accounts for the year 2000. Enron was described by the *Financial Times* as a 'virtual company': Enron bolstered its profits by 'booking income immediately on contracts that would take ten years to complete. It moved debts into partnerships it created and in effect controlled, even though defined by auditors as off-balance-sheet' (*FT*, 4 February 2002). Participants in the partnerships included most of the main US financial institutions, such as Merrill Lynch, J.P. Morgan, Citigroup, Lehman Brothers, Credit Suisse First Boston and GE Capital (*FT*, 5 February 2002). Enron used these entities to manipulate its accounts at the end of each quarter and employed financial derivatives and other complex transactions aggressively to the same end. It masked poorly performing assets with rapid deal making (*FT*, 4 February 2002). The construction of complex off-balance-sheet vehicles was a widely used practice in US financial firms in the 1990s: 'That this type of off-balance-sheet behaviour is a common feature of modern finance has raised a question for the entire banking sector' (*FT*, 2 February 2002). The leading accountancy firms were closely involved through their consultancy arms in advising on the construction of such schemes. They cast doubt on the degree of objectivity of the Big Five in undertaking their auditing work.

The most explosive period in the bubble in Enron's stock price growth was after the de-regulation of the credit derivatives industry and the launch of EnronOnline, 'the world's biggest web-based transactions system'. Enron conveyed an impression of a company perfectly suited to the new economy: 'Enron is a bull market machine. Its investor relations and culture – even its business model – were ideally suited to the confidence that pervaded Wall Street in the 1990s' (*FT*, 12 November 2001). One commentator said: 'Wall Street is a fashion show and Enron was fashionable. The analysts were not analysing. They were believing' (quoted in *FT*, 12 November 2001). Enron was regarded as the model of the 'new economy':

> For year after year, it was voted the most innovative company in America. Its peers also put it top of the list for the quality of its management. Business gurus, investment analysts and the media described it as one of the great companies of the century. It had a heavyweight board of directors, which appeared to tick off all the boxes for good corporate governance. Its auditors and financial advisors seemed beyond reproach. (*FT*, 15 December 2001)

Enron was recognized as lacking transparency, but even this was seen as a virtue by analysts: 'Its finances were very complex, very sophisticated. . . . There was an arrogance about the management that made many analysts loath to admit to the company that Enron's accounting was beyond them. . . . Nobody wanted to admit that because they could not get to the bottom of Enron's financial dealings, they could not recommend one of Wall Street's best-performing stocks' (*FT*, 12 November 2001). One analyst observed that the lack of transparency 'suggested dynamism: the company was growing so fast and conquering so many new and unsupervised areas that even Enron had a hard time explaining all it did' (*FT*, 12 November 2001). The bubble was self-feeding as Enron's market capitalization climbed from US$2 billion to nearly US$70 billion at the peak of the US stock market bubble. Once the bubble burst with the revelation of inappropriate use of off-balance-sheet vehicles, 'Enron's attributes, so useful in a bull market, suddenly became liabilities. Where the business's impenetrability had once given investors scope for optimism, it now left them to imagine some dreadful secret – or even a crime' (*FT*, 12 November 2001).

No sooner had the Enron affair begun to die down than fresh auditing scandals erupted. In late March 2002, the SEC indicted several senior officers of Waste Management with 'massive fraud'. Waste Management had been obliged to restate its earnings for 1998 by US$1.43 billion, 'the largest restatement in US history'. The SEC said: 'Defendants were allegedly aided in their fraud by the company's long-time auditor, Arthur Andersen, which repeatedly issue unqualified audit reports on the company's materially false and misleading financial statements' (quoted in *FT*, 27 March 2002). A further disaster awaited Andersen. In late June it was revealed that the telecommunications giant WorldCom had massively falsified its accounts. It boosted the company's reported profits for 2001 and the first quarter of 2002 by treating US$3.8 billion of costs as capital spending, a fraud of 'breathtaking simplicity' (*FT*, 27 June 2002). This was the largest reported fraud in corporate history. The outside auditing firm was, once again, Arthur Andersen: 'The sheer scale of the financial misstatement – almost $4 billion – makes auditor denials difficult, though not impossible, to swallow' (*FT*, 27 June 2002).

Questions about the accounting profession's role in the audit of large US companies were brought under further scrutiny by the case of Adelphia, the sixth-largest US cable operator. Adelphia filed for bankruptcy under Chapter 11 in June 2002, the fifth largest bankruptcy in US history. Five senior executives were arrested in July (*FT*, 25 July 2002). These included the company's founder, John Rigas, his two sons, and two others. The decline in the company's fortunes began in March 2002 when it was disclosed that it had large off-balance-sheet entities controlled by the Rigas family. The five executives were charged with orchestrating 'one of the biggest frauds ever to take place at a US public company'. US government officials declared that they had 'looted Adelphia on a massive scale, using the company as the Rigas family piggy bank', causing losses to investors of billions of dollars (*FT*, 25 July 2002).

The way in which de-regulation of financial services combined with incredible greed was well illustrated by the exposure of so-called 'spinning' during the collapse of WorldCom. This practice involved investment banks giving certain customers preferential access to stocks in initial public offerings (IPOs) in order to win their firm's investment banking business. During the 'IT frenzy' in the US, initial public offerings of IT firms were typically 'hugely undervalued when they went to market', rising strongly in price even on the first day's trading (*FT*, 29 August 2002). During the collapse of WorldCom it was revealed that WorldCom chief Bernie Ebbers personally (i.e. as an individual retail client) was allocated 800,000 shares in telecoms IPOs by Salomon Brothers. In one case, Ebbers received two-thirds of the entire retail allotment of share for a telecoms IPO. All the telecoms shares he was allocated 'rose sharply' on the first day's trading. He is estimated to have shown paper profits on the first day's trading alone of more than US$1 million for each of his 'investments' in Nextlink, McLeod USA and Qwest.

Arthur Levitt, the SEC's regulator at the time, was 'scathing' about the allocation: 'This is a practice I totally abhor, but the [SEC's] enforcement division was simply unable to find a violation of securities laws at the time' (quoted in *FT*, 19 August 2002). In 1999, under Levitt's chairmanship, the SEC examined the issue of allocations of shares in IPOs, and concluded that there was no case to bring against investment banks favouring clients, 'particularly as there was no evidence of the other side of the transaction, no *quid pro quo* for receipt of shares in a hot new company virtually guaranteed to rise in price'. Some SEC staff 'thought the process unethical', but 'no action was taken' (*FT*, 29 August 2002). Some securities lawyers argue that the investment banks were just 'serving their shareholders': 'The bank's business was being improved by attempting to please favored clients.' The lawyers said that there was 'no distinction to be made between companies receiving shares or senior executives being handed allocations as private clients'. Of course, 'it would be criminal behavior . . . if someone at the investment bank personally gained from the practice'. Arthur Levitt commented simply: 'It looks to me like commercial bribery' (quoted in *FT*, 29 August 2002). After the revelations at WorldCom it emerged that the practice had been widespread in Wall Street investment banks during the 1990s.

As the revelations of corporate fraud escalated in the year 2002, the Chairman of the Federal Reserve, Alan Greenspan, made his famous comment that the root of the breakdown in US corporate governance lay in the 'infectious greed' that had accompanied the 'irrational exuberance' of the late 1990s (*FT*, 20 July 2002). These sentiments recall those of J.K. Galbraith, writing about the Great Crash that followed the 'Great Bubble' in the US economy in the 1920s: 'American enterprise in the twenties had opened its hospitable arms to an exceptional number of promoters, grafters, swindlers, imposters, and frauds. This, in the long history of such activities, was a flood tide of corporate larceny' (Galbraith, 1992: 195). The same description seems apt for the late 1990s.

The boundary separating the legal from the illegal tends to be particularly blurred in financial services. In part, this is due to the unique potential for constructing extremely complex transactions, which may make it hard to determine the final nature of the action:

> [Because] the essence of insider abuse and fraud is deceit, it almost invariably requires false records and statements to be supplied to the regulators. Indeed, deliberate insider abuse of any kind by definition constitutes a breach of fiduciary duty to the institution. That such activities are rarely prosecuted speaks to the burden of proof required and the difficulties of prosecution. (Calavita et al., 1997: 23)

In part, the relative absence of prosecution for financial crime may be because the fact that risk is central to the sector makes it hard to evaluate whether a particular action is a consequence of an intention to defraud, incompetence or movements in asset values and market behaviour that could not reasonably be predicted. Is a loan made to a third party by a financial firm non-repayable because of poor risk evaluation, or because the creditor knew that the debtor had no intention of repaying? It is near impossible to prosecute many types of white-collar crime in financial institutions:

> There are a number of perfect or near perfect crimes that are available to insiders who wish to loot their banks. . . . [For example,] the bank insider could have a speculative project of his own. He could mention this project to prospective borrowers from the bank without ever saying that the provision of the loan was dependent on the borrower purchasing an interest in his project. Soon, the major borrowers from the bank (all of whom would default) would buy interests in his project. Another perfect crime. (Calavita et al., 1997: 21)

Conclusion

A significant minority of US opinion still clings to the hope that the US will turn away from the current path of development and take a different path that is more in tune with the real needs of the whole society. Richard Sennett concludes his study of the consequences of the changing nature of work in the USA as follows: '[A] regime which provides human beings no deep reasons to care about one another cannot long preserve its legitimacy' (Sennett, 1998: 148). The US economy has survived the downturn in the collapse in the stock market bubble relatively unscathed. However, should the USA encounter more serious economic turbulence, one can imagine that confidence in free market fundamentalism would be eroded, just as it was during the Great Depression.

While ideologues among the economics profession may support 'free market fundamentalism', and quote in their support Adam

Smith's 'invisible hand', the more deep-thinking economic theorists have persistently pointed out that Smith's invisible hand could by no means solve all economic problems. For example, Frank Hahn's lecture on the invisible hand cautioned that 'the limitations on the applicability of pure market theory are numerous and many of them quite serious' (Hahn, 1984: 132). He argues that these limitations have deep implications for practical economic policy:

> The predominant conclusion [about the invisible hand] must be that we are quite uncertain of what really is the case. The pretence that it is otherwise comes under the heading of religion or magic. Once the uncertainty is recognized it will greatly affect the set of rational or reasonable actions. Traditional theory . . . suggests that, exceptional and near-catastrophic circumstances apart, it will not in general be wise to put all your eggs in one basket or to give harsh pulls on levers, unless you are what economists call a risk-lover. . . . But risk loving itself is unreasonable. . . . [T]hese are the reasons why . . . the wishy-washy, step-by-step, case-by-case approach seems to me the only reasonable one in economic policy. (Hahn, 1984: 3)

It is precisely the 'wishy-washy', step-by-step, case-by-case approach that has governed China's philosophy of 'reform and opening-up' since the late 1970s. As we shall see in chapter 3, China's own long economic history has also exemplified a similar approach to relations between the state and market.

It is hard to imagine a less relevant philosophy for the deep challenges that China faces than the extreme form of 'market funda-mentalism' that has come to dominate mainstream US politics since the 1980s. The only part of Asia where these ideas have been sub-stantially implemented is Hong Kong. Even this affluent, highly devel-oped city-state, however, the massive beneficiary of the efforts of the Chinese government and people across the border, is experiencing its own deep problems. These include the emergence of deep social divisions; ecological failure; attacks on its prosperity due to the im-pact of global economic forces; deep misgivings about its long-run capability to compete on the 'global level playing field' with Shanghai; and a pervasive sense of loss of social cohesiveness in an intensely individualistic and materialist environment. This cannot serve as a suitable model to solve the challenges facing the 1.3 billion people on the Chinese Mainland. It would provide 'fuel on the fire' of the deep problems that the country faces at this stage in its development.

The left wing: Backwards to Maoism?

There is still a serious segment of domestic Chinese opinion, and a certain amount of international scholarly opinion, that can be called the 'left wing', and this is sympathetic to a return to the Maoist development path.

The relationship of the state to society and to the market was a central issue after the seizure of power by the Communist Party in 1949. In the early years after the revolution, in the cities the Party allowed a mixed economy, and in the countryside it allowed private agriculture alongside the development of mutual aid institutions to meet people's needs in health, education and finance. However, in 1953, the Party began the push towards 'socialist transformation'. By 1956, most farmers had entered collective farms, most of the industrial means of production had been nationalized, most prices were under direct state control, foreign assets had been expropriated and international trade was strictly regulated. For the next two decades, the market economy was driven underground. Indeed, during the Cultural Revolution, capitalism was likened to a 'dog in the water', to be 'beaten with a stick and drowned'.

In the sharpest contrast with the USSR, Chairman Mao led the Chinese Communist Party in an attempt drastically to attack social inequality. This amounted to nothing less than trying to transform people's work motivation, to overcome the classic 'principal–agent' problem, by liberating human productive energies from the link with material reward. 'Serve the people' (*wei renmin fuwu*) was the foundation of Maoist ideology. The phrase was first enunciated by Mao in 1944, in a speech at the memorial meeting in honour of Zhang Side.[22]

Mao believed that under the leadership of the Communist Party it would be possible to build a non-capitalist, humane society which provided the opportunity for the whole population to fulfil their human potential. It was a philosophy that was powerfully driven by the intention to restrict drastically the population's 'negative' freedoms to act in accordance with their individual wishes free of external restriction, while providing the maximum equality of opportunity for citizens to achieve their 'positive freedoms'.

During the Great Leap Forward and again in the Cultural Revolution, the Party leadership led the drive to reduce drastically inequalities in the workplace. It was accepted that, as in the USSR, it was necessary in the 'socialist' phase to stimulate workers' enthusiasm through the principle of 'from each according to their labour', which Marx termed 'bourgeois right':

> Under this mode of distribution, each and every person's labor is rewarded on the basis of an equal standard – labor is the measure and from that perspective [the reward] appears equal. But great differences exist in the conditions of individual laborers: some are stronger, some weaker; some have a higher cultural level, some a lower one; some have more mouths to feed, some fewer and so forth. Therefore, to use a unified measure of labor as the measure of distribution and to apply this to very unequal individuals must result in real inequality and differences of living standards. The peculiarities of bourgeois right manifest themselves; equal right will in fact be the premise of inequality. (Comrades, 1974: 596–7)

The explicit goal of the Party under Mao's leadership, especially during the Great Leap Forward (1958–9) and the Cultural Revolution (1966–76), was to push beyond the 'socialist' stage and towards the goal of a 'communist' society:

> In a socialist society, it is necessary to acknowledge the differences in the rewards for labor, but the differences ought not to be too great. We must actively create the conditions for communist society's stage, 'from each according to their abilities, to each according to their needs', and should constantly strive to lessen the three great differences and increasingly extirpate the influence of bourgeois right. (Comrades, 1974: 597)

Under Mao, the Party's avowed aims were those of 'gradually lessening differences' and 'gradually increasing the element of "distribution according to need"' (Comrades, 1974: 597). It was argued that various types of welfare measures and so forth were in reality the 'sprouts of communist distribution according to need': 'We ought to rationally and gradually shrink, not expand, the distance between the individual incomes of the masses of the people and those of the functionaries in the party, the national government, in industry, and in the people's communes' (Comrades, 1974: 598). The Party leadership advocated 'resolutely upholding the principle of the Paris Commune and opposing the system of high salaries (for the few)': '[This] has the advantage of promoting intimate relations between the party and masses, provides a style of plain living and hard struggle, and contributes the revolutionization of the thinking of many cadres' (Comrades, 1974: 597–8).

Mao believed that through overcoming the irrationality and selfishness of a class society, the Chinese people's productive capabilities could be released. On the eve of the Great Leap Forward in 1958, he said: 'Now our enthusiasm has been aroused. Ours is an ardent nation, now swept by a burning tide. . . . Our nation is like an atom. When this atom's nucleus is smashed, the thermal energy released will have really tremendous power. . . . [W]e shall catch up with Britain within fifteen years' (quoted in Selden, 1979: 382).

From the mid-1950s, when the collectivization of agriculture was accomplished and industrial planning implemented, through to the mid-1970s, China made great progress in many key aspects of social and economic development. The growth rate of national product was faster than in most developing countries.

In normal times, the mass of the people enjoyed a high degree of livelihood security. Most impressive of all, the country achieved enormous advances in health and education. For many economists, the key indicator of development are 'basic needs' in nutrition, health and education. By the mid-1970s, China's levels of infant mortality and child death rates had fallen to exceptionally low levels compared with other developing countries. Infant mortality had fallen to just 71 per thousand compared with 124 per thousand in other low-income countries (excluding India) and 81 per thousand in middle-income countries. Life expectancy at birth, arguably the most important single indicator of development, had risen from 36 years pre-1949 to 71 years in 1981, an extraordinary achievement (Nolan, 1995: 49). The system also provided a high degree of security, drastically reducing the age-old fear of an unforeseen personal, natural or economic disaster that was the reality for every farm family and for a large fraction of the urban workforce in pre-revolutionary China.

These achievements were applauded by numerous Western scholars as evidence that redistributive policies could enable low-income countries to achieve high levels of 'basic needs' long before average per capita incomes had risen to high levels.

Alongside these enormous achievements, however, the Maoist period also resulted in deeply problematic outcomes. Diversity of thought was crushed. Large numbers of people were imprisoned for their political views. Freedom of cultural expression was dramatically narrowed, causing large-scale damage to people's welfare. The intense political struggles to limit social differentiation caused immense suffering to innumerable participants.

Although growth rates were high, they were achieved in a highly inefficient way, with slow technical progress, a long-run fall in capital productivity, and stagnation in average per capita incomes after the mid-1950s. Apart from improvements in consumption of a narrow range of consumer durables (the 'four big goods' – watches, bicycles, radios and sewing machines), per capita consumption of most other items either stagnated or declined (Nolan, 1995: 49).

Although 'basic needs' indicators improved greatly, the World Bank estimates that the proportion of the population in absolute poverty remained at around 30 per cent in the mid-1970s, totalling around 270 million people, compared with around 190 million in 1957 (Nolan, 1995: 50).

Most disturbing of all, the utopian attempt to leap into a communist society during the Great Leap Forward resulted in a colossal man-made disaster: work incentives were eroded, production schedules were wrecked by the focus on political struggle, and ill-conceived schemes of capital construction (notably the massive movement to extend the amount of irrigation, and the ill-fated 'backyard iron and steel campaign') caused immense waste. The result was an estimated collapse in national output of around 35 per cent from 1958 to 1962. The collapse in farm output caused the biggest famine of the twentieth century, with as many as 30 million 'excess deaths' (Nolan, 1995: 48).

The Maoist period left many valuable legacies, and scored many fine achievements in development. However, the Chinese people paid a high price for the attempt to suppress market forces completely, to cut the country off from the global economy and society, to constrain drastically the dimensions of inequality, to eliminate material incentives, to limit cultural freedom radically and to lead the society in wild, nation-wide mass movements.

Summing up the task facing the Party in 1980, Deng Xiaoping said: 'The decade of the Cultural Revolution brought catastrophe upon us and caused profound suffering. . . . Had it not been for "Left" interference, the reversals of 1958, and especially of the Cultural Revolution, significant progress would certainly have been achieved in our industrial and agricultural production and in science and education, and the people's standard of living would certainly have improved to a fair extent' (Deng Xiaoping, 1980: 234). Deng emphasized the critical importance of preserving political stability: 'Without political stability it is impossible for us to settle down to construction. . . . The experience of the Cultural Revolution has already proved that chaos leads only to retrogression, not to progress, and that there must be good order if we are to move forward. Under China's present circumstances it is clear that without stability and unity we have nothing' (Deng Xiaoping, 1980: 236–7).

Chairman Mao is a towering historical figure, and in hindsight many aspects of the Maoist period appear attractive. However, although, for the sake of academic debate, it is tempting to emphasize the achievements of the period, many aspects of which are, indeed, deeply worthy of study, it is not a development path that many Chinese people wish to rejoin or to which China is likely to return. China cannot go back.

Conclusion

When a traveller reaches a crossroads in the middle of a long journey he must go somewhere. In which direction does China go? Does it turn to the 'left' and resolve to follow the path of tough, realistic 'primitive capitalist accumulation'? Does it turn to the 'right' and follow the path of US-style 'free market fundamentalism'? Does it try to return to the path of Chairman Mao in the Great Leap Forward and the Cultural Revolution? Each of these paths is deeply flawed. Indeed, adopting either of the first two alternatives may well produce the third path, as the only way out of the resulting chaos that would be highly likely to result. There is another way, namely to move beyond the crossroads by following broadly the same direction as has been followed over the past two decades, namely 'groping for the way forward' in an experimental, non-ideological fashion, which builds on China's long traditions of trying to find its own 'Third Way'.

3

China at the Crossroads
'Use the Past to Serve the Present' (Gu Wei Jin Yong)?

In their search for a way forward amidst the immense challenges that they confront, China's leaders can turn to the country's own past for a source of inspiration. They can use this rich history to provide intellectual nourishment for the attempt to persist in the non-ideological approach of trying to 'grope for a way forwards', an approach that 'seeks truth from facts', devising policies in a pragmatic, experimental fashion to solve concrete problems as they emerge. This approach means basically continuing along the broad path that has served the country so well up until this point since the late 1970s, despite the depth of the challenges that face the country at this point.

China's long-run economic dynamism

Western scholars mostly believe that Europe began significantly to overtake Asia in the late Middle Ages in terms of social organization and economic development, and that this process led inexorably to the Industrial Revolution. The monumental pioneering work of Joseph Needham in the field of technical progress (Needham, 1954–) demonstrated that China made great advances before the West in many important fields. Following his research, for many years the question that scholars asked was: 'Why did China not experience an "Industrial Revolution", despite having made much early technical progress?' (e.g. Nolan, 1993). The answer that most scholars have provided is that the 'totalitarian' traditional Chinese state crushed the development of the market economy (e.g. Balazs, 1964; Huang, 1990; Wittfogel, 1957).

Lin Yifu has argued:

> The curriculum of China's civil service examination, which emphasized the moral obligations of government officials to the emperor, and the built-in evaluation criterion along the ladders of officialdom, obstructed the incentives to learn mathematics and conduct experiments – both necessary for modern scientific research. Therefore, despite its early lead in scientific discovery and technological inventions, China had no indigenous scientific and industrial revolutions. The result was that the Western world, benefiting from the fruits of those revolutions, became wealthy, while China's previous prosperity disappeared. (Lin Yifu et al., 1996: 1)

This view is widely shared by people in the government and business community.[1]

A widely held corollary of this perspective is that China today should 'learn from the past' by substantially removing the state from an active role in the economy if it wishes the latter to grow rapidly and achieve prosperity for its people. Hong Kong, often called 'Adam Smith's other island', is invariably held up as the example of what the 'free market' could achieve for China if only the state would drastically reduce its role, and confine itself to the position of 'ring-master' for private enterprise.

The recent research of numerous Chinese economic historians has shown that the traditional Chinese economy was far more dynamic over a long period than had formerly been thought (see especially Li Bozhong, 1986, 1998, 2000; Xu Dixin and Wu Chengming, 2000). Increasingly, the key question has become: 'What factors permitted the Chinese economy to make sustained progress over more than 1,000 years?' To answer this question, we need to probe more deeply into the structure of traditional Chinese political economy, especially the relationship of state and market. By analysing this rich tradition, we can see key aspects of China's traditional system of political economy that can form the inspiration for understanding the possible solutions to the challenges that face the Chinese leadership today. They can provide a source of confidence to the leadership in resisting the strong pressures of free market economics that are proposed both within China and from the outside, especially from the USA, as the solution to these challenges. The most urgent of these challenges is to resolve the relationship of finance capital to the rest of the economy and society. Chinese history has deep lessons, not only for China itself, but also for the wider world, about the nature of the relationship between the state and economy and society.

China's long-term growth

Agriculture and property rights   The foundation of Chinese civilization was, and still is, agriculture. D.H. Perkins' (1968) meticulous account of the long-term development of Chinese agriculture between the fourteenth and the mid-twentieth century shows how the responsiveness of Chinese rice-based agriculture was able both to allow huge long-term population growth and absorb productively the sustained increase in farm labour force. Total population grew from around 100 million in the twelfth century to over 500 million in the early 1950s (Perkins, 1968). There were several elements in the long-term growth of Chinese farm output, enabling output per person to remain fairly constant over the long run. They included substantial increases in the cultivated area in the earlier period, but these were substantially exhausted by the late seventeenth century. The main path to increased output was an intensification of techniques to raise output per acre. These involved the spread of double-cropping rice, initially introduced in the eleventh century, huge long-term expansion of the irrigated area, the introduction of indigenous dryland crops into new areas, the spread of 'new' dryland crops from the New World, and ·powerful effects resulting from increased inter-regional trade and specialization, which continued strongly into the modern period (see especially Li Bozhong, 1998, on the impact of inter-regional trade on farm productivity in Jiangnan between 1620 and 1850).

It is widely thought that the key to the economic development of Western Europe lay in the 'unique' system of private property rights that developed in this part of the world. This view received its most powerful advocacy from Nobel Prize-winner Douglas North:

> Efficient economic organization is the key to growth; the development of an efficient economic organization in Western Europe accounts for the rise of the West. Efficient organization entails the establishment of institutional arrangements and property rights that create an incentive to channel individual economic effort into activities that bring the private rate of return close to the social rate of return. (North and Thomas, 1973: 1)

The development of private property rights is thought to have been caused by the growing population pressure on the limited supply of farmland. Land replaced labour as the relatively scarce resource. From this developed the concept of private property in physical assets that, it is argued, underpinned the entire edifice of early modern economic development in Western Europe:

> The pressure to change property rights emerges only as a resource
> becomes increasingly scarce relative to society's wants. . . . The abund-
> ance of land during the high Middle Ages made labour easily the most
> scarce, and hence the most valuable, factor of production. . . . [U]npro-
> tected land at the time was almost as abundant as air and of no more
> economic value. Labour and capital, the scarce factors of production,
> alone set the boundaries for all output. (North and Thomas, 1973: 30)

By the thirteenth century, arable land had reached the limits of
expansion with existing technology: 'Throughout the century the
rewards to labour declined while land provided ever greater returns
to its owners' (North and Thomas, 1973: 51).

'China' does not even appear in the index of North and Thomas
(1973). In fact, pressure of population on land occurred in China far
earlier than in Europe. As the political power of aristocrats declined
and their estates disappeared, this led to the growth of private property
in land, including, before long, the right of freed slaves to own their
own land. Before the Tang dynasty (618–907), 'large aristocratic
families dominated the countryside, administered huge rural estates,
and held their farm labourers in virtual slavery' (Eastman, 1988: 71).
During the Tang and Song dynasties, the power of the aristocratic
families gradually collapsed: 'With the collapse of the aristocrats'
political power and the disappearance of their estates, the peasants
working the fields gradually sloughed off their status as slaves, and
by about the fourteenth century, most of them had gained the freedom
to own and rent land and to move about at will' (Eastman, 1988:
71). By the seventeenth century at the latest, China was 'feudal' only
in the broad sense that the surplus was extracted mainly from peasants
by land rents, not in the narrow sense of a manorial, serf economy.[2]
These considerations invalidate the proposition that private property
in land was a uniquely European phenomenon that formed the basis
of wider concepts of private property, which in turn facilitated capitalist investment and innovation, which, in short, was responsible for
'the rise of the West' (North and Thomas, 1973).

Technical progress Joseph Needham (1954–) has documented the
enormous technical advances made in medieval China. From the tenth
to the thirteenth century, China set out along the path of the 'Second
Industrial Revolution' well before Europe. The list of technical innova-
tions independently developed in China includes such items as the
windmill, canal lock gates, mechanical clockwork, power transmis-
sion by driving belt, water-powered metallurgical blowing engines,
hemp-spinning machines, gear wheels, numerous naval inventions

(e.g. the stern-post rudder, watertight compartments) and water-powered trip hammers for forges (Needham, 1965: 222–4). A key feature of industrial advance in the European Middle Ages was the crank: '[T]he powers of the crank were widely used and appreciated throughout the Chinese Middle Ages. For 3–400 years before the time of Marco Polo it was employed in textile machinery for silk-reeling and hemp-spinning, in agriculture for rotary winnowing and water-powered flour-sifting, in metallurgy for the hydraulic blowing-engine, and in such humble uses as the well-windlass' (Needham, 1965: 224). Although the pace of technical progress slowed down after China's medieval 'Industrial Revolution', a steady stream of significant technical advances was made thereafter through until the nineteenth century (Xu Dixin and Wu Chengming, 2000), without making the leap to a full-fledged modern 'Industrial Revolution'.

Trade These technological developments were stimulated by the powerful long-term growth of both domestic and international trade. For long periods, the Chinese state was able to unite the vast territory of China into a single integrated market. Marco Polo provided a vivid description of the level of commerce on the Chang Jiang (Yangtse) in the thirteenth century:

> This river runs for such a distance and through so many regions and there are so many cities on its banks that truth to tell, in the amount of shipping it carries and the total volume and value of its traffic, it exceeds all the rivers of the Christians put together and their seas into the bargain. . . . I have seen in this city [Sinju] fully 5,000 ships at once, all afloat on this river. Then you may reflect since this city, which is not very big, has so many ships, how many there must be in others. For I assure you that the river flows through more than sixteen provinces, and there are on its banks more than 200 cities, all having more ships than this. . . . The amount of shipping it carries, and the bulk of the merchandise that merchants transport by it, upstream and down, is so inconceivable that no-one in the world who had not seen it with his own eyes could possibly credit. Its width is such that it is more like a sea than a river. (Polo, 1974: 170 and 209)

In the eighteenth century, Father Du Halde, the Belgian Jesuit priest wrote:

> [T]he particular riches of every province, and the ability of transporting merchandise by means of rivers and canals, have rendered the empire always very flourishing. . . . The trade carried on within China

is so great, that all of Europe cannot be compared therewith. (quoted in Ho Ping-ti, 1959: 199)

Foreign trade was a crucial part of the Chinese economy along the coastal regions. Although there were periods in which the central state tried to restrict trade with foreigners, such as the early Ming dynasty in the late fourteenth and early fifteenth century, for most of the last two thousand years, international trade operated free of government controls, other than the levying of import duties.

In his pioneering account of trade and economic development in South China before 960 AD, Wang Gungwu comments:

> The South China Sea was the main trade route of what may be called the Asian east–west trade in commodities and ideas. It was the second Silk Route. Its waters and islands straits were as the sands and mountain passes of Central Asia; its ports were like the caravanserais. It became to the southern Chinese what the land outside the Jade Gate was to the northern Chinese. (Wang Gungwu, 1998: 3)

Guangzhou remained at the centre of the thriving trade with Southeast Asia for the next thousand years, except during the relatively brief periods of government restriction on trade with foreigners.

Marco Polo writes of the city of Tinju, which made porcelain bowls that were exported all over the world (Polo, 1974: 239). He records that 'Zaiton' (Xiamen) is

> the port for all the ships that arrive from India laden with costly wares and precious stones of great price and big pearls of fine quality. It is also a port for the merchants of all the surrounding territory, so that the total amount of traffic in gems and other merchandise entering and leaving the port is a marvel to behold. (Polo, 1974: 237)

Shiba's account of the growth of the port city of Ningbo shows the importance of both domestic and international maritime trade in the city's growth (Shiba, 1977: 391–9). After Ningbo moved to its present site in the eighth century, it developed into an outport for the Lower Yangtse region and flourished for the next thousand years as a centre of both the coastal trade and the long-range trade with other regions of China, with Japan and with Korea. During the Southern Song (1127–1279), shipping flourished in Ningbo. The concentration of shipping and shipbuilding accelerated the economic specialization of the city's hinterland, stimulating the production and marketing of materials necessary for the transport industry. After restrictions on international trade were lifted in the mid-Ming dynasty in 1567, silver from Japan, Portugal and Spain poured into inland China via Ningbo. Numerous other ports up and down the long Chinese coast, such as Guangzhou and Xiamen, had similar paths of development.

Far from Europe dominating the long-term development of the world economy from the late Middle Ages onwards, it had little to sell that Chinese people wished to buy until well into the nineteenth century. The persistent pattern of international exchange over many centuries, right up to the early nineteenth century, was Chinese export of manufactured goods in return for specie, especially silver.

Mercantile capital in traditional China was highly developed. Marco Polo's *Travels* is replete with accounts of teeming mercantile activity, and innumerable cities in which there are 'merchants of wealth and consequence'. Brooks' (1999) study is focused on the extraordinary degree to which volumes of commerce advanced during the Ming dynasty (1368–1644), with a pervasive impact on the culture of the period. In the late eighteenth century, there were reported to be about 5,000 sea-going ships in the ports of Shanghai and Zhapu, with a total weight estimated at around 550,000 tons. Large merchants were reported to each own fleets of more than 100 ships employing over 2,000 people (Xu Dixin and Wu Chengming, 2000: 364). By the mid-eighteenth century, 'native trade in all but the isolated interior regions of China was dominated by three groups of prominent traders, the Hui-chou merchants of Anhui, Shansi merchants, and Fukienese merchants from the Ch'uan-chou–Chang-chou region' (Shiba, 1977: 403).

For several hundred years prior to the nineteenth century, Foshan was the centre of the flourishing iron trade in Guangdong province, with products 'marketed far and wide: up and down the coast of China and all over Southeast Asia' (Wagner, 1998: 73). Merchants came from all over China, 'including the wealthy merchants from the provinces of Shanxi and Shaanxi in the north, who traded throughout China. Remains left by the outsiders must have dotted the Chinese coast' (Faure, 1996: 6). These were increasingly challenged by the merchants from Ningbo, of whom 'several thousand' had settled in Shanghai by the end of the eighteenth century (Shiba, 1977: 436).

Industry   The textile industry was much the most important in traditional China, as it was in early modern Europe. Towards the end of the Ming dynasty (1368–1644), cotton replaced hemp and silk as the principal fabric for daily wear. The spinning and weaving of cloth became the largest handicraft industry (Xu Dixin and Wu Chengming,

2000: 213). By the early nineteenth century, there were around 60–70 million peasant households engaged in the occupation as a subsidiary activity to farming (Xu Dixin and Wu Chengming, 2000: 217). Around one-half of the cloth was for self-consumption and one-half for sale on the market. Of the marketed cloth, it is estimated that around 15 per cent entered long-distance trade.

By the early Qing (1644–1911), in the late seventeenth and early eighteenth century, there were many examples of large-scale businesses (Xu Dixin and Wu Chengming, 2000: 250–98), especially in the metallurgical industries. In the iron industry many big private enterprises emerged as the market economy expanded. One of the largest was the Guangdong merchant, Ho Xi. In the early eighteenth century, he was recorded as owning sixty-four iron mines employing 130,000 workers. In the manufacture of iron from iron ore, there were several examples of large iron works that employed two or three thousand workers. Large copper mines also often employed several thousand workers. One report even records a copper mine in which as many as 700,000 were employed. Although this is thought to have been somewhat exaggerated, there are many reliable reports from the early Qing of copper mines with many thousands of employees. In the coal industry, there are frequent references to large mines with many hundreds or even several thousand employees. However, examples of large-scale businesses were not confined to the metals and mining sector.

In the porcelain industry in the sixteenth century, Jingdezhen was reported to have up to 50,000 people employed in the different branches of the industry. Most of these were employed in private kilns, with around 100–200 employees per kiln (Xu Dixin and Wu Chengming, 2000: 314). In the salt fields of Sichuan there were many large businesses. Reliable evidence from the early nineteenth century records that in the large saltworks at Fushun and Jianwei, there were 'several hundred thousand' employees and in the smaller ones, 'several tens of thousands' (Xu Dixin and Wu Chengming, 2000: 338). In Imperial times, Foshan, 'the city of iron and steel' (in Guangdong), was estimated to have a population of close to a million people, 'mostly of the working class' (Wagner, 1998: 73).

Urbanization   G. William Skinner's pathbreaking research (Skinner, 1977: 286) showed that late Imperial China had a high level of urbanization for a pre-industrial society. In the nineteenth century there were estimated to have been a total of 35,000 'standard' and 'intermediate' market towns. Above this dense local trading structure were a further 2,300 'central market towns', 932 'cities' and 26 huge 'metropolitan trading systems', which in turn formed 8 great 'economic systems'. Among these were cities of a size and level of sophistication that far exceeded those of contemporary European cities until late in the latter's economic development.

The Tang dynasty (618–907) capital, Chang An, was the 'largest, richest and grandest city in the world of that time' (Boyd, 1962: 51). The vast eleventh-century painting *Ch'ing ming shang he tu* shows in minute detail the city of Kaifeng, the capital of the Northern Song dynasty up until around 1127. It provides a unique visual insight into the immense richness of trade, calmness of atmosphere, cultural profusion and effectiveness of government administration, as well as the beauty and sophistication of architectural arrangement in a large medieval Chinese city.

Marco Polo's long account of Hangzhou ('Kinsai') around 1280 (Polo, 1974: 213–22) reveals him to have been overwhelmed by the city's size (the greatest extent of its walls was about 15 miles, and that of the inner city walls, about 8 miles); booming trade ('as for the merchants, they are so many and so rich and handle such quantities of merchandise that no one could give a true account of the matter'); highly developed civic infrastructure (including '12,000 bridges, mostly of stone' and 'fully 3,000 public baths'); effective government administration ('when [the guards] find a man who is unable to work on account of illness, they have him taken to one of the hospitals, of which there are great numbers throughout the city, built by the ancient kings and lavishly endowed'); and a flourishing manufacturing and service economy ('the city has twelve main guilds . . . [and] each of these guilds has 12,000 establishments, that is to say, workshops'). Marco Polo considered Hangzhou to be 'without doubt the finest and most splendid city in the world'.

In the 1950s there took place an intense battle over the nature of the capital city Beijing under communism. This stimulated deep reflection over the nature of Chinese cities. Old Beijing was one of the architectural marvels of the world, 'moat enclosing moat, wall behind wall, and compartment opening within compartment, a hierarchy reflecting every gradation of power and influence'. It was 'possibly the greatest single work of man on the face of the earth' (Tang, 2003). Even before 1949, leading intellectuals, including architects and town planners, had demanded the preservation of Old Beijing at all costs.

The most influential figure in the battle over the development path of Beijing was Liang Sicheng, China's leading architect and town planner.[3] Liang was deeply versed in both traditional Chinese and Western architectural traditions. He had studied extensively in the West, and was familiar with leading Western architects and urban planners such as Le Corbusier and Frank Lloyd Wright. Liang argued against the Soviet city planners and the Beijing city government, urging them to consider deeply the significance of Beijing. He argued for 'redeveloping Beijing as a living city', while 'preserving it as a historic city'. As a historic city, Beijing occupied a special place in Chinese and world history:

> The whole form of Beiping [Beijing] is not only a rare example across the world, but also a masterpiece of art. Many of the buildings within and without the city are themselves too the most invaluable pieces in their own part of the history of architecture and art. Needless to say, many of the rest of the cultural relics and architecture are overwhelmingly art with rich historical meanings. Altogether, they constitute a huge 'historical art museum'.

In Liang's view, preservation of this heritage was 'beneficial to the people's soul, the nation and, eventually, humankind' (quoted in Tang, 2003).

Japanese plans in the 1940s had intended to develop the city's production capability outside the boundaries of the historic centre. Liang Sicheng and his supporters also made this a centrepiece of their plans for the growth of production in the 'living city'. Liang believed that bringing modern industry into the heart of a city was the root cause of 'sick cities'.

In terms of residential spaces, like other Chinese cities, Old Beijing had 'no centre or focal point around which the whole composition is arranged', but rather 'a long progression in one direction of a diffusion and balance of elements throughout the composition': 'In Peking and in many other [Chinese urban] ensembles, there is no climax, but rather a series a series of architectural events leading to one objective after another and then on beyond. . . . The subtle balance and interdependence between the constituent parts of a composition is a striking quality in Chinese planning' (Boyd, 1962: 73).

Liang argued that the way in which the traditional Chinese city was planned enabled the provision of a 'place where people can live and work in peace and contentment' (*anju leye*) (quoted in Tang, 2003). Important buildings formed an 'ensemble of walled enclosures', and even an urban house was typically a walled enclosure. The traditional Chinese city was organized as a series of 'cells' arranged in an orderly fashion, typically around a north–south and an east–west axis, 'the whole and parts being built up of south-facing axial walled enclosures' (Boyd, 1962: 50). Buildings were mostly single-storey.

Towns were almost all surrounded by city walls: 'From the walls, or any other vantage point, the city spread out below like an undulating sea of roofs, many of them over-topped by the trees in their court-yards, and out of this level mass an inner walled enclosure and the receding line of more important buildings stood out visibly' (Boyd, 1962: 73). In Liang Sicheng's view, the achievement of traditional Chinese urban planning was to 'affect the residents' morality', and help to 'maintain good social order'.

Liang Sicheng's battle to save Old Beijing was defeated. Under Chairman Mao the city walls were demolished. Large parts of the old city were demolished to be replaced by Soviet-style apartment blocks and industrial enterprises. Nevertheless, by the end of the Cultural Revolution there was still a substantial part of Old Beijing left. The destruction of the old city continued apace under the influence of the emerging market economy and, especially, the fast-growing domin-ance of the automobile. This in turn was stimulated by the assertion of the rights of individuals (in the early stages, this was mainly through their work units) to use automobiles, and the failure of the city gov-ernment to provide high-quality public transport. From being argu-ably the world's most magnificent city in 1949, by the turn of the twenty-first century, a combination of Maoist 'planning' and the market economy had turned the city into one of the ugliest, most polluted and most unpleasant cities in the world. Most of China's other ancient cities fared little better. Few physical phenomena could more powerfully symbolize the dangers to Chinese people's welfare that arise from both the 'left' (Chairman Mao) and the 'right' (the dominance of individual 'freedom' and market forces).

Jiangnan Jiangnan was much the most developed area of China in the late Ming and early Qing. This is the Delta Region of the Yangtzi River. In 1815 it had a population of around 26 million (Li Bozhong, 1986), out of a total Chinese population of around 330 million (McEvedy and Jones, 1978: 167). This compares with a European population in 1820 of around 190 million, including 31 million in France, 25 million in Germany and 14 million in Great Britain (Cipolla, 1973: 747). By the end of the seventeenth century, Jiangnan was the world's biggest exporter of textiles and fibres and was more highly commercialized and urbanized than any other part of the world (Li Bozhong, 1986). Over many centuries Jiangnan's agriculture became steadily more intensified, with improvements in yields per crop, increases in multiple-cropping and rising real value of output per unit of farmland (Li Bozhong, 1986: 4–16).

By the late sixteenth century, textiles had become the largest single part of the Jiangnan industrial economy. Nanjing was the centre of the silk industry. In the 1840s there were nearly 200,000 people engaged in the industry, with more than 35,000 looms (Li Bozhong, 1986: 21). Songjiang prefecture was the most highly developed part of China in terms of the production of cotton cloth for the market, and Suzhou, the country's most important commercial centre, 'teemed with cloth merchants and was also a dyeing centre' (Xu Dixin and Wu Chengming, 2000: 171). During the Qing about 90 per cent of the marketed cotton cloth produced in Jiangnan was exported to other parts of China or abroad. In the eighteenth century, the fastest growth rates of exports were to Europe: between 1786 and 1798, the export of 'Nankeens' (cloth woven in Nanjing and other places in Jiangnan) to Western Europe and the Americas increased almost fivefold (Li Bozhong, 1986: 27).

The level of urbanization in Jiangnan in the late eighteenth century may have been as high as 35–45 per cent, if the residents of small towns are included (Li Bozhong, 1986: 51). Around 5,000 sea-going ships were based in Jiangnan, with a tonnage that was 2.8 times that of British ships of all kinds in 1700 (Li Bozhong, 1986: 53). The proportion of people who obtained some kind of education was 'very high by pre-modern standards', with a relatively high fraction of ordinary workers educated to a basic level. Jiangnan's farmers and craftsmen were 'full of commercial awareness', and 'organized their production with an eye to the changing markets'. Its entrepreneurs 'organized their business activities in order to maximize profits' (Li Bozhong, 1986: 58).

Chinese economic development in comparative perspective   Paul Bairoch (1982) has compared national output in different parts of the world historically. He estimates that in 1750, China's share of global manufacturing output stood at 33 per cent, compared with 25 per cent in India/Pakistan and just 18 per cent in the 'West'. Bairoch estimates that in 1800, China's per capita GNP was US$228 (at 1960 prices) compared with US$150–200 for England and France (Bairoch, 1982). Up until the nineteenth century, the dominant view of China among European intellectuals was of a country that was materially superior to Europe. As late as 1798, Malthus declared China was the richest country in the world (Dawson, 1964: 7). Western travellers praised the quality of its roads and the cleanliness of its cities. In his description of the McCartney mission to China in 1793, Sir George Staunton says that 'in respect to its natural and artificial productions, the policy and uniformity of its government, the language, manners, and opinions of the people, the moral maxims, and civil institutions, and the general economy and tranquillity of the state, it is the grandest collective object that can be presented for human contemplation or research' (quoted in Dawson, 1964: 7).

As Europe entered the Industrial Revolution, however, and China encountered severe political and economic difficulties, so China's role in the global economy drastically changed. By 1913 its share of world manufacturing output had fallen to under 4 per cent, while that of the 'West' had risen to 82 per cent (Bairoch, 1982). It was only with this dramatic change of fortune that the predominant image of China shifted to one of a stagnant, impoverished despotism.

State and market in Chinese development

We have seen that over the long sweep of history China has had epochs of corrupt rule and collapse of law and order. However, it is impossible to understand Chinese socio-economic development over the long term without examining the role of the Chinese state in facilitating the growth and technical progress of the Chinese economy.

The bureaucracy The key feature of the traditional Chinese state was a combination of a hereditary emperor with a large professional civil service, selected mostly by competitive examination.[4] The early Han rulers (202 BC–AD 9) were the first to achieve real unification of the Chinese state. They instituted a professional civil service, which was essential to guard against rivals and foreign incursions. It is estimated that in the late eighteenth century there were around 27,000 professional civil servants, with a further 750,000 or so people who were members of the local 'gentry' (*shenshi*) (Feuerwerker, 1976: 42–3), 'who dealt with many interests of their local communities for which the official government had no time' (Michael, 1964: 60). The local foundation of the bureaucracy was the county magistrate, who typically administered an area with a population 'upwards of 100,000' (Will, 1990: 87). There were around 1,200–1,300 counties in the eighteenth century. Whereas the magistrate was appointed by the empire, most of the day-to-day administrative tasks were in the hands of 'a mass of subordinate agents', who were 'in theory nominated or confirmed by the magistrate', but were 'almost entirely outside the control of the central administration' (Will, 1990: 87).

The examination system was the key to the ideological domination exercised by the bureaucracy. A vastly greater number sat the exams for the civil service than were allowed to pass them. In the late eighteenth century, the gentry consisted of those candidates who had passed the local examinations at the level of either *shengyuan* (estimated to number 406,000 in the late eighteenth century) or *jian sheng* (31,000 people). Those who had the higher level exams at the level of *gongsheng* (27,000), *juren* (18,000) or *jinshi* (2,500) were eligible for appointment as professional members of the civil service (Feuerwerker, 1976: 42). Around one-half of these succeeded in obtaining such appointments.

The dominant ideology of bureaucratic rule was conveyed continuously through the examination system. The competitive examination system was an excellent means for thoroughly indoctrinating ambitious commoners, compelling the talented sons of officials and bureaucratic families to submit to the most comprehensive professional ideological training (Wittfogel, 1957: 351). Ideology was the key to the system's long-term stability and cohesion. One of the most striking features of pre-nineteenth-century China is the universality and the depth of commitment to the basic social values of Qing society as expressed in the dominant Confucian ideology (Feuerwerker, 1976: 11). Among the Confucian elite there were few dissenters or 'Sunday Confucians'. The Confucian belief system was 'the root of morality itself' (Feuerwerker, 1976: 11).[5]

Feuerwerker considers that 'though he might sometimes be hard-pressed to earn his livelihood, the Confucian was rarely "alienated"' (Feuerwerker, 1976: 11). The function of Confucianism was to supply 'the source and definition of the ultimate values which provided the individual personality with the means for managing [his or her] "existential" tensions', and which 'gave a meaningful coherence to the central social values that defined the structure of society' (Feuerwerker, 1976: 13). Feuerwerker evaluates the Qian Long period of rule (1735–96) as follows: 'Basic beliefs, operational values, and social institutions . . . were highly integrated and mutually reinforcing, because through the reign of Ch'ien Long [Qian Long] the system did work – for the political and social elite in any case – to nourish mind and body generously in a society as glorious as that of any previous Chinese imperial age' (Feuerwerker, 1976: 11). The over-riding values were those of 'the primacy of order and stability, of co-operative human harmony, of accepting one's place in the social hierarchy, of social integration' (Feuerwerker, 1976: 15).

China's long tradition of political philosophy emphasized that the sole test of a good ruler is 'whether he succeeds in promoting the welfare of the common people. . . . This is the most basic principle in Confucianism and has remained unchanged throughout the ages' (Lau, 1979: 32 and 37): 'These common people are the touchstone by which the Three Dynasties were kept to the straight path' (Confucius, 1979: 37). In order to serve the interests of the mass of the people, the bureaucracy must gain the trust of the masses: 'Only after he has gained the trust of the common people does the gentleman work them hard, for otherwise they would feel ill-used' (Confucius, 1979: 154). If the bureaucracy becomes corrupt, losing its moral foundation, the result is disaster for social order: 'Those in authority have lost the Way and the common people have for long been rootless' (Confucius, 1979: 155).

Pierre-Étienne Will (1990) has provided a uniquely detailed account of the practical operations of the Chinese bureaucracy in relation to famine avoidance and relief in the eighteenth century. His monumental study of this critical area of state activity concludes with an overall evaluation of the capability and intentions of the bureaucratic apparatus (Will, 1990: 271–2). The conclusions of his study run counter both to 'the scornful attitude and vaunting attitude of Western superiority in the treaty port era', as well as to the 'profound pessimism that is rarely absent from the writings of Chinese bureaucrats'. Will shows that the bureaucratic system had proved highly durable. It had been elaborated over a long period of time, was nourished by a venerable tradition, and had reached an advanced stage of inventiveness and complexity. This system could and did work relatively well: 'With intelligent guidance it was possible to make effective use of the hundreds, if not thousands of sub-bureaucrats available in each county' (Will, 1990: 272).

Will singles out the example of Fan Guancheng (1698–1768) as a 'perfect exemplar of those "technical" high officials who specialized in a well-defined range of problems' (Will, 1990: 14). After a year spent as governor of Zhejiang province, he brought back to Zhili (today's Hebei province) samples of potatoes, along with a team of specialists who were to teach the North Chinese how to grow them. In 1765 he presented a series of woodcuts to the Emperor on the cultivation of cotton. He sponsored the publication of *The Book of Rivers and Water Conservancy in Zhili*. He was responsible for the drainage of the marshy areas near the Shandong frontier and along the Ziyahe (Hejian province) and their successful conversion to wheat land. Most notably, he was responsible for the creation of a 'vast and dense network of "charity granaries" across the whole of Zhili', in response to an Imperial directive of 1746 (Will, 1990: 15). In 1753 he codified the practices into a text to be used by local magistrates in running 'charity granaries'. During 1743–4 he was sent to co-direct full-time the famine-relief operations in Zhili. Ten years later he compiled a long and detailed text on the subject. This was one of the longest and most detailed accounts of a specific famine-relief operation. It was used as a handbook to guide other bureaucrats in famine relief (this topic is further analysed on pp. 134–8).

Ruling China's vast population was not simply accomplished by ideological means, important as these were. The Imperial government had a mighty army. Its main function was not international war, but, rather, maintaining order within the empire. The survival of the state was, literally, a matter of life and death: 'A displeased person may become pleased, an unhappy man may become happy again, but a State, once destroyed, cannot be restored' (Sun Wu, 1996: 136). A critical function of the bureaucracy was dispensing justice. In Confucius' view, social order was to be achieved as far as possible by ideology, but, if that failed, in the end, there should no compunction about keeping social order through force: 'The Master said "Guide them by edicts, keep them in line with punishments, and the common people will stay out of trouble but will have no sense of shame. Guide them by virtue, keep them in line with the rites, and they will, besides having a sense of shame, reform themeselves"' (Confucius, 1979: 63).

China's merchants occupied a subordinate ideological and political role. They were placed at the bottom of the bureaucracy's official ranking of social strata, behind the scholars, farmers and artisans. There was no official representation of the merchants' interests in either the local or the central government. However, the fact that the merchant's political standing was degraded did not mean that trade itself was regarded as undesirable. The successful merchant's wealth 'had always drawn covetous awe if not respect' (Faure, 2001). If merchants wished their families to enter the ruling bureaucratic class, their children needed to go through the laborious and highly competitive examination system. The consequence was thorough absorption of the ideology of the ruling scholar-bureaucrat elite. The merchants were allowed to perform their essential function of stimulating economic interaction through expanding the division of labour, facilitated by trade, but were firmly kept in their place in terms of the political power structure and the ideology that underpinned that structure.

Law   During the long periods in which it functioned relatively effectively, the Chinese state provided a framework of law and order and
protection for property rights within which powerful long-term economic development took place and was matched by corresponding
technical progress. Chinese merchants never were able to develop
the independence from the state that began to develop in increasingly
autonomous towns in late medieval Europe (Balazs, 1964). However, the control exercised by the state ensured that in periods when
the central government functioned well, the cities provided a secure
environment in which to conduct business, not only because they
were peaceful, but also due to an environment in which their property
rights were protected by the state. For example, Marco Polo's account
of 'Kinsai' (Hangzhou), the largest commercial city in China during
the Yuan dynasty, under the Mongols, noted: 'Fronting on each of
these squares are two palatial buildings, one at either end, in which
are the officers of the magistrates appointed by the king to impose
a summary settlement if any dispute arises among the traders or
inhabitants of these quarters' (Polo, 1974: 216). It is unimaginable
that such huge quantities of merchandise could have been stored and
traded without security that the corresponding contracts were legally
enforceable, or that robbery of the merchants' property was illegal.

William Rowe (1984) has provided a vivid account of commercial development in the city of Hankow. Before 1850, Hankow was
already one of the largest and most sophisticated trading centres of
China, and indeed of the world. In late Imperial Hankow there were
all manner of written commercial agreements. These ranged from
shipping orders (*ch'uan-piao*) to bills of lading (*pao-tan, ch'ing-tan*)
to promissory notes (*p'ing-p'iao, chieh-chu*) to contracts of sale (*ting-
tan, ch'eng-tan*), all of which were routinely circulated and enforceable in Hankow. Indeed, without them the bulk trade of the port
would hardly have been conceivable. Local officials in late Imperial
Hankow played a consistent and conscientious role in guaranteeing
the repayment of debts. One estimate for 1874 suggests that fully
90 per cent of all legal cases brought before the local magistrate by
petition concerned failure to meet credit obligations. Local records
provide abundant evidence of the administration's availability as a
recourse for commercial creditors (Rowe, 1984: 168).

The army   The most important function of the Imperial state was to
provide long periods of relative peace and stability over the vast
territory under its rule. Although, as we have seen, there were terrible
periods of state disintegration, for long periods, at the beginning and

end of dynasties, China was distinguished from the rest of the world by the fact that the central authorities were able to establish peaceful conditions over vast territories. Even in the midst of long dynasties, such as the Ming, China had the world's largest army (Huang, 1981: 160). An important part of central government expenditure was on troops to control outlying regions and fight off threats from surrounding foreign countries should they engage in war with China. However, a large part of the central government's military outlays was spent on stationing garrisons of troops in the cities within areas under stable central rule. Ultimate authority over the army was exercised by the Emperor. However, in routine matters, the provincial governors and their bureaucracy were entitled to give orders to army commanders (Huang, 1981: 162). Their subordinates, on garrison duty in local districts, were 'at the beck and call of the Civil Service magistrates and prefects' (Huang, 1981: 175).

This system has usually been interpreted only in relation to the authoritarian aspect of central rule. However, the economic significance of the huge army and its wide network of local garrisons goes far beyond this. The local army garrison was typically heavily engaged in civilian duties. For example, during the Ming dynasty, a force of 120,000 officers and men was responsible for organizing the transport of grain along the Grand Canal to Beijing (Huang, 1981: 161). In peacetime, the local army garrison in Ningbo was 'not infrequently assigned [by the civilian authorities] to work on water-control and reclamation projects that directly benefited the city' (Shiba, 1977: 421).

Most importantly, the presence of so many troops also provided a source of security for economic activities during the long periods in which they were under effective control from the civilian authorities. They provided merchants with the confidence to undertake trade that far exceeded that in other parts of the world until modern times. The normally peaceful environment over wide areas provided a powerful incentive to those with capital to undertake long-term investments. It also enabled the entire territory of China to form a single unified free trade area. The degree of state interference in trade was small, in normal times confined mainly to taxation of a small number of key items. Estimates for the eighteenth century show that only around 7 per cent of national income went into the central government budget, of which the vast bulk, 74 per cent, came from the land tax and just 14 per cent came from the domestic and international customs revenue (Nolan, 1993: 17). Therefore, long before any other comparable region of the world, China was able to enjoy for a long period the powerful 'Smithian' stimulus of specialization, the division of labour, the rapid spread of best-practice techniques and powerful incentives to accumulate capital.

Money   In the traditional Chinese economy, exchange was almost always a monetary transaction (King, 1965: 42). For over two thousand years, the Chinese government was aware of the importance of money to a sound economy. One of its ongoing struggles was to ensure that the money supply was not debased and that the quantity of money corresponded to the current economic needs. The first explorations of a quantity theory of money are probably those expounded in the *Book of Guan Zi*, written more than 200 years BC (Hu Jichuang, 1984). The concept of legal tender, with a specified form, weight and degree of fineness, first appeared in China in writings of the second century BC. As early as the second century BC, Song Hongyang, minister of finance under the Western Han dynasty (206 BC–AD 24), paid great attention to unifying the monetary system for the whole country: 'With unified currency, people's faith in currency will not be divided; and where coins are exclusively issued from above, there will be no grounds for public distrust of the coinage' (quoted in Hu Jichuang, 1984: 45).

Marco Polo was fascinated by the control exercised by the central authorities over the supply of money. During the Yuan dynasty (1271–1368), the Mongol rulers were the first economy in the world to have paper money. He was amazed that 'all the peoples and populations who are subject to [the Great Khan's] rule are perfectly willing to accept these papers in payment, since wherever they go they pay in the same currency, whether for goods or for pearls or precious stones or gold or silver. With these pieces of paper they can buy anything and pay for anything' (Polo, 1974: 148).

The central government tried persistently to maintain central control over the amount and nature of currency in circulation. Detailed accounts from the early Qing dynasty in the late seventeenth and early eighteenth centuries show the way in which the central government constantly monitored the state of money supply, frequently changing the specified weight and composition of coins in response to changing economic conditions, and attempting to maintain a constant exchange rate between copper cash and silver coinage (King, 1965: 133–43). Although local authorities had significant areas of discretion in monetary policies, including even county-level authorities, the central government established basic common features by edict, by a common source of monetary ideas, by similar training of officials, and by the frequent transfer of officials from one post to another (King, 1965: 43–4). In times of central weakness, there were large problems with monetary policy, with periods of serious debasement of the currency.

Water control[6]   The most important single function of the state in traditional China was water control, for drainage and irrigation, as well as for transport. It is a peculiarity of Chinese geography, in terms both of climate and of the nature of the crops most suited to Chinese conditions (especially rice), that in both North and South China, water control is crucial to liberating the productive potentialities of the soil:

> In the loess region in the northwest, the problem is primarily one of canal irrigation; in the Yangtze and Pearl River valleys, it involves the continuous drainage of the fertile but swampy land and the maintenance of a complicated system of drainage and irrigation; while in the Lower Yellow and Hwai River valleys the problem is essentially one of flood control. (Ch'ao-ting Chi, 1936: 12)

Large water control projects were almost exclusively public, organized either directly by the central government, or by lower levels of the bureaucracy. Water control activities carried a grave moral imperative for government officials, with a responsibility similar to national defence: '[B]uilding embankments on the Yellow River is like constructing defenses on the frontier, and to keep watch on the dike is like maintaining vigilance on the frontier' (a high official of the Ming dynasty, quoted in Ch'ao-ting Chi, 1936: 73).

One of the Qing dynasty's outstanding government water control officials commented as follows on the state's function in this respect:

> As to the construction and repair of canals in the interior, for the purpose of letting various people share in the benefits, the expenses are heavy and maintenance difficult. Although the officials could not do the work without burdening the people, *yet, if it is left to the people, not only could it not be undertaken by one man or a single family, but it could easily give rise to quarrels; furthermore [their meagre] resources would usually face quick exhaustion.* (K'ang Chi-t'ien, quoted in Ch'ao-Ting Chi, 1936: 71, emphasis added)

The central administration had important functions in inter-district water projects or projects with large expenses. For example, the construction of transport canals, involving tens of thousands of labourers, working under the corvée system, would usually be carried out under an Imperial edict and supervised by an Imperial commissioner. In the Ming and Qing dynasties, the construction of the embankment of the Yellow River was in the charge of a special official ranking high in the bureaucratic hierarchy.

The Grand Canal was by far the greatest transport infrastructure achievement of the traditional Chinese state. Under the dynasties of Sui, Tang, Song, Yuan, Ming and Qing, the Grand Canal played a significant part in providing a transport system linking the productive south with the political north. It engaged the attention of the best minds of China for more than ten centuries, and demanded countless millions of lives and a large portion of the wealth of the country for its improvement and maintenance.

The Grand Canal was constructed in disconnected sections at different periods in Chinese history before Emperor Yang Di of the Sui dynasty (605–18) completed it by connecting the various waterways running north–south and adding long sectors in the north and south. The Sui Grand Canal was a north–south as well as an east–west trunk line of communication. It consisted of five sections. The first was the Pien Canal, constructed in 605 and bridging the Yellow River and the Huai (Hwai) River. The construction mobilized over a million men and women from the prefectures to the south of the Yellow River and north of the Huai River. Along the bank of the canal, an Imperial road was constructed and planted with willows. The canal not only combined the navigation facilities of the Yellow River and Huai (Hwai) River into one system, but wove the tributaries of both rivers into a network of water-routes, covering a section of the North China plain which historically has been most important. The economic and military significance of the Pien Canal in Chinese history cannot be exaggerated.

The second section of the Grand Canal was called Shanyangtu, linking the Huai River with the Yangtze River. Restored by the founder of the Sui dynasty, Wen Di, in 587 to facilitate the transportation of tax grain, Shanyangtu was improved by his son Yang Di from 605. The improvement work mobilized over 100,000 inhabitants of the territory south of the Huai River. Roads were constructed along both banks of the canal and planted with elms and willows. The third section, known as Jiangnan He, was built by the order of Yang Di in 610. It extended from Zhenjiang in Jiangsu province to Hangzhou in Zhejiang province. Jiangnan completed the southern terminus of the Grand Canal and enabled Yang Di and his successors to tap the wealth of the south-eastern coast of China. The construction of the fourth section, Kwantun Canal, from Chang An to Tungkwan, established the direct water-route communication between the capital Chang An and Hangzhou. The fifth section was Yungchi Canal, completed in 608. It provided a direct link between the Hai He basin and central Yellow River valley, and between the Yangtze valley and Qiantang basin. It provided a direct means of communication from Hangzhou to the present city of Beijing.

The Sui Grand Canal can properly be called the artificial waterway system of the Sui, Tang and Song dynasties. It was frequently restored, modified and improved during the Tang (618–907) and Northern Song (960–1127) dynasties. During the Tang dynasty, the grain transport system was established between the north and south of China. The Tang officials engaged in both the administration of the transport service and the maintenance and improvement of the waterways. The improvements in the Tang dynasty culminated in the monumental achievement of Liu Yen, who, upon his appointment in 764 as Transport Commissioner of the Yangtze and Huai Rivers, deepened the Pien River, and adopted with improvements the system suggested by his predecessor, Pei Yao-ch'ing:

> Special boats were constructed to suit the different conditions and floating capacities of the various sections of the canal. The Kiang or Yangtze boats were to reach Yangchou, the Pien boats to reach Hoyin, and the Ho boats to reach the mouth of the Wei. The Wei boats would finally carry the cargoes to the Ta Ts'ang, the great granary at the capital. Transit granaries were established along the rivers and canals to facilitate changes of boats and to provide for bad navigation conditions which might necessitate waiting. (Ch'ao-ting Chi, 1936: 127)

The reconstruction and extension of the Grand Canal became one of the major tasks of the Yuan administration.[7] When the Yuan dynasty chose Beiping, called Dadu, as the capital, the Sui Grand Canal that had been designed to serve the capital at Chang An during the Sui and Tang dynasties was no longer convenient. Moreover, the long period of fighting between the Southern Song dynasty and the Tatar dynasties had inflicted great damage upon the Canal. In certain periods of the Yuan dynasty, ocean transport became very important. However, there were tremendous risks associated with this form of transport, in terms of human and property losses, and therefore the Yuan dynasty still relied chiefly on inland canals. Marco Polo presented a vivid description of the Yuan Grand Canal:

It is the Great Khan who has had this water-way constructed from Kwa-chau to Khan-balik. He has made a huge canal of great width and depth from river to river and from lake to lake, and made the water flow along it so that it looks like a big river. It affords passage for very large ships. By this means it is possible to go from Manzi as far as Khan-balik. It is equally possible to go by land; for alongside the waterways there runs a causeway. So that there is a way . . . by land and water alike. (Polo, 1974: 210)

The Grand Canal was maintained and improved during the Yuan dynasty and the later dynasties, the Ming and Qing, during which time it served as the main avenue of communication between north and south in these dynasties.

At a local level, too, government officials had a highly important role in water control. For almost any local water works beyond the capacity of the peasants of a single village, the magistrate intervened with the delegation of the duty of mobilizing forced labour, supervising the construction of local works, and regulating the use of water by rival villages. Like the other levels of the government bureaucracy, there was a heavy moral burden upon local officials to ensure that the innumerable local water control activities were provided at an adequate level. In the words of Ku Shih-lien, an early Qing dynasty scholar and official, the ideal magistrate 'is an official close to the people, and flood and drought should be of as much concern to him as pain or sickness of his person'. Such an official should make extensive visits to the countryside during the slack season: 'He should survey the topography of the region, ask about conditions of drainage, and investigate sluices and locks. . . . All these affect the conditions of the public treasury and the welfare of the people and must be carefully considered by the magistrate' (quoted in Ch'ao-ting Chi, 1936: 72).

Li Bing, the governor of the Qin dynasty (221–207 BC), has been considered the father of the irrigation system in Sichuan province and his work has been considered an immortal achievement by Chinese historians. At the centre of this system was the Du Jiang Dam (Du Jiang Yan). The Dam divided the Min River into two main streams, each of which branched out into many minor canals. The Dam and canals provided people transportation, irrigation and power supply for centuries to come: 'It is no exaggeration to say that the Ch'engtu [Chengdu] plain owes its fertility and economic sufficiency to this water-control system' (Ch'ao-ting Chi, 1936: 97).

The local water transport system in ancient China was closely analysed in Shiba's study of Ningbo: '[W]aterways extended out from

Ningpo [Ningbo] like the spokes of a wheel' (Shiba, 1977: 427).
Along these waterways, major commercial products of the region
and transit goods for exports came to the hub of Ningbo. Along the
same waterways, the commodities moved from Ningbo out toward
the peripheries of its trading area:

> The Yung River was deep enough to let large ocean-going junks sail
> upstream to the wharves along Chiang-hsia. In the Yu-yao River there
> were constant streams of lorchas plying between Chiang-hsia and Ts'ao-
> o. From the western plains, sampans sailed to the wharves near the
> west gate via two canals – His-t'ang and Chung-t'ang. Small boats could
> enter the city freely through a sluice near the west gate. In similar
> fashion, sampans from the southwestern plains sailed to the south gate
> via the Nan-t'ang, and small boats went into the city through a sluice
> near the south gate. Sampans and rafts from farther south in Feng-hua
> county came to the wharves outside the east gates via the Feng-hua
> River and its tributaries. As these were shallow rivers that tended to
> dry up, however, boats often preferred to break their journey and
> switch to canals, especially the Nan-t'ang, which ran parallel to the
> Feng-hua River. From the eastern plain, sampans plied to the wharves
> near the east gates via three canals – Ch'ien-tang, Chung-t'ang, and
> Hou-t'ang. (Shiba, 1977: 427)

Famine relief   Famine relief in the Chinese empire included famine
investigation, providing relief funds, supplying relief grain, controlling
prices, and strengthening and rebuilding production (Will, 1990).[8]
Many of the measures to fight famine demonstrated subtle strategies
by the state in providing relief to the poor and the capability of the
state in using the market to combat famine problems. Many of the
measures adopted anticipate the analysis of famine made by modern
writers such as A.K. Sen. The 'detailed and formalized procedures for
combating famine' were permitted by 'the sophistication, centralisa-
tion, and stability of the [Chinese] bureaucratic system' (Will, 1990:
4). In addition, local gentry had a prominent part in fighting famine
and distributing relief:

> Famine prevention and relief operation for the most seriously affected
> groups are indeed among the classic tasks of the Chinese bureaucracy,
> an integral part of the paternalistic conception of power that informed
> the Confucian ethic: to 'feed' the people to better 'educate' them. Yet
> in most cases it is impossible to isolate the State administration from
> the segments of society that were inextricably bound up with it to
> form a power structure of which it was only the visible capstone. The
> gentry . . . were the most prominent part of the local power structure

that took over at the point where the regularly appointed bureaucrats left off, below the level of the county (*xian*). (Will, 1990: 4)

Will explained the rationale for collective action: 'It was to the advantage of both the bureaucrats and the holders of local power, headed by the great landowners and the gentry, that appropriate measures be taken to prevent the ruin of the economy and social disorder, and this was certainly a powerful factor for cohesion within the global power system' (Will, 1990: 5).

In Will's view, there was nothing fundamentally new in the methods of famine control proposed in the official regulations of the eighteenth century. Indeed, 'most of these methods had been formulated as early as the Song period, and many of the recommended procedures – surveys of the disaster and its victims, the regular distribution of grain, public soup kitchens, and so forth – had been practised for centuries, albeit on a smaller scale, by the local notables and landlords in co-operation with the bureaucracy' (Will, 1990: 74).

Since the Ming dynasty (1368–1644), classification schemes had been proposed to determine the true economic conditions of the disaster victims and to give priority to the poorest. In 1742, a single system of classification scheme was established and adopted in Zhili, Will's focus, a year later. The scheme distinguished two categories of poor people: the 'very poor' and the 'less poor'. The numerous criteria for the classification concerned what immediate means each household had for dealing with the problem of subsistence.

After a natural disaster had occurred, the 'preliminary survey of damages' was conducted to measure the crop losses compared with normal years and to establish an average rate of damage for each village. The county administration distributed the forms for registering through the *baojia* system[9] the extent of damage to land during a natural disaster. This preliminary survey provided the 'provisional registers' for the final survey for which the magistrate was personally responsible. The survey of damages was then followed by the 'relief survey' to identify the households that could not survive without help from the state. Again, the village chiefs and *baojia* heads drew up the preliminary registers 'containing general comments on the situation of the families examined and proposing their classification as "very" or "less poor"' (Will, 1990: 115). This was to be verified and rectified by the investigators, who, together with the magistrate, wrote up the 'certificate of aid' before their subjects.

To discourage fraud and encourage co-operation during the damage and relief survey, efforts were made to provide information and explanation about regulation, thus publicizing each stage of the relief operation to the population. In order to gain the population's confidence, investigators, the magistrate and high-ranking officials who were in charge of the relief operation were advised to have close personal contacts with the subjects. Secretaries, employees in the magistrate's office (*yamen*), village chiefs or *baojia* heads who might be tempted to meddle with the survey and attempt to influence its findings to their own profit were promised punishment such as the *cangue* (a wooden halter worn around the neck) or flogging (Will, 1990: 120).

The Chinese bureaucracy devised and implemented subtle strategies in providing food relief to the disaster victims. Owing to the time spent on surveying damages and relief as well as on transporting supplies, there was a lag before the 'main relief' could arrive at the disaster areas. To tackle this problem, the state's regulations provided a palliative in the form of 'preliminary relief' (*xianzhen*, also called 'emergency relief', *jizhen*, or 'appeasement relief', *fuxu*), consisting of one month's worth of food distribution on the spot, without distinction between 'very' and 'less' poor. In the case of major floods, 'emergency relief' was distributed immediately, since the final survey had to be put off until the waters had receded and the inhabitants had returned to their villages: 'Better still, the officials travelling through the countryside to investigate the situation were enjoined to look for people who could not even wait for the arrival of the "preliminary relief" and to give them grain or money on the spot: this was called the "special relief".' Finally, 'selective relief' could be made available for villages and towns in areas adjoining the disaster areas where the losses were below 60 per cent (Will, 1990: 129–30).

The usual rule was to give half of the relief in kind and half in money, as was seen in Zhili in 1743–4. Private business took over when grain was available locally or nearby at a reasonable price and when the scope of disaster was limited. However, when 'the area and the duration of the disaster were such that private trade, even with the help of tax exemptions and other subsidies, could no longer ensure the provisioning of famine-stricken regions' (Will, 1990: 133), the administration took charge of both transporting and distributing aid.

In principle, government relief was to be given monthly to peasants and state students. The administration saw helping the peasant family cultivating a small farm with its own hands 'another form of aid to further agricultural production' (Will, 1990: 134). As for the students, 'it was out of the question to let potential bureaucrats starve to death' (Will, 1990: 135). In practice, the authorities appreciated the need for a certain degree of flexibility. In urban areas where neither survey nor distribution was available, widows, old people and the disabled poor could have themselves inscribed on the lists of neighbouring villages. The authorities also recognized the impact of disaster upon the living conditions of the boatmen when the Grand Canal froze over, upon non-agricultural craftsmen such as blacksmiths and carpenters, as well as upon wage labourers. With these people in mind, 'the administration took advantage of the crisis to set up various public works projects' (Will, 1990: 137).

The government took complete control of the monthly distributions and it also encouraged other forms of aid to help to fill in the gaps in relief: 'The fact that appeals for private funds and charitable initiatives, and indeed for the organizational abilities of the elites, went hand in hand with purely administrative endeavors can never be stressed enough' (Will, 1990: 137). For example, in the eighteenth-century regulations, the soup kitchens were assigned an auxiliary role. Encouraged and supervised by the administration, the local gentry made efforts to establish, manage and provision soup kitchens. They were designed first and foremost to help the poorest people survive until public distributions could begin and after the public distributions ended. Soup kitchens also provided aid to the social categories 'that were statutorily excluded from regular public relief', such as city dwellers, landless villagers and the old and sick, whose monthly allocations were not sufficient. Vagabonds, beggars and vagrants of all kinds were also among those being helped. Soup kitchens 'could also help prevent the exodus of the poorest people from places that had not been declared disaster areas and that accordingly did not get relief'. The administration limited its role to 'giving "encouragement", to endorsing the volunteers . . . , to performing spot checks, to ensuring public order, and finally to rewarding directors' (Will, 1990: 140).

The details of relief supplies to Zhili during 1743–4 demonstrated that, among other things, the administration used the market as a medium for distributing its relief. For transporting relief, the central administration ordered the official in charge of receiving and shipping cereals in the metropolitan areas to hire boats. They also rented annually the flat-bottomed barges from their owner-captains. For relief grain, the capital granaries provided part of the supplies. In addition, the Zhili provincial government used its own funds to import grains from outside the province. For example, a special provincial grant was made available to purchase black soybeans from Fengtian, where there was a good harvest in 1743. In 1744, two purchasing campaigns were launched to restore the local granaries to the pre-crisis level. The first purchase was proposed by the Governor-General of Zhili and was conducted in two prefectures in Henan province. The second purchase was approved by the Emperor and was carried out in various prefectures in Zhili and Henan, where the harvest was good. An additional purchase was made in areas close to the Canal in Henan and Shangdong, where prices of grain were reportedly low. All of these purchases were made at the current market prices.

Famine administration also benefited from the grain tribute system. The network of navigable waterways linked with the Grand Canal enabled the shipment of food relief to reach the disaster areas. The grain tribute reserves in the capital area helped partially ease famine in Zhili because the reserves were 'deliberately maintained above the level required to supply the court, the bureaucracy, and the army'. Also, the yields from the tribute were regarded as 'a safety reserve that would enable the government to take effective steps to aid the population – as long as the size of the famine-stricken area did not exceed a certain threshold' (Will, 1990: 172). In addition, '[s]urpluses were regularly redirected to the local granaries of the provinces where the tribute was levied' (Will, 1990: 191).

Commodity price stabilization   From early in Chinese history, the Chinese state was deeply interested in ways to stabilize the prices of basic commodities. From very early on, China's bureaucrats were aware of the dangers of speculation for ordinary people's livelihood. This parallels the modern interest in 'commodity price stabilization'. As early as in the Warring States Period (475–221 BC), Fan Li's price policy held that fluctuations in the price of grain should be kept within a certain range so that it could benefit both production and distribution. The government participated in the grain trade not to make a profit but rather to reduce fluctuations in the grain price: 'To take measures to stabilize the price of grain so as, in turn, to stabilize the prices of all other goods and keep market places free from commodity shortages – this is the proper way to rule a state' (Fan Li, quoted in Hu Jichuang, 1984: 17).

In the first century of the Eastern Han dynasty (AD 25–220), Emperor Wang Mang set up a benchmark price system in municipal cities (Hu Jichuang, 1984: 48–9). Each designated municipal government was required to establish a benchmark price for important commodities such as grain, cloth and silk. This price was determined on the basis of the price of the commodity concerned during the mid-months of the four seasons of the lunar calendar year. It was observed by the public as the standard price for an important commodity. The price of the commodity was allowed to fluctuate within a limit of 10 per cent above the benchmark with no specific lower limit. In each mid-month, the benchmark price might be readjusted.

The municipal government regulated the commodity price by economic means. When the price for a certain commodity rose above the upper limit, the municipal government intervened by selling the same commodity in the market. The government did not generally interfere when the price fell below its par 'because it was only concerned with solving the problem of rising prices'. However, when 'the market prices of certain daily necessities fell far below par and sales became sluggish, the government bought the goods at prices sufficient to cover the production costs so as to prevent the sellers from suffering too great loss' (Hu Jichuang, 1984: 50).

Marco Polo described the provision of grain in the Yuan dynasty (1271–1368). When the harvests were plentiful and the price of crops was cheap, 'the Great Khan accumulates vast quantities of corn and every kind of grain and stores them in huge granaries'. When some crops failed and there was dearth of grain, he drew on these stocks: 'If the price is running at a *bezant* for a measure of wheat, ... he supplies four measures for the same sum. And he releases enough for all, ... and this he does throughout all parts of his empire' (Polo, 1974: 157).

Will (1990) provides a meticulous account of the way in which in the Qing dynasty in the eighteenth century the bureaucracy intervened in the rice market to protect the livelihood of the masses from price fluctuations and speculation. The government established a vast network of 'evernormal granaries' (*changpingcang*) across the country in order to stabilize grain prices. In addition to maintaining emergency reserves, the purpose of the *changpingcang* was 'to cushion the impact of seasonal price fluctuations by buying up grain immediately after the harvest, when prices were low, and reselling it at a low price during the lean period before the new harvest came in'. The 'evernormal granaries'' spring sales and autumn purchases were supposed to even out prices by compensating for the weakness of the private sector or by competing with it when it tended to take advantage of and speculate on seasonal and/or regional price differentials (Will, 1990: 182).

Although there were statutory limits on reduced-price sales, provincial governors were recommended to be flexible in cases of crisis or emergency. In principle, the reduced-price sales were a 'public relief measure for the benefit of families classified as "poor"' (Will,

1990: 185). These sales were most effective when stocks were made available especially to deal with crisis on a larger scale: 'Compilations like the *Qingchao wenxian tongkao* repeatedly mention the shipping of major quantities of grain "above quota" to such and such a place "for reduced-price sales"' (Will, 1990: 186). In such cases, the sales of public grain became 'one of several strategies available to the State to combat a subsistence crisis' (Will, 1990: 186).

The stock of grain entrusted to *changpingcang* comprised both government purchase and private contributions: 'Private contributions played an important part in the initial buildup of evernormal reserves during the late seventeenth and early eighteenth centuries, but public purchases accounted for the larger part of the grain stored by the counties from the 1730s, and for virtually all of it by the late 1760s' (Will, 1990: 190).

There were fluctuations in the performance of *changpingcang*: '[T]ypically, each period was marked by an effort on the part of the central government to update the granaries' operations and place them under tighter control.' This was followed by 'a gradual deterioration at the local level until the next tightening of control'. The evernormal granary system 'functioned reasonably well in the *Yongzheng* and (most of) the *Qianlong* years' during the Qing dynasty (Will, 1990: 188). The technical standards of *changpingcang* 'represented the last word in technology at the time' (Will, 1990: 189).

Data on the provincial quotas in 1748 indicated the government's high degree of sensitivity to the regional differences in *changpingcang*. It was clear that large quotas were set up for poor provinces and regions with poor transport systems. The highest quota was for Gansu, where the wars waged against the western Mongolian federations, 'combined with the poverty and remoteness of the area, created enormous problems in keeping grain prices down and providing relief'. Comparable levels were reached only in a few other provinces – Yunnan in the southwest, the most mountainous province of the empire, and the coastal and mountainous provinces of Fujian and Guangdong, 'which were also "enclaves" of sorts, since it was difficult to provide them with surpluses from the Yangzi valley other than by sea' (Will, 1990: 194). Zhejiang's was also high because it was called on from time to time to help fill the needs of Fujian.

Tax policy   The idea of cultivating the sources of taxes was expressed by the disciple of Confucius, Ran Qiu, in the fifth century BC: 'How can a prince suffer destitution when the common people are enjoying abundance? And how can a prince enjoy abundance while the common people are suffering destitution?' This implies, according to Hu Jichuang, that the state needs to let people carry on their productive activities without impediments so that the state revenue may be replenished. This doctrine was strictly observed by Confucians as the golden rule of public finance for 2,000 years (Hu Jichuang, 1984: 6).

The first set of principles of taxation in Chinese history was developed by Fu Xuan in the third century. Fu Xuan emphasized that taxes should be levied in a most equitable way; tax revenue should be 'used economically and for the public'; there should be 'certainty' and 'stability' in the taxes levied. The point of 'certainty' means the system of taxation should be definite and the rate of tax should be fixed (Hu Jichuang, 1984: 59–60). In the eighth century, Liu Yan, the well-known financier of the Tang dynasty, observed two principles in his taxation policy. He insisted that the imposition of taxes should be limited to those that 'can be knowingly taken without the people grumbling', or to those that 'do less harm to the people'. He also stressed that taxes should be 'imposed upon things urgently needed by the people' because the quantity of such things (commodities) sold would be considerable and these commodities would become a plentiful and stable source of taxes (Hu Jichuang, 1984: 66–7). Owing to these policies of taxation, Liu Yan 'miraculously restored the prosperity of the Tang empire following the destruction resulting from the rebellions that lasted from 756 to 762' (Hu Jichuang, 1984: 66). However, in 821, Li Jue, a minister of the interior of the Tang dynasty, opposed the increase of taxes on tea. He pointed out: 'To impose a heavy tax on commodities which are urgently needed by the people will greatly raise their market prices by reason of the shifting of taxation, and the poor people will thus be made to suffer' (Hu Jichuang, 1984: 71). As early as the third century, the taxable capacity of different categories of tax-payers was identified. According to the land-tax system then, the male adult was the taxable standard, followed by the female adult and the quasi-adult at a lower rate. After the end of the fifth century, new criteria were introduced, including the tax-payers' age and their possessions in labour power such as farm cattle, slaves and maidservants. In the Tang dynasty, Yang Yan abandoned this approach of determining taxable capacity based on the tax-payers' physical strength and their possessions in labour power. He adopted instead the method of levying taxes according to the wealth of a family. Thus China became the first country to apply this method to the land tax (Hu Jichuang, 1984: 70–1).

A tax levied on profits that is similar to the modern income tax was implemented in the first century by Emperor Wang Mang of the Eastern Han dynasty. He levied a tax of 10 per cent on the profit made by tradesman in the cities. In the seventeenth century, Wang Yuan suggested a new system of taxation in commerce that was more concrete and analogous to modern income tax. In Wang Yuan's view, businessmen (all working people other than those who till the land) should be classed into two categories, shopkeepers and itinerant merchants, each of which should follow a specific procedure in taxation (Hu Jichuang, 1984: 94–6). For the shopkeepers, the tax should be fixed at 10 per cent of their monthly profit, which would be estimated in advance on the basis of 1 per cent of the total capital. The annual rate of taxation would be 1.2 per cent of the original capital. The tax would be paid at the end of each year and recorded on the certificate issued by the county office. The shopkeepers would be required to renew their certificate if there were changes in the trade or the original capital. Moreover, in order to prevent the shopkeepers from concealing part of their capital, Wang Yuan proposed to classify them into nine grades on the basis of capital. A shopkeeper of any grade would be granted the privilege of dressing like an official of the ninth rank if his tax payment exceeded a specific amount. If he paid more, higher privileges would be granted.

Police and fire-fighting   In the Southern Song dynasty (1127–1279), fire-fighting was seen as a responsibility of bureaucratic government. Official regulations specified that every city of average size should be equipped with water tanks, watchtowers and other fire-fighting facilities in each quadrant of the city and/or in the vicinity of major government buildings (Shiba, 1977: 421). Army personnel commanded by a military official served in the police and carried out fire-fighting duties. By the thirteenth century, Ningbo's militia commanded by an officer recruited from among the principal families of the city took over the responsibilities of police and fire-fighting. In the mid-nineteenth century, Ningbo established twelve fire stations 'through private initiative', in which Hui-chou merchants played a leading role. Shiba noted: 'Each station, equipped with a watchtower and an alarm drum, had as its responsibility a particular quarter of the city. Costs were covered by levies on those renting out houses and apartments at the rate of three per cent of rental income, and a station's management was in the hands of houseowners resident in the area of its responsibility' (Shiba, 1977: 422). The city's fire-fighting system was thus 'markedly improved' (Shiba, 1977: 421).

Conclusion: The 'Third Way' in Chinese history

Even economists who have been powerful advocates of the dynamic power of the market in promoting economic development have sometimes acknowledged the frequency with which market failure necessitates state intervention. The more subtle have distinguished between the different ways and levels of market failure in different countries, at different stages of development, and confronting different challenges in the international economy. Criticism of market failure needs also to be tempered by sharp awareness of the potentialities for state failure. There is nothing intrinsically good or bad about either the state or the market. Each has its advantages and disadvantages in serving human needs: '[T]he state should be treated essentially like the market – a necessary, but imperfect and occasionally dangerous way of achieving socio-economic goals' (Suzy Paine, quoted in Nolan, 1988: 18). Historically, the state has proved as flawed and as dangerous as the market: 'Awareness of the actual evils of and intrinsic limitations of both the state-owned and state-controlled economy and the market mechanism should be central to socialism' (Suzy Paine, quoted in Nolan, 1988: 18).

One of the most insightful analyses of this issue is contained in the *Wealth of Nations*, in which Adam Smith deeply criticized wasteful government expenditure, and was meticulous in considering the great variety of ways in which public goods might be financed. However, he was explicit about the potential importance of state intervention to act in the overall interests of society where markets failed:

> The third and last duty of the government [apart from establishing peace and maintaining law and order] is that of erecting and maintaining those public institutions and those public works which, though they may be in the highest degree advantageous to a great society are, however, of such a nature, that the profit could never repay the expence to any individual or small number of individuals, and which it therefore cannot be expected that any individual or small number of individuals should erect or maintain. The performance of this duty requires too very different degrees of expence in the different periods of society. (Smith, 1776, Vol. 2: 244)

Smith's formulation leaves open the door for greater or lesser state intervention depending on the particular circumstances that confront a given country or region in a particular epoch.

The relationship of the traditional Chinese state to the market for over one thousand years approximates the approach indicated by

Adam Smith. Through its activities the state strongly encouraged the development of the traditional market economy. Indeed, one answer to the 'Needham question' of why China failed to achieve an 'Industrial Revolution' despite a high level of technical development is precisely that markets were so highly developed that any local bottlenecks could almost always be met through the market mechanism, across the great Chinese 'free trade area' (Nolan, 1993). The state stepped in where markets failed, not only in respect of immediate growth issues, but also in relation to the wider issues of social stability and cohesion. It nurtured and stimulated commerce, but refused to allow commerce, financial interests and speculation to dominate society. When the state performed its role most effectively, it intervened in a non-ideological, pragmatic way:

> The best of all rulers is but a shadowy presence to his subjects; next comes the ruler they love and praise; next comes one they fear; next comes one with whom they take liberties. The best ruler is leisurely and carefree, seldom issuing orders. . . . When his task is accomplished and his work done, The people all say, 'It happened to us naturally'. (Lao Zi, 1963: ch. 17)

Behind the edifice of authoritarian Imperial rule was a pervasive morality based on the necessity of all strata of society observing their duties in order to sustain social cohesion, to achieve social and political stability and to ensure social sustainability. When these functions were operating effectively, there was 'great harmony' (*da tong*), a prosperous economy and a stable society. When they were operating poorly, there was 'great turmoil' (*da luan*), economic retrogression and social disorder: 'When the way prevails in the empire, fleet-footed horses are relegated to ploughing the fields; when the way does not prevail in the empire, war-horses breed on the border' (Lao Zi, 1963: ch. 46).

The moral target: Marrying the hedgehog and the snake

Francis Fukuyama has argued that democratic capitalism constitutes the 'final form of human government', and that its global reach represents the 'triumph of the Western idea' (Fukuyama, 1992). The current US government endorses such a view and has dedicated its international relations efforts to achieving such a goal. In the early twenty-first century, advanced oligopolistic capitalism has produced a uniquely powerful mechanism for propelling forward human initiatives to meet people's wants. Goods and services are provided with an improving quality, falling costs and real prices. Technical progress has advanced as never before. This system has proved uniquely effective in meeting people's wants as consumers. However, the experience of the USA, where this system has reached its apogee, has demonstrated that it is deeply deficient in meeting human needs as producers, as consumers and in their relations with each other. The virtually untrammelled free market in the USA which re-emerged in the late twentieth century is unable to satisfy fundamental human needs for self-fulfilment and security. It accentuates individual insecurity and social disintegration. The central task of Chinese political economy in the years ahead is to find a way to marry the 'hedgehog' of market dynamism with the 'snake' of social cohesion.

Adam Smith and the contradictions of the free market economy

Introduction Adam Smith provides a principal source of inspiration for free market economists across the world. In almost every discussion about the general direction of China's economic reforms, someone will refer to the so-called 'fact' that Adam Smith demonstrated the superiority of the free market as a form of socio-economic organization. Thus, it is argued, Adam Smith 'proved' that the ultimate direction for China's economic reforms (the 'other bank' in China's journey across the river) is the unfettered free market.

In fact, Smith himself had grave doubts about the ability of the free market to meet human needs. He believed that the market was a two-edged sword, with unique dynamic qualities, but also with deep in-built contradictions, though he did not use this word to describe them. Free market economists rarely, if ever, acknowledge his penetrating and realistic analysis of the inherent contradictions of the market economy. In fact, Smith has left a rich legacy of ideas in this sphere which are even more relevant to the pressing issues that face the world today than they were when he wrote his key works.

The *Wealth of Nations*, first published in 1776, is the most influential book in the history of economics, arguably more so even than Marx's *Capital*. It is a huge work of more than one thousand pages. Apart from specialist scholars of Smith, few people read the whole text. Few economics undergraduates read the book. Indeed, many professional economists, while freely making use of the idea of the 'invisible hand', have never read any part of it. It is widely assumed that the *Wealth of Nations* 'proves' that the free market, guided by the 'invisible hand', is the best arrangement for organizing economic life. Smith's other great work was the *Theory of Moral Sentiments*, published in 1759, and revised by Smith in 1761. Many economists have never heard of this work. Fewer still have read it. Far from being an 'early work', which was superseded by the *Wealth of Nations*, the *Theory of Moral Sentiments* is intellectually inseparable from the former. While their main topic is different, they share the same fundamental passion about the moral foundations of social life. At the heart of each of these books is an explicit recognition of fundamental contradictions within the market economy. Smith demonstrated that the free market is an immensely powerful force for impelling economic progress, but one that has deep in-built contradictions. He gave little clue as to how these might be resolved, but felt it was his duty to point them out.[10]

In the *Wealth of Nations*, Smith identified two powerful drivers of economic progress: the division of labour and the accumulation of capital. The foundation of Smith's 'growth model' was the division of labour, discussion of which occupies the first few chapters of the *Wealth of Nations*. Smith declared: 'The greatest improvements in the productive powers of labour, and the greatest part of the skill, dexterity and judgement with which it is any where directed, or applied, seems to have been the effects of the division of labour' (Smith, 1776, Vol. 1: 7). Smith considered that the fundamental driver of the accumulation process was the pursuit of profit: 'It is only for the sake of profit that any man employs a capital in the support of industry' (Smith, 1776, Vol. 1: 477). The possessor of capital directs his stock of capital towards those industries that yield the greatest profit and are, therefore, 'likely to be of the greatest value': '[B]y directing that industry in such a manner as its produce may be of the greatest value, he intends only his own gain, and he is in this, as in many other cases, led by the invisible hand to promote an end which was no part of his intention' (Smith, 1776, Vol. 1: 477).

Smith believed that these principles were the key to 'economic development', or the 'wealth of nations':

> Little else is required to carry a state to the highest level of opulence from the lowest level of barbarism, but peace, easy taxes, and a tolerable administration of justice.[11] . . . The natural effort of every individual to better his own condition, when suffered to exert itself with freedom and security, is so powerful a principle that it is alone, and without

any assistance, not only capable of carrying on the society to wealth and prosperity, but of surmounting a hundred impertinent obstructions with which the folly of human laws encumbers its operation. . . . (Smith, 1776, Vol. 2: 49–50)

The system appears to be an elegant, harmonious integration of individual self-interest and social interests. However, this is far from the case. Alongside Smith's rigorous analysis of the growth process was a deep awareness of the internal contradictions of that same process. Both the division of labour and the pursuit of profit contained deep internal contradictions from an ethical standpoint, the one from the perspective of man as producer, and the other from the perspective of man as consumer.

Man as producer   While the division of labour promoted productivity growth, the basis for long-term improvements in the 'wealth of nations', it also has deeply negative consequences for the mass of the population. Smith believed that people are born with relatively equal capacities for self-expression and self-realization. He considered that people's capability for self-realization was largely dependent on their social environment, especially their work environment, not on inherited differences:

> The difference of natural talents in different men is, in reality, much less than we are aware of; and the very different genius which appears to distinguish men of different professions, when grown up to maturity, is not upon many occasions so much the cause as the effect of the division of labour. The difference between the most dissimilar characters, between a philosopher and a common street porter, for example, seems to arise not so much from nature, as from habit, custom and education. (Smith, 1776, Vol. 1: 19–20)

In the course of industrial advance, opportunities arise for a greatly enhanced division of labour which were not present in agriculture: 'The nature of agriculture, indeed, does not permit of so many subdivisions of labour, nor of so complete a separation of one business from another, as manufactures' (Smith, 1776, Vol. 1: 9). Smith believed that the advantages of the enhanced division of labour included increased worker dexterity and reduced time lost in passing from one task to another, on account of greater occupational specialization; the greater possibility for applying mechanization to specialist tasks; and the associated opportunities for technical progress in the production of new types of machines by specialist machine-makers

(Smith, 1776, Vol. 1: 9–14). However, a major advantage of the enhanced division of labour was the possibility it presented for 'saving time' by increasing the labourer's work intensity:

> The habit of sauntering and of indolent and careless application, which is naturally or, rather, necessarily acquired by every country workman who is obliged to change his work and tools every half hour, and to apply his hand in twenty different ways almost every day of his life; render him almost always slothful and lazy and incapable of any vigorous application even on the most pressing occasions. (Smith, 1776, Vol. 1: 12)

For Smith, the division of labour was a two-edged sword. It promoted the advance of productivity, but at a high price. He was brutally realistic about its consequences for the mass of workers:

> In the progress of the division of labour, the employment of the far greater part of those who live by labour, that is the great body of the people, comes to be confined to a few very simple operations, frequently to one or two. But the understandings of the greater part of men are necessarily formed by their ordinary employments. The man whose life is spent in performing a few simple operations, of which the effects too are, perhaps, always the same, or very nearly the same, has no occasion to exert his understanding, or to exercise his invention in finding out expedients for removing difficulties which never occur. He naturally loses, therefore, the habit of such exertion, and generally becomes as stupid and ignorant as it is possible for a human creature to become. (Smith, 1776, Vol. 2: 302–3)

Smith warned: 'But in every improved and civilized society, this is the state into which the labouring poor, that is, the great body of the people, must necessarily fall, unless government takes some pains to prevent it' (Smith, 1776, Vol. 2: 303). The only 'solution' that Smith was able to offer to this deep contradiction was the establishment of 'little schools' in each parish or district, 'where children may be taught for a reward so moderate even a common labourer may afford it' (Smith, 1776, Vol. 2: 306).

Smith thought that great inequality and class conflicts were unavoidable in a society based on private property: 'Wherever there is great property, there is great inequality. For one very rich man, there must be at least five hundred poor, and the affluence of the few supposes the indigence of the many' (Smith, 1776, Vol. 2: 232). He warned that without a substantial 'trickle down' of the fruits of economic progress to the mass of the population, a society would be morally unsatisfactory and at risk due to social instability:

> Servants, labourers, and workmen of different kinds, make up by far the greater part of every great political society. But what improves the circumstances of the greater part can never be regarded as an inconvenience to the whole. No society can surely be great and flourishing of which the far greater part of the members are poor and miserable. It is but equity besides, that they who feed, clothe, and lodge the whole body of the people, should have have such a share of the produce of their own labour as to be themselves tolerably well fed, cloathed and lodged. (Smith, 1776, Vol. 1: 88)

However, Smith believed that it would be difficult to obtain co-operative solutions to the great differences of socio-economic interests in an economy like that of Britain in the late eighteenth century: 'The affluence of the rich excites the indignation of the many, who are often driven by want, and prompted by envy, to invade his possessions' (Smith, 1776, Vol. 2: 232). He concluded that it was a critical duty of the state to protect property-owners, upon whom rested the key instruments for economic progress: 'The acquisition of valuable and extensive property, therefore, necessarily requires the establishment of civil government. . . . Civil government presupposes a certain subordination . . . [which] gives some men some superiority over the greater part of their brethren' (Smith, 1776, Vol. 2: 232).

Smith considered that the realities of the labour market were basically antagonistic: 'The workers desire to get as much as possible, the masters to give as little as possible. The former are disposed to combine in order to raise and the latter in order to lower the wages of labour' (Smith, 1776, Vol. 1: 74). In late eighteenth-century Britain, the balance of power in the labour market was tipped decisively towards the masters:

> The masters, being few in number, can combine much more easily; and law, besides, authorizes or at least does not prohibit their combinations, while it prohibits those of the workmen. We have no acts of parliament against combining to lower the price of labour; but many against combining to raise it. In all such disputes, masters can hold out much longer. . . . Many workmen could not subsist a week, few could subsist a month, and scarce any a year without employment. (Smith, 1776, Vol. 1: 74–5)

Smith believed that class stratification was a necessary condition of economic progress, facilitating the accumulation of capital and the division of labour. However, he acknowledged that this contained the high possibility not only of class conflict, but also of 'corruption of moral sentiments', through the construction of social values that justified 'neglect of the poor and mean': '[T]he disposition to admire, and almost to worship, the rich and powerful, and to despise, or at least, to neglect persons of poor and mean condition, though necessary to maintain the distinction of ranks and the order of society, is at the same time, the great and most universal cause of the corruption of our moral sentiments' (Smith, 1761: 61).

Man as consumer   One of the central forces in Smith's growth model was the accumulation of capital, and that the central motive for the application of capital was to obtain profit derived from the use of capital. He believed that behind this lay an even deeper psychological drive, namely the desire to acquire 'wealth and greatness'. However, Smith considered that this fundamental driving force of economic progress contained its own 'deception', or in-built contradiction:

> The pleasures of wealth and greatness . . . strike the imagination as something grand and beautiful and noble, of which the attainment is well worth all the toil and anxiety which we are apt to bestow upon it. And it is well that nature imposes upon us in this manner. It is this deception which rouses and keeps in continual motion the industry of mankind. (Smith, 1761: 183)

Smith enumerates the dramatic effects of the application of this 'industry', impelled by the 'deception' of the pursuit of 'wealth and greatness':

> It is this which first prompted them to cultivate the ground, to build houses, to found cities and commonwealths, and to invent and improve all the sciences and arts, which ennoble human life; which have entirely changed the whole face of the globe, have turned the rude forests of nature into agreeable and fertile plains, and made the trackless and barren ocean a new fund of subsistence, and the great high road of com-munication to the different nations of the earth. The earth by these labours of mankind has been obliged to redouble her natural fertility, and to maintain a greater number of inhabitants. (Smith, 1761: 183–4)

It is deeply paradoxical that the driving force for economic progress should be considered to be a 'deception'.

Smith believed that the pursuit of 'wealth and greatness' was a 'deception' because, beyond a certain modest level of consumption, additional consumption brought no increase in happiness, and often brought unhappiness:

> In the langour of disease and the weariness of old age, the pleasures of the vain and empty distinctions of greatness disappear.... Power and riches then appear to be, what they are, enormous and operose machines contrived to produce a few trifling conveniences to the body, consisting of springs the most nice and delicate, which must be kept in order with the most anxious attention, and which, in spite of all our care are ready every moment to burst into pieces, and to crush in their ruins their unfortunate possessor. (Smith, 1761: 183–4)

Smith compared 'power and riches', to 'immense fabrics' which 'require the labour of life to raise':

> [They] threaten every moment to overwhelm the person that dwells in them, and which while they stand, though they may save him from some smaller inconveniences, can protect him from none of the inclemencies of the season. They keep off the summer shower, not the wintry storm, but leave him always as much, sometimes more exposed than before, to anxiety, to fear, and to sorrow; and to diseases, to danger and to death. (Smith, 1761: 184)

Smith was deeply critical of the pursuit of 'frivolous consumption', believing that it brought no increase in happiness:

> How many people ruin themselves by laying out money on trinkets of frivolous utility?... All their pockets are stuffed with little conveniences.... They walk about loaded with a multitude of baubles.... If we consider the real satisfaction which all these things are capable of affording, by itself and separated from the beauty of the arrangement which is fitted to promote it, it will appear in the highest degree contemptible and trifling.... [W]ealth and greatness are mere trinkets of frivolous utility, no more adapted for procuring ease of body or tranquillity of mind than the tweezer-cases of the lovers of toys. (Smith, 1761: 180–1)

Smith thought that the only worthwhile social goal was the pursuit of happiness. In his view, this was to be attained through 'tranquillity', not the pursuit of 'power and riches': 'Happiness is tranquillity and enjoyment. Without tranquillity there can be no enjoyment; and where there is perfect tranquillity there is scarce anything which is not capable of amusing' (Smith, 1761: 150). According to Smith, the attainment of happiness did not require high levels of consumption:

> [I]n the ordinary situations of human life, a well-disposed mind may
> be equally calm, equally cheerful, and equally contented.... [I]n the
> most glittering and exalted situation that our ideal fancy can hold out
> to us, the pleasures from which we propose to derive our real happiness,
> are almost always the same with those which in our actual though
> humble situation, we have at all times at hand and in our power....
> [T]he pleasures of vanity and superiority are seldom consistent with
> perfect tranquillity, the principle and foundation of all real and satis-
> factory enjoyment. (Smith, 1761: 149–50)

Smith believed that a good society was one in which people attained
happiness through fulfilling basic human needs, not in the vain pursuit
of unlimited wants. He considered that there was a clear choice:

> Two different roads are presented to us, ... the one by the study of
> wisdom and the practice of virtue, the other, by the acquisition of
> wealth and greatness; ... the one of proud ambition and ostentatious
> avidity, the other, of humble modesty and equitable justice; ... the
> one more gaudy and glittering in the colouring, the other more correct
> and exquisitely beautiful in its outline. (Smith, 1761: 62)

Smith considered that human psychology required social cohesion
as the foundation of a good society in which all citizens could achieve
happiness:

> All the members of human society stand in need of each other's
> assistance.... Where the necessary assistance is reciprocally afforded
> from love, from gratitude, from friendship, and esteem, the society
> flourishes and is happy. All the different members of it are bound
> together by the agreeable bonds of love and affection, and are, as it
> were, drawn to one common centre of mutual good offices. (Smith,
> 1761: 85)

The foundation of such cohesion was 'benevolence':

> [T]o feel much for others and little for ourselves, to restrain our selfish,
> and to indulge our benevolent affections, constitutes the perfection of
> human nature; and can alone among mankind produce that harmony
> of sentiments and passions in which consists their whole grace and
> propriety. (Smith, 1761: 25)[12]

Benevolence, not the pursuit of 'wealth and greatness', allows the
construction of a sense of duty, which, in its turn, enables the realization of social cohesion:

The regard to those general rules of conduct, is what is properly called a sense of duty, a principle of the greatest consequence in human life, and the only possible principle by which the bulk of mankind are capable of directing their actions. . . . Without this sacred regard to general rules, there is no man whose conduct can be much depended upon. . . . By acting according to the dictates of our moral faculties, we necessarily pursue the most effectual means for promoting the happiness of mankind. (Smith, 1761: 161–3 and 166)

Smith believed unless a society was 'just', there was a grave danger that it would disintegrate into chaos:

Justice, on the contrary, is the main pillar that upholds the whole edifice. If it is removed, the great, the immense fabric of human society, that fabric which to raise and support seems in this world, if I may say so, to have been the peculiar and darling love of Nature, must in a moment crumble into atoms. (Smith, 1761: 86)

Conclusion Smith's analysis of the market mechanism was an attempt to lay bare the fundamental laws governing economic development. At the same time that he sought to identify these principles, he devoted scrupulous attention to the underlying contradictions of the market economy. He did believe that the free market was the fundamental driver of economic progress. However, he demonstrated that this driving force contained deep internal contradictions from the point of view of people as both producers and consumers. In respect to both issues, Smith insisted that the dynamism of the free market economy should be considered alongside its deep ethical shortcomings. He was unable to answer satisfactorily how the latter shortcomings could be resolved, but his intellectual honesty and driving sense of moral purpose led him to lay bare these contradictions clearly and passionately.

His analysis of the contradictions of the market economy is highly relevant to fundamental issues facing the world today. These include the nature of work for almost one billion people in developing countries employed as 'lumpen labour' in the non-farm sector for US$1–2 per day; class conflict between capital and labour in developing countries that are still in the early phase of capitalist industrialization; the 'degradation of work' for a large fraction of the service sector workers in rich countries, who work under intense pressure from 'remorseless monitoring' made possible by modern information technology, in order to increase 'labour intensity'; the erosion of a sense of social cohesion as 'state desertion', in order to provide a 'good investment environment' for global capital, becomes widespread across countries at all levels of development; widespread consumer fetishism promoted by the immense marketing expenditure of global giant firms and commercialized global mass media; and even the very sustainability of life on the planet as fast-growing parts of developing countries move towards the immense per capita consumption levels of the advanced capitalist countries.

Adam Smith's penetrating analysis is of the deepest significance in China's search for a moral touchstone to help the country grope its way forward in the years ahead. It is deeply misleading to use Smith as if he provided unqualified support to the free market.

The market and morality, East and West

For many political commentators, the struggle over the meaning of 'freedom' is essentially a battle between American and European conceptions of the term. For example, Will Hutton believes that there is 'only one source of countervailing power and values [to the US]: Europe' (Hutton, 2002: 184). This Euro-centred perspective ignores the efforts of the rest of the world, not least China, to try to address the same issues. As we have seen, the central preoccupation of Chinese political practice over, literally, thousands of years has been the attempt to find a function for the state, and nurture a social ethic that enables the economy and society to operate in a way that serves that whole social interest. The core of this approach to political theory and practical politics is the desire to establish social cohesion in the interests of all members of society, no matter what position they occupy. These ideas had their foundation in the writings of Confucius (c.551–479 BC). *The Analects* (*Lun Yü*) is by far the most influential book in Chinese history, providing the moral foundations for the Chinese state for over 2,000 years.[13]

Confucius' ideas were developed during a time of rapid and drastic social change, without equal in Chinese history before the twentieth century (Graham, 1964: 29). During this period rapid social change undermined all accepted principles of government and standards of conduct (Graham, 1964: 55). Confucius and his successors found themselves in a world in which traditional methods of government and standards of conduct were ceasing to apply. In seeking for a solution to the practical problems of social and political chaos, they looked back with regret to the stable feudal order of the early Chou, in which there had been an accepted code of *li*, 'rites', and 'manners' regulating social relationships (Graham, 1964: 29). This way of behaving was the 'Way of the ancient kings'. The recovery of the *Dao*, or Way, became the central theme in Chinese philosophy.

Confucius and his followers were concerned with practical problems rather than interested in abstract philosophical debate for its own sake. They sought ideas that were practically useful for society: 'If we can make any safe generalization about the whole of Chinese philosophy, it is that interest has always centred on human needs, on the improvement of government, on morals, and on the value of human life' (Graham, 1964: 28). Chinese philosophical thinking is the kind of thought 'least conquerable by logicians' and 'too complex to be laid out in all its inter-relations', even when it concerns the most trivial everyday matters: 'When we try to convince someone else we can only pick out key phrases in our thought in order to guide him in the same direction and try to fill in the gaps when he refuses to make the leaps, but without hope of achieving full logical rigour' (Graham, 1964: 54). Graham considers that the Chinese philosophers have tended to distrust over-logical thinkers who insist on filling in all gaps, seeing them as 'triflers with unimportant questions' and 'gross simplifiers of important ones' (Graham, 1964: 55).

Philosophers in the Confucian tradition tend not to waste their time on logic-chopping without practical issue. The Chinese philosophers, following the Confucian tradition, have been 'much more impressed by the opposite extremes of intelligence, the aphoristic genius which guides thought of the maximum complexity with the minimum of words' (Graham, 1964: 55). This method of thinking was influenced by the fact that Chinese words are uninflected and their functions marked only by particles and by word-order, 'so that there is a much more complete illusion of looking through language at reality as though through a perfectly transparent medium' (Graham, 1964: 55).

Confucius and Adam Smith express themselves in different ways. However, from a comparison of the key ideas in Confucius' *Analects* and Smith's key works, the *Theory of Moral Sentiments* and the *Wealth of Nations*, we can see that there are powerful common themes concerning the relationship of the individual to society; the importance of maintaining social cohesion in order to serve the interests of the whole society; the function of morality in maintaining social cohesion; the relationship of material consumption to human happiness; and the function of education in a good society. The same ideas can be found in numerous other parallel sets of thinkers in China and the West. However, I have chosen to concentrate on Confucius and Adam Smith as they are uniquely influential within their respective cultures. Unwittingly, they occupy a broad common ground, across centuries and across cultures.

The relevant ideas of Confucius and Smith on different topics are set out in detail in the table (pp. 157–65). The common theme of these writers is that the market is not an intrinsically moral entity that should be allowed to dominate society. Restraint of selfishness, or 'benevolence', is the moral foundation of both philosophies, not the pursuit of individual self-interest. Both emphasize reciprocal social obligations and duties as the foundation of a good society. Both regard the pursuit of wealth and position as damaging to individual fulfilment. Both regard education as the foundation of self-fulfilment and the morality that forms the cement for social cohesion. Both regard individual happiness as the prime goal of a successful society, but they each believe that this is not to be achieved through the pursuit of ever greater material consumption. Rather, they both consider that this can be achieved through the contentment derived from living according to the ethical norms that have evolved in order to sustain a high level of social coherence. Each is scathing of the possibility for happiness from high levels of material consumption.

Groping for a way forward

The historical roots of China's development path   Especially since the Second World War, different parts of Western Europe have made valiant efforts to try to find a 'Third Way' between planning and the free market. Despite heavy attack from the forces of globalization, most Western European nations are still trying to find their own 'Third Way'. However, it is wrong to think that Europe alone offers an alternative to the globalization of American free market fundamentalism. Most of the developing world is debating intensely how best to respond to the forces of globalization and US 'free market fundamentalist' ideology. The Far East, and China in particular, has a huge potential contribution to make towards global thinking about how to devise a socially cohesive society that satisfies material and spiritual needs. China's own recent history under Chairman Mao's leadership provides a vivid illustration of the dangers of excessively simplistic and utopian approaches to this goal. However, it is hard to imagine the establishment of social cohesion without a strong role for the state.

China is struggling to cope with a series of immense, inter-related challenges: the development challenge, which arises from the fact that it is a huge poor country still firmly locked [*continues on p. 165*]

Social cohesion, East and West: Confucius and Adam Smith

Benevolence

'[T]o feel much for others and little for ourselves, to restrain our selfish, and to indulge our benevolent affections, constitutes the perfection of human nature; and can alone among mankind produce that harmony of sentiments and passions in which consists their whole grace and propriety.' (*TMS*: 25)

'All the members of human society stand in need of each other's assistance. . . . Where the necessary assistance is reciprocally afforded from love, from gratitude, from friendship, and esteem, the society flourishes and is happy. All the different members of it are bound together by the agreeable bonds of love and affection, and are, as it were, drawn to one common centre of mutual good offices.' (*TMS*: 85)

'To return to the observance of the rites through overcoming the self constitutes benevolence. If for a single day a man could return to the observance of the rites through overcoming himself, then the whole Empire would consider benevolence to be his. However, the practice of benevolence depends on oneself alone, and not on others.' (*Lun Yü*, XII: 1)

'A man who finds benevolence attractive cannot be surpassed. . . . Is there a man who, for the space of a single day, is able to devote all his strength to benevolence?' (*Lun Yü*, IV: 6)

'What can one do with the rites who is not benevolent? What can a man do with music who is not benevolent?' (*Lun Yü*, III: 3)

'A gentleman must be strong and resolute for his burden is heavy and the road is long, for his burden was benevolence and the road only came to an end with death.' (*Lun Yü*, VIII: 7)

'Do not impose on others what you yourself do not desire.' (*Lun Yü*, XII: 2)

Benevolence (cont'd)

'For gentlemen of purpose and
men of benevolence while it is
inconceivable that they should
seek to stay alive at the expense
of benevolence, it may happen
that they have to accept
death to have benevolence
accomplished.' (*Lun Yü*, XV: 9)

'Benevolence is more vital to the
common people than even fire
and water. In the case of fire
and water, I have seen men die
by stepping on them, but I have
never seen any man die by
stepping on benevolence.'
(*Lun Yü*, XV: 136–7)

Pursuit of wealth and social position

'[T]he disposition to admire,
and almost to worship, the rich
and powerful, and to despise,
or at least, to neglect persons
of poor and mean condition,
though necessary to maintain
the distinction of ranks and
the order of society, is at the
same time, the great and
most universal cause of the
corruption of our moral
sentiments.' (*TMS*: 61)

'Two different roads are
presented to us, . . . the one by
the study of wisdom and the
practice of virtue, the other, by
the acquisition of wealth and
greatness; . . . the one of proud

'The gentleman seeks neither a
full belly nor a comfortable
home.' (*Lun Yü*, I: 14)

'There is no point in seeking
the views of a gentleman who,
though he sets his heart on the
Way, is ashamed of poor food
and clothes.' (*Lun Yü*, IV: 9)

'If one is guided by profit in
one's actions, one will incur
much ill-will.' (*Lun Yü*, IV: 12)

'If wealth were a permissible
pursuit I would be willing even
to act as a guard holding a whip
outside the market place.' (*Lun
Yü*, VII: 12)

Pursuit of wealth and social position (cont'd)

ambition and ostentatious avidity, the other, of humble modesty and equitable justice; . . . the one more gaudy and glittering in the colouring, the other more correct and exquisitely beautiful in its outline.' (*TMS*: 62)

'[T]he candidates for fortune too frequently abandon the paths of virtue; for unhappily, the road which leads to the one, and that which leads to the other lie sometimes in very opposite directions. . . . But, though they should be so lucky as to attain this wished-for greatness, they are always most miserably disappointed in the happiness which they expect to enjoy in it.' (*TMS*: 64–5)

'Power and riches then appear to be, what they are, enormous and operose machines contrived to produce a few trifling conveniences to the body, consisting of springs the most nice and delicate, which must be kept in order with the most anxious attention, and which, in spite of all our care are ready every moment to burst into pieces, and to crush in their ruins their unfortunate possessor. . . . How many people ruin themselves by laying out money on trinkets of frivolous

'With Yu I can find no fault. He lived in low dwellings while devoting all his energy to the building of irrigation canals.' (*Lun Yü*, VIII: 221)

'Extravagance means ostentation, frugality means shabbiness. I would rather be shabby than ostentatious.' (*Lun Yü*, VIII: 36)

'In the eating of coarse rice and the drinking of water, the using of one's elbow as a pillow, joy is to be found. Wealth and rank attained through immoral means have as much to do with me as the passing clouds.' (*Lun Yü*, VII: 88)

'It is shameful to make salary your sole object, irrespective of whether the Way prevails in the state or not.' (*Lun Yü*, XIV: 1)

'If a man remembers what is right at the sight of profit, is ready to lay down his life in the face of danger, and does not forget sentiments he has repeated all his life even when he has been in straitened circumstances for a long time, he may be said to be a complete man.' (*Lun Yü*, XIV: 12)

'It is more difficult not to complain of injustice when poor

Pursuit of wealth and social position (cont'd)

---

utility? . . . All their pockets are stuffed with little conveniences. . . . They walk about loaded with a multitude of baubles. . . . If we consider the real satisfaction which all these things are capable of affording, by itself and separated from the beauty of the arrangement which is fitted to promote it, it will appear in the highest degree contemptible and trifling. . . . [W]ealth and greatness are mere trinkets of frivolous utility, no more adapted for procuring ease of body or tranquillity of mind than the tweezer-cases of the lovers of toys.' (*TMS*: 183–4, 180–1)

'The pleasures of wealth and greatness . . . strike the imagination as something grand and beautiful and noble, of which the attainment is well worth all the toil and anxiety which we are apt to bestow upon it. And it is well that nature imposes upon us in this manner. It is this deception which rouses and keeps in continual motion the industry of mankind. It is this which first prompted them to cultivate the ground, to build houses, to found cities and commonwealths, and to invent and improve all the sciences and

than not to behave arrogantly when rich.' (*Lun Yü*, XIV: 10)

'The gentleman devotes his mind to attaining the Way and not to securing food. The gentleman worries about the Way, not about poverty.' (*Lun Yü*, XV: 32)

Pursuit of wealth and social position (cont'd)

arts, which ennoble human life; which have entirely changed the whole face of the globe, have turned the rude forests of nature into agreeable and fertile plains, and made the trackless and barren ocean a new fund of subsistence, and the great high road of communication to the different nations of the earth. The earth by these labours of mankind has been obliged to redouble her natural fertility, and to maintain a greater number of inhabitants.' (*TMS*: 183–4)

Commonly held ethical values are the foundation of a cohesive social order

'Justice, on the contrary, is the main pillar that upholds the whole edifice. If it is removed, the great, the immense fabric of human society, that fabric which to raise and support seems in this world, if I may say so, to have been the peculiar and darling love of Nature, must in a moment crumble into atoms.' (*TMS*: 86)

'The regard to those general rules of conduct, is what is properly called a sense of duty, a principle of the greatest consequence in human life, and the only possible principle by which the bulk of mankind

'Of the things brought about by the rites, harmony is the most valuable. Of the ways of former kings, this is the most beautiful, and is followed alike in matters great and small, yet this will not always work: to aim at harmony without regulating it by the rites simply because one knows about harmony will not, in fact, work.' (*Lun Yü*, I: 12)

'The rule of virtue can be compared to the Pole Star which commands the homage of the multitude of stars without leaving its place.' (*Lun Yü*, II: 1)

*Commonly held ethical values are the foundation
of a cohesive social order (cont'd)*

are capable of directing their actions. . . . Without this sacred regard to general rules, there is no man whose conduct can be much depended upon. . . . By acting according to the dictates of our moral faculties, we necessarily pursue the most effectual means for promoting the happiness of mankind.' (*TMS*: 162–3 and 166)

'The gentleman has morality as his basic stuff and by observing the rites puts it into practice, by being modest gives it expression, and by being trustworthy in word brings it to completion. Such is a gentleman indeed.' (*Lun Yü*, XV: 18)

'For the gentleman it is morality that is supreme.' (*Lun Yü*, XVII: 23)

Civilization, specialization and human creativity

'In the progress of the division of labour, the employment of the far greater part of those who live by labour, that is the great body of the people, comes to be confined to a few very simple operations, frequently to one or two. But the understandings of the greater part of men are necessarily formed by their ordinary employments. The man whose life is spent in performing a few simple operations, of which the effects too are, perhaps, always the same, or very nearly the same, has no occasion to exert his understanding, or to exercise his invention in finding out expedients for removing difficulties which never occur. He naturally loses, therefore, the habit of such exertion, and

'The gentleman is no vessel.' (*Lun Yü*, II: 12)*

Civilization, specialization and human creativity (cont'd)

---

generally becomes as stupid and ignorant as it is possible for a human creature to become. . . . But in every improved and civilized society, this is the state into which the labouring poor, that is, the great body of the people, must necessarily fall, unless government takes some pains to prevent it.' (*WN*, Vol. 2: 302–3)

The family, education and ethics

'There is scarce any man, however, who by discipline, education, and example, may not be so impressed with a regard to general rules, as to act upon almost every occasion with tolerable decency and through the whole of his life to avoid any considerable degree of blame.' (*TMS*: 163)

'Do you wish to educate your children to be dutiful to their parents, to be kind and affectionate to their brothers and sisters? Put them under the necessity of being dutiful children, of being kind and affectionate brothers and sisters: educate them in your own house. From their parents' house they may with propriety go out every day to attend public schools: but let their dwelling, be always at home. . . .

'It is rare for a man whose character is such that he is a good son and obedient as a young man to have the inclination to transgress against his superiors. The gentleman devotes his efforts to the roots, for once the roots are established, the Way will grow therefrom. Being good as a son and obedient as a young man is, perhaps, the root of a man's character.' (*Lun Yü*, I: 2)

The family, education and ethics (cont'd)

Domestic education is the institution of nature; public education, the contrivance of man.' (TMS: 222)

'[T]he state of society does not place the greater part of individuals in such situations [as naturally form in them almost all the abilities and virtues which that state requires] and some attention of government is necessary to prevent almost the entire corruption and degeneracy of the great body of the population.' (WN, Vol. 2: 302)

Tranquillity and happiness

'[I]n the ordinary situations of human life, a well-disposed mind may be equally calm, equally cheerful, and equally contented. . . . [I]n the most glittering and exalted situation that our ideal fancy can hold out to us, the pleasures from which we propose to derive our real happiness, are almost always the same with those which in our actual though humble situation, we have at all times at hand and in our power. . . . [T]he pleasures of vanity and superiority are seldom consistent with perfect tranquillity, the principle and foundation of all real and

'Is it not a pleasure to have learned something, to try it out at due intervals? Is it not a joy to have friends come from afar?' (Lun Yü, I: 1)

'Be stimulated by the Odes, take your stand by the rites, and be perfected by music.' (Lun Yü, I: 8)

'The Master talked of music to the Grand Musician of Lu saying, This much can be known about music. It begins with playing in unison. When it gets into full swing, it is harmonious, clear and unbroken. In this way it

Tranquillity and happiness (cont'd)

satisfactory enjoyment.' (*TMS*: 149–50)	reaches the conclusion.' (*Lun Yü*, III: 23)
'Happiness is tranquillity and enjoyment. Without tranquillity there can be no enjoyment; and where there is perfect tranquillity there is scarce anything which is not capable of amusing.' (*TMS*: 150)	'When the Master was singing in the company of others and liked someone else's song, he always asked to hear it again before joining in.' (*Lun Yü*, VII: 32)
	'The gentleman is easy of mind, while the small man is full of anxiety.' (*Lun Yü*, VII: 37)
	'When Chih, the Master Musician, begins to play and when the *Kuan chu* comes to an end, how the sound fills the ears.' (*Lun Yü*, VIII: 15)
	'In the late Spring, after the Spring clothes have been newly made, I should like to go bathing with friends in the River Yi and enjoy the breeze on the Rain Altar, and then go home chanting poetry.' (*Lun Yü*, XI: 26)

* That is, he is no specialist, as every vessel is designed for a specific purpose (Lau, 1979: 64).
TMS: Adam Smith (1761), *The Theory of Moral Sentiments*
WN: Adam Smith (1776), *The Wealth of Nations*
Lun Yü: Confucius (1979), *The Analects (Lun Yü)*

into the 'Lewis phase' of development; the challenge of globalization and the global business revolution; the challenge from the transition from the administrative planning system; the ecological challenge; the military and ideological challenge from the USA; the challenge of the transformation of the Chinese Communist Party; the psychological challenge from frantic socio-economic change in the context of the one-child policy; as well as the challenge and urgent danger from the threat of financial crisis. While trying to manage this turbulent process, China's leaders are groping for a way to combine the virtues of the market with the attainment of desirable social objectives. The state is central to resolving these difficulties.

In this struggle, the USA's current mission to spread the individualistic, materialistic, anti-state philosophy which glorifies the finance-dominated free market threatens deeply China's hopes to negotiate a way through the massive challenges it faces. The consequence of the currently dominant US free market fundamentalism both within the USA and in its international relations is to undermine social coherence, by denigrating the useful functions of the state. It strives to establish a society based on minimizing the government's functions in order to maximize individual freedom and rights. Adopting such a philosophy would gravely endanger China's development. In the turbulent environment faced by China, a sense of social coherence and a central role for the government is the *sine qua non* of system survival, let alone successful development for China's 1.3 billion citizens.

In seeking for a moral framework to guide its development, China can look back to its long history of state activity to try to make the market serve common social purposes. It can also look back to its experience under communism from 1949 to the late 1970s, when the experiments with market reforms began. China's state-owned enterprises and rural people's communes were deeply problematic in terms of their ability to compete with capitalist firms. Their inefficiencies were a huge handicap in advancing the people's material standard of living. They greatly limited the horizons of their participants through severe constraints on migration from job to job and region to region. They contained their own serious inequalities. However, China's state enterprises and rural people's communes provided an exceptional example of social cohesion and security. In many rural areas, and in the urban areas, they provided a secure environment for workers in their daily lives, with security of employment, of housing, health and educational provision. 'Serve the people' (*wei renmin fuwu*) was the foundation of Maoist ideology.

China can learn from thinkers elsewhere, not least in the USA, who have deeply considered these issues, albeit that their voice is given only limited attention today, or that these voices from the past, such as Adam Smith's, are presented in a distorted fashion. China can currently find only limited support from continental Europe's political leaders in groping for its development philosophy, and none from the USA's leaders. The USA's currently dominant conception of 'freedom' is explicitly hostile to such a philosophy. The Chinese leadership must look mainly to the country's own past to try to find a philosophical direction that can provide the country and the Party with 'moral cement' and confidence in the face of enormous ideological challenges.

Jiang Zemin In his speech of 1 July 2001 to celebrate the eightieth anniversary of the Chinese Communist Party (see chapter 1), Jiang Zemin, Party General Secretary, emphasized that China should look to the past to serve its current needs for a philosophical foundation:

> We must inherit and develop the fine cultural traditions of the Chinese nation. . . . With regard to the rich cultural legacies left over from China's history of several thousand years, we should discard the dross, keep the essence and carry forward and develop it in the spirit of the times in order to make the past serve the present (*zuodao gu wei jin yong*).

Jiang also emphasized that the task facing China was to nurture social cohesion by stressing the importance of culture and morality as well as material advancement:

> We must realize that we would lose the common objective of struggle and reject the accepted code of conduct if we only value material gains and money without thinking of ideals and moral standards. We should combine the rule of law with the rule of virtue in order to lay a lofty and ethical foundation for good public order and a healthy environment. We should advocate patriotism, collectivism and socialism among all people, combat and resist money-worship, hedonism, ultra-egoism, and other decadent ideas.

He underlined that the goal of the Party was to achieve an 'all-round development of man'. He reiterated that the Party's traditions were to serve the ordinary people: 'All the Party's work must take the fundamental interests of the overwhelming majority of the people as the supreme criterion.'

Jiang stressed that the Party must give special emphasis to the least well-placed to lead fulfilling lives: 'Leading organs and leading cadres at all levels should pay particular attention to those who have encountered temporary difficulties in their work and life, put their problems on the top of the agenda for special consideration and solution and make proper arrangements for their employment and daily life.' He also laid great stress on the crucial importance of maintaining strong Party leadership in order for China to survive the current stresses as an intact society: 'It is vital to uphold the central-ized leadership and unity of the Party and the state and safeguard the authority of the Party Central Committee. . . . No localities, depart-ments and institutions should be allowed to go their own way.'

Hu Jintao In the early days following his election in November 2002 to the post of Party General Secretary (he became President in March 2003), Hu Jintao chose to make his first major speech at Xibaipo, a poor village in Hebei province at which the Party held a critical meeting on the eve of the Communist victory in 1949. He brought with him several members of the Party Central Committee. His speech was made on 6 December 2002, but not published in *Renmin Ribao* (*People's Daily*) until 2 January 2003. In the speech he repeatedly stressed that the Party, especially the leading cadres, should not feel complacent about the enormous achievements since the start of the reforms, because the Party and the country still faced so many complex challenges both at home and abroad. He emphas-ized through innumerable repetitions the fact that it was necessary for the Party to follow the path of 'plain living and hard struggle' (*jianku fendou*) for a long period ahead. He used the phrase over sixty times in the space of a relatively short speech. He stressed that China had only reached the 'lower stage' of a 'small comfort' (*xiao-kang*) society,[14] and that it still had far to go before it truly reached such a society for every segment of the Chinese people:

> Our Party, especially the leading cadres, should keep firmly in mind our country's basic condition and our Party's solemn mission, and establish for the Party and people over the long term the ideology of 'plain living and hard struggle' (*jianku fendou*). We must deeply un-derstand that in upholding the importance of 'plain living and hard struggle', the key point is to soberly understand our country's basic situation. Our country is today and will be for a long time to come, in the primary stage of socialism, in which the primary social contradic-tion still is that between the need to increase the people's material and cultural needs and the backward state of social production. Alongside the struggle objective of comprehensively establishing a 'small com-fort' (*xiaokang*) society, the Sixteenth Party Congress deeply analysed the pressing problems and difficulties that we face, and made clear to the whole Party and the whole population the need for plain living and hard struggle over a long period of time.

Ours is a developing country with almost 1.3 billion people. The productive forces, technology and educational level are still relatively backward. We have a long road to travel in order to achieve industrialization and modernization. Our population's standard of living has, generally speaking, attained the level of 'small comfort'. However, the level of 'small comfort' that we have attained is still low, incomplete, and the development level is extremely unbalanced. Consolidating and raising our present level of 'small comfort' still needs a long period of plain living and hard struggle.

Compared with the world's advanced level, our country's economic, technological and national defence strength is still greatly lacking. We still face pressure from the fact that the advanced countries have the upper hand in technology and other respects. On the international front we face a complex and ever-changing situation. Domestically, we face complex and difficult reform, with heavy construction tasks. We carry the heavy burden of our Party's historical mission. Consequently, we can have no reason for becoming intoxicated with what we have already achieved, and slackening our efforts. We can have no reason for being complacent, conservative and standing still. We can have no reason for being satisfied with the present situation, and forgetting the need to forge ahead.

The whole Party, especially the leading cadres, as well as every level of the Party, must in a clear-headed and sober way recognize that the intense international struggle provides us with an urgent challenge. They must in a clear-headed and sober way recognize the arduousness and complexity of the responsibility that we carry. They must in a clear-headed and sober way recognize the difficulties and risks we face in our work. They must raise their awareness of the suffering that lies ahead. They must prepare for times of danger. They must thoroughly understand the extreme importance of plain living and hard struggle. They must firmly establish the ideology of long-term 'plain living and hard struggle' for the Party and the people. (Hu Jintao, 2003)

In his speech at Xibaipo, Hu Jintao placed great stress on the need for the Communist Party to relate closely to the difficulties faced by ordinary Chinese people. This also was a task of the utmost importance necessitating 'plain living and hard struggle' for Party members. He also stressed the critical need for the Party to take extremely seriously the instruction of Chairman Mao: 'serve the people' (*wei renmin fuwu*). To achieve this, Party members need to go deeply among the mass of the population to understand their difficulties, especially among the poorest and most disadvantaged groups:

The whole Party, and especially the leading cadres, must keep firmly in mind the aim of serving the people (*wei renmin fuwu*) with their heart and soul. They must steadfastly work for the broad mass of the people. 'Plain living and hard struggle' are the basic colour of a Marxist political party. It is also the unavoidable demand for holding firmly to power for the people, and for, from start to finish, forming the leading core for socialist construction with Chinese characteristics. Only through upholding plain living and hard struggle and installing the popular masses in our hearts, from start to finish breathing together with the mass of the people, sharing their fate, and linking our hearts with theirs, can we ensure that our Party is linked flesh and blood with the mass of the people. Only then can we increase our resistance to the penetration of decayed thinking. Only then can we uninterruptedly go with the times and open up our creativity.

If we cast aside the work style of plain living and hard struggle, and covet material comforts, if we are unwilling to carry on with hard work, if we are indifferent to the masses' sickness and suffering, if we turn a deaf ear to the cries of the masses, then we will inevitably be separated from the masses. We must keep firmly in mind the Party's aim, upholding plain living and hard struggle. These two are intimately connected. Only by keeping firmly in mind the aim of serving the people can we preserve the revolutionary will and the revolutionary character and morals that constitute plain living and hard struggle. Only by upholding plain living and hard struggle can we wholeheartedly attain the aim of serving the people.

The basic purpose of holding fast to plain living and hard struggle is to strive unremittingly to serve the interests of the broad mass of the people, uninterruptedly doing a good job at safeguarding, promoting and developing the masses' interests. This also is the inevitable requirement of putting into practice Jiang Zemin's important thinking of the 'three represents'. Every level of the Party must thoroughly uphold entering the basic level, and entering the lives of the masses, listening attentively to the cries of the masses. They must concern themselves with the masses' sickness and suffering. They must always place in their hearts the masses' safety and changing circumstances. Their authority must be at the service of the people. Their feelings must be concerned for the people. Their interests must work for the people.

It is especially important to be concerned about those of the masses who encounter difficulties in their livelihood and production, to enter into the impoverished areas and go to the enterprises that are in difficulties. It is especially important to go among the poor masses, including the workers who have lost their jobs, the poor population in the villages, and the poor residents of the cities. We should leave no stone unturned in order to help them resolve their difficulties. Through work which is concrete and effective, we should work with the utmost care for the masses' interests, and lead the masses to construct their own happy life.

Just before and just after Hu Jintao made his speech at Xibaipo, Wen Jiabao, China's Vice-Premier (he become Premier in March 2003), and newly elected member of the Standing Committee of the Politburo, made highly publicized visits to poor people in Guizhou and Shanxi, including both the rural population and the urban laid-off workers. He spoke strongly of the urgent need to solve the problems of the poorest people in Chinese society, and the need to establish and a society of all-round 'small comfort' (*xiaokang*) (*Renmin Ribao* [*People's Daily*], 24 November 2002 and 5 January 2003).

Chairman Mao   Today, on the one hand, China faces the dangers of hubris and over-confidence. It is the last remaining fast-growing substantial part of the world economy. It received US$53 billion in FDI in 2002, making it, as noted above, the largest recipient of FDI in the world. On the other hand, the leadership faces an immensely challenging situation both at home and abroad. It is highly significant that the new Chinese leadership under Party General Secretary Hu Jintao should have turned for inspiration to Chairman Mao's 1949 speech on the eve of the revolution. Mao deeply emphasized that victory over the KMT was just the start of a 'long march of ten thousand *li*':

> After several decades, the victory of the Chinese people's democratic revolution, viewed in retrospect, will seem only like a brief prologue to a long drama. A drama begins with a prologue, but the prologue is not the drama. The Chinese revolution is great, but the road after the revolution will be longer, the work greater and more arduous. This must be made clear now in the Party. (Mao Zedong, 1949: 374)

Mao stressed the dangers of complacency: 'With victory, certain moods may grow within the Party – arrogance, the airs of a self-styled hero, inertia and unwillingness to make progress, love of pleasure and distaste for continued hard living' (Mao Zedong, 1949: 374). He warned further:

> With victory, the people will be grateful to us and the bourgeoisie will come forward to flatter us. It has been proved that the enemy cannot conquer us with force of arms. However, the flattery of the bourgeoisie may conquer the weak-willed in our ranks. There may be some communists, who were not conquered by enemies with guns and bullets; they will be defeated by sugar-coated bullets. (Mao Zedong, 1949: 374)

Mao emphasized that in the period ahead, private capitalism would have a vital role to play in the development of the national economy:

'In this period, all capitalist elements in the cities and countryside which are not harmful but beneficial to the national economy should be allowed to exist and expand. This is not only unavoidable but economically necessary' (Mao Zedong, 1949: 368). However, Mao also emphasized that the existence and expansion of capitalism in China would not be 'unrestricted and uncurbed as in the capitalist countries'. He advocated the adoption of Sun Yat-sen's policy of 'regulation of capital': '[C]apitalism will be restricted from several directions – in the scope of its operation and by tax policy, market prices and labour policy. We shall adopt well-measured and flexible policies for restricting capitalism in each place, each industry and each period' (Mao Zedong, 1949: 368). In the period ahead, Mao believed:

> Restriction versus opposition to restriction will be the main form of class struggle in the new democratic state. It is entirely wrong to think that at present we need not restrict capitalism and can discard the view of 'regulation of capital'; that is a Right opportunist view. But the opposite view, which advocates too much or too rigid restriction of private capital or holds that we can simply eliminate private capital very quickly, is also entirely wrong; this is a 'Left' opportunist or adventurist view.

Mao argued that 'in the interest of the whole national economy and in the present and future interest of the working class and all the labouring people' China should not 'restrict the private capitalist economy too much or too rigidly', but, rather, should 'leave room for it to exist and develop within the framework of economic policy and planning of the people's republic' (Mao Zedong, 1949: 368).

In terms of politics, Mao emphasized that while the Communist Party should be 'led by the proletariat' and be 'based on the worker-peasant alliance', it was also necessary that the Party 'unite with as many as possible of the representatives of the urban petty bourgeoisie and national bourgeoisie who can co-operate with us and with their intellectuals and political groups' (Mao Zedong, 1949: 372). He emphasized that the Party's policy should 'regard the majority of non-Party democrats as we do our own cadres, consult with them sincerely and frankly to solve problems that call for consultation and solution, give them work, entrust them with the responsibility and authority that go with their posts and help them to do their work well' (Mao Zedong, 1949: 373). He urged the Party to 'oppose the two deviations, the Right deviation of accommodation and the closed-door and

perfunctory "Left" deviation, and adopt an entirely correct attitude'
(Mao Zedong, 1949: 373).

Li Bai   In 759, Li Bai wrote a poem about leaving the town of Baidi,
in the upper reaches of the Chang Jiang (Yangtse River), and travelling
'one thousand *li*' down the river to Jiangling. The river flows rapidly
down through the Three Gorges, with swift currents passing over
dangerous shoals. During the journey, the monkeys cry out unceasingly
from both the left and the right banks of the river. But the 'quick
craft' must negotiate its way down the middle of the river to find its
safe path, not veer to one bank or the other. The boat of Chinese
reform and opening-up has left 'Baidi', but it still has far to go before
it reaches 'Jiangling'. The river is swift and the dangers are great.
Turning back against the swift-flowing current is almost impossible.
It will require great skill to complete the journey safely.

Zhao ci Baidi cai yun jian,	朝辞白帝彩云间
Qian li Jiangling yi ri huan,	千里江陵一日还
Liang an yuan sheng ti bu zhu,	两岸猿声啼不住
Qingzhou yi guo wan chong shan.	轻舟已过万重山

Early in the morning, leaving Baidi town, splendid amidst the clouds,
In one day returning 1,000 *li* back to Jiangling,
On either river bank, monkeys screech unceasingly,
The quick craft has already passed by the serried ranks of 10,000
mountains.

Li Bai

4

Conclusion

If, by the 'Third Way', we mean a creative symbiotic inter-relationship between state and market, then we can say that China practised its own 'Third Way' for two thousand years. This was the foundation of its hugely impressive long-run economic and social development. The Chinese 'Third Way' was not simply an abstract set of rules about intervening with the market, but was a complete philosophy that combined comprehensive thought about concrete ways of both stimulating and controlling the market, with a deeply elaborated system of morality for rulers, bureaucrats and ordinary people. When the system worked well, the philosophical foundation was supplemented by non-ideological state actions to try to solve practical problems that the market could not solve. It is a complete misunderstanding (not least, by Karl Marx) to view the traditional Chinese state as a stagnant 'Oriental despotism'. Confucianism produced a deeply developed concept of 'duty' which was the foundation of social prosperity and collective action. The fact that the system went through regular cycles when these principles were poorly observed, rulers and bureaucrats were corrupt and the economy and society foundered should not blind us to the underlying coherence of and lasting benefit from this integrated system.

China today is groping for its own Third Way in totally different circumstances from those in Europe in recent decades. Europe was already industrialized and militarily strong, contained a mass of powerful, globally competitive firms and was able to assert strong controls over international capital movements until the 1970s without incurring international pressure to do otherwise. China today is painfully weak militarily compared with the USA. The vast mass of the population are still poor farmers and will remain so for a long period ahead. The country is still firmly locked into the 'Lewis phase' of development. The 'global middle class' constitutes a tiny fraction of the population. The economy is increasingly 'dependent' in the classic sense used by Latin American economists in the past. The high value-added modern sector of the economy is more and more dominated by international capital, with over US$400 billion in accumulated investments, forming complete production systems within China, and accounting for over one-half of the country's export earnings. China faces intense pressure to liberalize its financial system comprehensively as the price for participation in the international economy.

Europe tried to pursue a 'Third Way' in order to build a civilized society after it had already industrialized and developed. China is trying to construct a 'Third Way' while it is still in the midst of economic development and industrialization, with a huge rural surplus labour force, amidst a turbulent international environment, and with a surging flow of foreign capital into the country. China's leaders are trying to construct a civilized society in this uniquely challenging setting.

In the early twenty-first century, China cannot step outside the mainstream of world history. It cannot close itself off from the main trend in international economics and politics. It cannot turn round and go back to the Maoist period. However, system survival necessitates that it uses the market as the servant of the development process, not the master, as if the market possessed an intrinsic moral value, which the current US leadership and Western propagandists for the unfettered free market believe to be the case. In this effort China's leaders can make common cause with powerful streams in international thought that have gone against the current mainstream. They have at certain periods been highly influential both in the West, including even in the USA, and in the Far East outside the Chinese mainland.

At the heart of the thinking of the most powerful advocate of the dynamic force of the market economy, Adam Smith, was a deep awareness of the damaging impact of unfettered market forces. Smith understood the contradictions at the heart of the capitalist system. We have seen that his efforts to build a moral philosophy based on controlling the market rather than letting it dominate society closely parallel the most fundamental issues in China's own philosophical tradition. Central to this long tradition was a belief that commerce and finance should be nourished, but not allowed to dominate society and control the political system, either centrally or locally.

However, Smith gave no answers to the deep contradictions that he identified.

Writers such as Fukuyama (1992) and Ohmae (1990) argue that the collapse of communism and the rise of the global corporation have produced an end of ideological conflict. Yergin and Stanislaw (2000) have chronicled the 'withdrawal of the state from the commanding heights, leaving it more and more to the realm of the free market', across a wide swathe of countries. However, they conclude their book with a prescient warning about the market: '[I]f its benefits are regarded as exclusive rather than as inclusive, if it is seen to nurture the abuse of private power and the specter of raw greed, then surely there will be a backlash – a return to greater state intervention, management and control' (Yergin and Stanislaw, 2000: 398).

Can free market fundamentalism prevent a 'Chinese Financial Crisis'? Can it solve the problem of the rapid rise in social inequality within China? Can it solve the problems of the Chinese farm economy? Can it enable China's large firms to compete on the 'global level playing field'? Can it help China to deal with the massive international relations challenge? Can it solve the Chinese environmental crisis? Can it provide China with an ethical foundation for building a socially cohesive society? Anglo-Saxon free market fundamentalism, which reached its modern apogee in the 1990s, offers no hope for sustainable global development, at the level either of ecology, society or international relations. China's numerous deep socio-economic challenges each require creative, non-ideological state intervention with the market to solve the innumerable practical problems that the market alone cannot solve. The biggest challenge of all is in the relationship between China's financial system and that of the global economy, since this has the greatest potential in the near future to trigger system disintegration.

In groping for its own system survival, China can make a powerful contribution to global system survival. In tackling these problems, it can look to its own long history of nurturing market forces while simultaneously placing them under control, in the service of the whole society, in order to achieve a socially cohesive overall political economy. It must creatively adapt these traditions to the particular difficulties facing the country today, namely dealing with the challenges of globalization in the context of a huge and still poor developing country, firmly rooted in the 'Lewis phase' of 'economic development with unlimited supplies of labour'.

If China is able to marry the 'snake' of the global market economy with the 'hedgehog' of its ancient past, as well as its recent history, especially that of the Chinese Communist Party, it will be able to offer a way forward for a stable, socially cohesive society within the country. If it fails to do so, the entire Chinese system of political economy may collapse. This would be devastating, not only for China, but also for the whole global political economy. At the very least, China may be condemned to a long period of harsh social control to contain the surging tensions of the country's high-speed growth. During the Asian Financial Crisis, China had to take a 'choice of no choice' (*mei you xuanze de xuanze*) to survive by 'cutting the trees to save the forest' (i.e. making GITIC bankrupt). If it wishes the system to survive today, it must also take the 'choice of no choice' to re-establish social cohesiveness, confidently using its own past traditions and the best traditions from outside the country.

If China were to 'choose' the path of 'state desertion' and free market fundamentalism, it would lead to uncontrollable tensions and social disintegration. Full liberalization of international financial firm competition inside China and full liberalization of international financial flows is the most dangerous area through which this disintegration might occur. A crisis in the financial system would fan the flames amidst the 'combustible material' in all other sectors of society, into which the long tentacles of the financial system extend. The 'choice' to increase and make more effective the role of the state to solve the intensifying socio-economic challenges facing the country can only succeed if the Chinese state today, with the Communist Party at its core, as in periods of greatest prosperity in the past, can radically improve its level of effectiveness, and eliminate rampant corruption. State improvement, not state desertion, is the only rational goal for Chinese system reform. This is the 'choice of no choice' for China's system survival.

By taking the 'choice of no choice', China's own survival can contribute to global survival and sustainable development, by offering a beacon as an alternative to the US-dominated drive towards global free market fundamentalism. This is a crossroads not only for China, but also for the whole world.

Epilogue: The Conclusion of *The True Story of Ah Q*

'A number of men in long coats and short jackets put a white vest of foreign cloth on him. It had some black characters on it. . . . At the same time his hands were tied behind his back, and he was dragged out of the *yamen* [magistrates' office]. Ah Q was lifted onto an uncovered cart, and several men in short jackets sat down with him. The cart started off at once. In front were a number of soldiers and militiamen shouldering foreign rifles, and on both sides were gaping spectators, while what was behind Ah Q could not see. Suddenly it occurred to him: Can I be going to have my head cut off? Panic seized him and everything turned dark before his eyes, while there was humming in his ears as if he had fainted . . .

Ah Q took another look at the shouting crowd. At that instant his thoughts revolved like a whirlwind. Four years before, at the foot of the mountain, he had met a hungry wolf which had followed him at a set distance, wanting to eat him. He had nearly died of fright, but luckily, he happened to have an axe in his hand, which gave him the courage to get back to Weizhuang. He had never forgotten that wolf's eyes, fierce yet cowardly, gleaming like two will-o'-the-wisps, as if boring into him from a distance. Now he saw eyes more terrible than the wolf's: dull yet penetrating eyes that, having devoured his words, still seemed eager to devour something beyond his flesh. And these eyes kept following him at a set distance. These eyes seemed to have merged into one, biting into his soul.

"Help. Help!"

But Ah Q never uttered these words. All had turned black before his eyes, there was buzzing in his ears, and he felt as if his whole body were being scattered like so much light dust.

As for any discussion of the event, no question was raised in Weizhuang. Naturally all agreed that Ah Q had been a bad man, the proof being that he had been shot; for if he had not been bad, how could he have been shot? But the consensus of opinion in the town was unfavourable. Most people were dissatisfied, because a shooting was not such a fine spectacle as a decapitation; and what a ridiculous culprit he had been too, to pass through so many streets without singing a single line from an opera. They had followed him for nothing.'

(Lu Xun, 1944: 139–43)

Notes

Preface

1. A study of this large topic is under preparation and will be published in due course.

Prologue

1. It should be noted that the first phase of rural reform did not end with the privatization of farmland. Instead, as Deng Xiaoping emphasized in his comments, land was still collectively owned. It has been collectively owned throughout the whole reform period right up to the present day. The Rural Land Contracting Law of 2002 represents the latest stage in a long and complex reform of rural land rights. The new law reaffirmed, in a detailed fashion, what began as a broad policy pronouncement in 1993, that farmers are entitled to thirty-year (one generation) land-use rights, which are long enough to recover the value of nearly every kind of agricultural investment (*South China Morning Post*, 12 February 2003). The enormous care that has been to taken to experiment with rural land rights in a way that tries to both preserve farmers' incentives and maintain social cohesion is a major reason that socio-economic problems in the countryside have not been more severe. It is hard to imagine how disastrous would have been the consequences of a policy of outright land privatization in the late 1970s and 'betting on the strong'.
2. Neville Maxwell was well known and respected in China for his definitive book on the India–China border dispute, entitled *India's China War*, as well as for his analysis of the Chinese rural economy. The delegation consisted of Neville Maxwell, Keith Griffin, Roger Hay, Ashwani

Saith, Marsh Marshall and myself. The delegation was accompanied throughout by Wang Gengjin, Deputy Director of the Rural Economics Research Institute of the Chinese Academy of Social Sciences.

3. These points are not taken from an official record of the meeting. They are from my own notes made at that meeting.

4. Data in this and the following two paragraphs are from SSB, *ZTN*, 2002.

5. I cannot detect any basis in logic or evidence in the arguments expounded by Sachs and Woo (1994) that China's extraordinary performance compared to the former USSR can be explained by the 'advantages of backwardness' compared with the former USSR's disadvantage of 'over-industrialization'. Can the 'advantages of backwardness' explain simultaneously the slow growth of South Asia, the erratic growth of Latin America or the disastrous failure of development in most of Sub-Saharan Africa at the same time as explaining China's explosive growth? For a more detailed critique of the Sachs and Woo argument, see Nolan, 1998.

6. It should be cautioned that there is a considerable element of double-counting in these figures, but it is impossible to accurately identify its extent. Even taking this into account, there has still been a remarkable rise in the total stock of FDI in the Chinese Mainland plus Hong Kong.

Chapter 1 The Challenges to China's Economic and Political Stability: Can China Build a Sustainable and Civilized Modern Economy?

1. Just 8.9 per cent of the total number of rural households, or approximately 71 million people, had an average per capita income of over US$600 (RMB5000) per year.

2. The issue of safety of 'global citizens' within the safe havens of 'Treaty Port'-style compounds was brought sharply to the forefront by the attack in May 2003 upon the expatriate compounds in Saudi Arabia. After the attacks, one banker commented: 'Everyone thought they were safe in the compounds. That illusion has now been shattered' (*FT*, 14 May 2003).

3. These included tariffs, which fell gradually but still were significant in many sectors at the end of the 1990s; a wide range of non-tariff barriers, including limitations on access to domestic marketing channels, requirements for technology transfer and to sub-contract to selected domestic firms as the price for market access; government procurement policy; government selection of the joint venture partners for major international joint venture projects; preferential loans from state banks; and privileged access to international stock markets with listing in Hong Kong and New York.

4. These included tariff and non-tariff barriers, restrictions on foreign direct investment, preferential purchase policy by state-owned utilities,

government defence procurement contracts, government-subsidized
R&D, government-sponsored rationalizations of different industries
and a 'flexible', pragmatic competition policy which allowed the growth
of oligopolistic competition.

5. In 1999, total IT hardware sales in China reached US$20 billion,
    including mobile infrastructure and handsets; traditional fixed line and
    broadband switching equipment; optical cable/optical cable fibre; and
    SD and DWDM products. It is estimated that 90 per cent of the IT
    hardware by value was supplied by the global giants (including Nokia,
    Motorola, Ericsson, Cisco, Siemens, Alcatel and Lucent) through either
    imports or their large production networks within China.

6. For example, in oil and petrochemicals, for many years the policy was
    to increase the autonomy of large production units. Then policy shifted
    totally towards centralized control over large production units.

7. For example, while control was being centralized in the oil and petro-
    chemical industry, China Aviation Industries Corporation was, incom-
    prehensibly, being broken up into two separate entities, each of which
    was even less able than before to compete with the global giants.

8. Despite the rapid growth, in 2001, China still accounted for only 18
    per cent of the total stock of FDI in developing countries (UNCTAD,
    2002), significantly below its share of population. Latin America's total
    stock of FDI in 2001 stood at US$693 billion, 75 per cent greater than
    that of China. Latin America's population (509 million) is only 37 per
    cent of that of China.

9. In the mid-nineteenth century, the term 'workshop of the world' was
    used to describe the British economy. However, the sense in which this
    term was used in relation to the British economy is entirely different
    from that currently being used to describe China. At that point, Britain
    was, by far, the world's dominant economy, producer of a large fraction
    of the world's most advanced capital goods.

10. Measured in PPP dollars, it is the second largest (World Bank, *WDR*,
    2001), which greatly overstates the true size of its national product.
    This measure also inflates its energy efficiency.

11. In addition, a substantial fraction of China's huge exports of electrical
    goods (US$85 billion in 2001) were produced by indigenous Chinese
    firms acting as 'Original Equipment Manufacturer' suppliers to the
    global giants.

12. Sun Zi distinguished between 'local agents' (*yinjian*), 'planted agents'
    (*neijian*), 'dare-to-die agents' (*sijian*), 'converted agents' (*fanjian*) and
    'messenger agents' (*shengjian*).

13. China is currently engaged in a large-scale, multi-billion dollar pro-
    gramme, with extensive support from the central government, to intro-
    duce coal liquefaction to convert coal into oil. This has the potential to
    reduce greatly the country's environmental damage from direct coal-
    burning as the main source of primary energy, as well as reducing

China's dependency on imports of primary energy below the levels they would otherwise reach.

14. In North China water charges are just RMB1.3 (US$0.16) per cubic metre on average, compared with RMB2.9 in Beijing (*FT*, 20 February 2003). It was reported that the unit price of water would be decided by the provincial governments and municipalities on a case-by-case basis.

15. Even as the US was preparing to attack Iraq, in late February 2003, in his speech to the American Enterprise Institute, President Bush announced his intention to encourage 'regime change' across the whole of the Middle East: 'A new regime in Iraq would serve as a dramatic and inspiring example of freedom to other nations in the region' (quoted in *FT*, 1 March 2003).

16. The influence of the neocons upon US foreign policy was complicated by the strongly pro-Israel stance of many of their members: 'Most of the first generation of neocons were Jewish; just about all of the later neocons were. Israel looms large for many of them . . . who are closely identified with the hardline policies of the Likud Party. But to others, Israel is one of a number of democracies such as Britain whose continued wellbeing is in American interests' (*FT*, 6 March 2003).

17. In its listing prospectus in July 2002, BOC (HK) referred to the 'Kaiping incident', acknowledging that there had been 'embezzlement or misappropriation of funds from the BOC's Kaiping branch amounting to approximately US$500 million, from 1993 to 2001' (BOCI, 2002: 168). Initial reports had suggested that as much as US$725 million had gone missing (*FT*, 16 March 2002, and *FEER*, 30 May 2002).

Chapter 2 China at the Crossroads: Which Direction?

1. In fact, calculation of the precise extent of the private, collective and state economy has become extremely complicated due to the comprehensive change in the nature of property rights towards mixed ownership structures. What is certain is that the state-owned sector no longer dominates the economy.

2. Chang (2002) has catalogued the widespread absence of political democracy and social welfare institutions across the wide spectrum of today's rich countries during the early phase of their industrialization.

3. In 2001 Transparency International ranked China 59th out of the 102 countries on its 'corruption index'.

4. See Nolan, 1995, and Chang, 2002, for summaries of the evidence on this point.

5. It should be noted that there is little evidence that material living standards declined. However, in view of the extremely low level of wages at

the start of the process, determined substantially by the huge relative size of the rural reserve army of labour, this is hardly surprising.

6. In fact, a substantial contribution to the rise in real wages in late Victorian Britain was made by the fall in the price of basic consumer goods due to the 'improvement' (i.e. for British consumers) in the country's terms of trade, as vast new tracts of territory were opened up to supply food and raw materials, using new transport technologies, notably the railway, refrigeration and steam shipping.

7. Brazil's liberalization has led to dominant positions in most industries being taken by local subsidiaries of multinational giants. Among the top twenty-five 'Brazilian' firms, fourteen are global giants, including (in descending order of revenue within Brazil in 2001) Volkswagen (2), GM (3), Fiat (5), Unilever (7), Bunge Foods (9), Phillip Morris (10), Nestlé (11), Ford (12), Cargill (13), Daimler Chrysler (16), Siemens (20), Ericsson (21), BASF (22) and Motorola (24).

8. For example, at the meeting of the 21st Century Forum in Beijing in the year 2000, Prof. Dwight Perkins, of Harvard University, who has been notable for his sophisticated and deeply informed defence of China's incremental economic reform strategy, argued that the WTO would provide a crucial contribution to China's system change by drastically reducing the scope for corrupt state activity.

9. A succession of Chinese free market economists have argued that China must accept the 'pain' that is involved if the country is to construct a suitable environment for the market economy to develop. For example, Li Yining, of Beijing University, argued in 2001, in a speech that was widely circulated on the internet:

> China can obtain 'genuine gold' from opening up, particularly towards the advanced countries. Joining the WTO is the last chance for China's state-owned enterprises to fight their way out from their desperate situation and rise to a new level from their predicament. It is only a matter of time before China joins the WTO and experiences 'pain'. The later that China joins, the more pain it will experience, so why not do so now happily?

10. Karl Wittfogel's monumental study, *Oriental Despotism* (1957), had as its underlying theme the argument that the Chinese and Soviet regimes were both directly descended from their respective 'despotic' systems in imperial times.

11. From early in the history of the USA, there has been tension between the conception of the 'manifest destiny' of the white majority population and the rights of other civilizations. From 1791 until 1850, no fewer than eighteen new states entered the Union: 'National boundaries made little difference to expansion; in Florida, Louisiana, Texas, and other areas, American settlers rushed in to claim land under the jurisdiction

of Spain, France, Mexico, and Indian tribes, confident that American sovereignty would soon follow in their wake' (Foner, 1998: 50). Sitting Bull, the leader of the Sioux Indians, proclaimed: 'The life my people want is a life of freedom' (quoted in Foner, 1998: 51). However, the Native American idea of freedom was 'incompatible with that of western settlers, for whom freedom entailed the right to expand across the continent and establish farms, ranches and mines on land that the Indians considered their own. Indian removal – accomplished by fraud, intimidation and violence – was indispensable to the triumph of manifest destiny and the American mission of spreading freedom' (Foner, 1998: 51). Thomas Jefferson was clear that the vast Louisiana purchase from France in 1830, which doubled the then size of the 'Empire of Liberty', would 'push far into the future the dreaded day when an overpopulated, class-divided America would cease to be the home to freedom' (Foner, 1998: 50). This massive territorial expansion depended on the 'energetic exercise of public authority' (Foner, 1998: 53).

12.   In the 1890s, women's rights advocate Abigail Dunaway advocated increased Asian immigration under the campaign slogan 'Hire a China-man', in order to liberate American women from the burden of housework (Foner, 1998: 137).

13.   It is an extreme irony that one hundred years later, the AEA should have become the vehicle for conveying the most stultifying form of orthodoxy, which eliminated from the subject of 'economics' anything other than formal mathematical modelling, largely based on free market models, leaving the subject far removed from the open-minded analysis of the real world from which the Association originally derived its inspiration.

14.   Green's ideas on 'positive freedom' far precede similar notions propounded by such late twentieth-century philosophers as Isaiah Berlin (1969) or A.K. Sen (e.g. Dreze and Sen, 1989).

15.   In fact, as Foner points out, Hayek's views were far more complex than the interpretation they were given by the New Right. *The Road to Serfdom* endorsed measures that later conservatives would 'denounce as tantamount to socialism' – a minimum wage, laws limiting maximum hours of work, antitrust enforcement, and a social safety net guaranteeing all citizens' basic needs of food, shelter and clothing (Foner, 1998: 236).

16.   There is a close relationship between religion and the neoconservative New Right in the USA. The USA remains a country of 'widespread, intense and often fundamentalist religiosity', and in the depth and extent of its religious belief, it 'stands alone among advanced countries'. Americans are 'the most churchgoing in Protestantism and the most fundamentalist in Christendom' (Gray, 1998: 126). In 1991, 69 per cent of the adult population belonged to a church, and 42 per cent attended weekly church services, far higher than in any other industrialized

nation. Just under 70 per cent of Americans believe in the devil, compared with a third of British people, a fifth of French people and an eighth of Swedish people (Gray, 1998: 126). George W. Bush opens every Cabinet meeting with prayers, and it was widely reported that Tony Blair and George W. Bush, both 'born-again' Christians, prayed together prior to the attack on Iraq.

In his masterly study *The Art of Loving* (1957), Erich Fromm advanced a prescient analysis of the relationship between religion and 'free market fundamentalism', though he did not, of course, use the latter term (Fromm, 1957: part 3, 'Love and its Disintegration in Contemporary Western Society'). Fromm believes that a major change occurred in advanced capitalism with the move from an emphasis on saving to one on spending, 'from self-frustration as a means for economic success to consumption as the basis for an ever-widening market, and as the main satisfaction for the anxious automatized individual'. Fromm believes that this change accounts for the huge rise in the influence of Freudian ideas, which advocated the 'the full and uninhibited satisfaction of sexual desires' as the basis for mental well-being and happiness: 'Not to postpone the satisfaction of any desire became the main tendency in the sphere of sex as well as in that of material consumption.' In fact, 'the complete satisfaction of all instinctual needs is not only not a basis for happiness, it does not even guarantee sanity' (Fromm, 1957: 72).

In the advanced free market economy, 'daily life is separated from any religious values'. It is devoted to 'the striving for material comforts, and for success in the personality market'. The principles on which this secular society is built are 'those of indifference and egotism (the latter often labelled as "individualism" or "individual initiative"' (Fromm, 1957: 88). Fromm characterizes this as an 'infantile dependence on an anthropomorphic picture of God without the transformation of daily life according to the principles of God' (Fromm, 1957: 81).

In Fromm's view, in the advanced free market economy, man has 'transformed himself into a commodity; he experiences his life energy as an investment with which he should make the highest profit, considering his position and the situation on the personality market'. In these circumstances, man is 'alienated from himself, from his fellow men and from nature'. His main aim is 'profitable exchange of his skills, knowledge and of himself, his "personality package" with others who are equally intent on a fair and profitable exchange'. In the 'religious revival' the belief in God has been 'transformed into a psychological device to make one better fitted for the competitive struggle': 'Make God your partner' means to 'make God a partner in your business, rather than to become one with Him in love, justice and truth. . . . God has been transformed into a remote General Director of the Universe, Inc.; you know that he is there, he runs the show . . . , you never see him, but

you acknowledge his leadership while you are "doing your part"'
(Fromm, 1957: 82–3).

17. Similar views deeply influenced Western attitudes to the Muslim world.
Maxime Rodinson observes: 'Some European scholars . . . endeavour
to show that this religion [Islam], by forbidding those who hold it to
engage in any progressive economic intitiative, dooms them to stagnation. . . . The conclusion to be drawn is that these (Muslim) peoples
must be vigorously combatted, in the interest of the progress of civilization' (Rodinson, 1974: 3). Between 1757 and 1919, it is estimated that
there were ninety-one acquisitions of Muslim territory by non-Muslim
governments (Huntington, 1996: 210). By 1920, there were only four
Muslim countries that were independent of some form of non-Muslim
rule. Rodinson demonstrates that in fact the medieval Islamic peoples
achieved considerable economic progress, establishing long-lasting and
sophisticated commercial systems. A mainly commercial indigenous
bourgeoisie took root from the eighth century AD (second century AH);
'attaining an important social position', 'winning the respect of other
strata by causing their activities to be accepted as respectable and praise-
worthy' and 'imposing the values that were bound up with these activities' during the ninth century AD (third century AH); and becoming a
'socio-economic factor of the highest importance' in the tenth and eleventh centuries AD (fourth century AH) (Rodinson, 1974: 55). Rodinson
argues that 'if primitive accumulation of capital never attained the
European level', then 'this was due to factors quite other than the
Muslim religion' (Rodinson, 1974: 57).

18. It is estimated that the top 10 per cent of the US income distribution
accounts for an income equal to that of the poorest 43 per cent of the
whole world (UNDP, *HDR*, 2002: 19).

19. The core of the campaign success of George W. Bush was a hugely
successful fund-raising machine. At the heart of this was a small group
of 'Pioneers', each of whom pledged to raise at least US$100,000 for
the last (1999/2000) presidential campaign (*FT*, 20 May 2003). For
the 2003/4 presidential campaign, the Pioneers have each been asked
to raise at least US$200,000. In July 2000, the Bush campaign was
forced to reveal the names of 212 of the Pioneers, including such people
as Kenneth Lay, the former chairman of Enron, and Maurice 'Hank'
Greenberg, the chairman of AIG. In 2003 it seemed likely that they
would be pressed to reveal the names of a further 312 Pioneers. Of the
212 who were initially revealed, 43 had been offered public offices,
including 19 who were appointed to ambassadorships. Two of the
Pioneers were given seats on the President's intelligence advisory board.

20. The centrepiece of the Bush budget for 2003 was a range of tax cuts,
including elimination of taxes paid by 'investors' on dividends. According to the Tax Policy Centre, the fifth of the population with the
lowest income would receive less than 1 per cent of the benefit, the

middle fifth would receive 6 per cent, and the top fifth, 78 per cent. More than a quarter of the tax benefits would go to the 1 per cent with the highest income. Households earning more than US$100,000 would get 79 per cent of the benefit of elimination of double taxation of dividends (*FT*, 8 February 2003).

21. Within Texas, Enron was a huge political donor, spending 'more than US$4.8 million on more than 89 Texas lobbying contracts' (*FT*, 9 February 2002). Enron was the leading corporate donor to the re-election campaigns of Texas Supreme Court judges between 1993 and 2001. The donations were alleged to have totalled about US$134,000 and were made at a time when Enron was a party to six petitions for review before the court: 'It still shocks people, even in Texas, that judges take money from people who have cases in their courtrooms' (*FT*, 22 January 2002). It also 'supported former staffers moving into public office to maintain links with the government' (*FT*, 9 February 2002).

22. Mao said: 'The Chinese people are suffering; it is our duty to save them and we must exert ourselves in the struggle. . . . [W]e have the interests of the people at heart and the sufferings of the great majority at heart, and when we die for the people it is a worthy death' (Mao Zedong, 1944: 178).

Chapter 3 China at the Crossroads: 'Use the Past to Serve the Present'?

1. For example, Antony Leung, Financial Secretary of Hong Kong Special Administrative Region, has said: 'China was unable to give birth to capitalism in historical times. China's non-competitive tendencies hindered the development of the market' (speech at the Royal Institute of InternationalAffairs, London, 26 November 2002).

2. See, especially, Dobb, 1976, for an extensive discussion of the broad and the narrow interpretation of the term 'feudal'.

3. Liang Sicheng's father was Liang Qichao, one of the major figures in the late Imperial reform movement known as the 'Hundred Days'. Between 11 June and 21 September 1898, the Emperor Kuang Hsu, advised closely by Liang Qichao and Kang Youwei, issued more than forty reform edicts dealing with almost every conceivable subject. Almost none of them was implemented, but the episode was highly significant in the history of late Imperial China. Both Liang Sicheng and his father, Liang Qichao, were at one time professors at Qinghua University. Liang Sicheng was the founder of Qinghua's Department of Architecture in 1946.

Liang Qichao and Kang Youwei were leading proponents of the deeply influential philosophy of 'Chinese studies as the essence' (*zhongxue wei ti*), and 'Western studies for usefulness' (*xixue wei yong*) (Levenson, 1968). Liang Qichao was deeply versed in Western philosophy: 'No other Chinese scholar this century has given more serious attention to Western political theory or written more prolifically about it than has Liang' (Twohey, 1999: 45). Liang Qichao visited America for seven months in 1903. This had a profound impact on him. Thinking in Social Darwinist terms, Liang concluded that American laissez-faireism and liberal democracy were a source of short-term dynamism, but of long-term weakness: 'Over the long-term, the gradual displacing of group interests in favour of individual interests, or what Liang saw as the prevailing trend in America, would only lead to an uncooperative and disunited nation that would be unable to compete with other nations' (Twohey, 1999: 51). Liang believed also that, although the American system had 'the power to make America immensely strong', there 'would be a price to pay for other nations, especially because of the threat of American imperialism, increasingly evident in American foreign policy'. His trip to America convinced him that 'the divergent nature of different classes made any kind of consensus impossible'. Liang concluded that 'group dynamism was more important than individual dynamism', and that 'authoritarianism and government intervention were far superior to liberal democracy and laissez-faireism in the long-term' (Twohey, 1999: 51). Liang Qichao asked: 'Was it not best for the state to rise above societal conflicts for the sake of maintaining order?' (Twohey, 1999: 51). In answer, he asserted that, at China's stage of development, 'strong leadership and a strong state were the major signposts to be followed along the Chinese road of development' (Twohey, 1999: 51).

   After his visit to the USA, Liang Qichao never wavered from his view that the US model of political economy was unsuitable for China. Even in the wake of the failed liberal reforms of 1898, which he had championed, Liang Qichao remained deeply afraid of the 'chaos' and 'troubled times' (*ju luan si*) that the absence of an authoritarian leadership and the proliferation of regional leaders could bring to China. He believed that only a strong state authority would be able to eliminate poverty in China and would hold the key to sustained Chinese unity, to peace and tranquillity (*shen ping si*) (Twohey, 1999).

4. At the end of the Qing dynasty, there was a substantial increase in the number of lower-level positions in the civil service that were sold in order to meet the state's pressing budgetary needs.

5. There is, of course, endless debate about the meaning of 'Confucianism'. It encompasses not only the key ideas of Confucius himself, but also those of innumerable thinkers who subsequently interpreted and transformed his ideas in response to the changing circumstances around them. A key reason for the longevity of Confucianism in China is the fact that while the basic social values did not change, in practice 'they

were implemented by a combination of detailed prescriptive regulation and discretionary flexibility' which 'allowed over the centuries for creative response to social strains and gradual change within the tradition' (Feuerwerker, 1976: 17).

6. The information in this section is all from Ch'ao-ting Chi's classic account (1936).

7. The Yuan Grand Canal consisted of six sections: the T'unghui Canal, running from the capital to T'ungchou; the Po Ho, connecting T'ungchou with Chihku; the Yu Ho, extending from Chihku to Linch'ing; the Huit'ung Canal, flowing from the Hsuch'en district in Tungch'ang to Linch'ing; the Yangchou Grand Canal, running southward from the Huit'ung Canal at Shantsako (in Linhsien in Shantung province); and the Chinkiang Canal, running from Chinkiang to the Luchen Dam in Chang-chou.

8. Will (1990) provides a meticulous account of famine relief in late Imperial China.

9. *Baojia* was the system by which households were organized into groups with responsibilities for performing various social obligations and for self-administering the affairs of the group members.

10. Smith's idea of human collective activity unwittingly damaging their own interests anticipates later Marxist analysis of the notion of 'alienation'.

11. This famous sentence in fact is not contained in the *Wealth of Nations*. It is from Adam Smith's *Essays*, quoted in Edwin Cannan's Introduction to the 1904 'Cannan' edition of the *Wealth of Nations* (Smith, 1776: xl).

12. Smith's ideas on basic needs and happiness find their modern echo in Abraham Maslow's research published in the early 1940s (*Motivation and Personality*). Maslow (1987) concluded that there was a pyramid of human needs, at the base of which were 'basic needs' such as food, water and basic material comforts. Next were safety and security needs. Then came love and belongingness, including the desire to feel accepted by the family, the community and colleagues at work. After that came the need for esteem, both self-esteem and other people's respect and admiration. Finally, at the apex, came 'self-actualization', at which point 'people achieved the happiness that came from becoming all they were capable of becoming': 'At this level people might seek knowledge and aesthetic experiences for themselves and help others achieve self-fulfilment' (*FT*, 8 March 2003). Recent 'happines studies' support Maslow's proposition. They show that, while people on very low incomes become significantly happier when their earnings rise, once they reach a 'quite modest' level of income – as little as $10,000 per year – further increases in earnings 'bring little extra happiness', and can even be associated with falls in happiness.

13. Lao Zi's *Dao De Jing* (*Tao Te Ching*) has also been immensely influential, but despite its great importance, it is the ideas of Confucius that
were to 'dominate the moral consciousness of China from the victory
of his school in the second century BC down to the present day' (Graham,
1964: 31).

14. The phrase '*xiaokang*' (small comfort) society was used in ancient
times in the Book of Poetry (*Shi Jing*) and the Record of Rites (*Li Ji*)
(Liu Fang and Li Zhenming, 2003). In these works it is possible to
distinguish between a society with '*da tong*' (Great Harmony) and one
with '*xiaokang*' (Small Comfort). It was first used by Deng Xiaoping in
1979 in discussion with the visiting Japanese Prime Minister, Ohira
Masayoshi. Deng said that the term depicted the process of modernization with Chinese characteristics. Afterwards, Deng reaffirmed the '*xiaokang*' concept several times. He said that in the achievement of the
'Three Steps' for modernization, reaching '*xiaokang*' defined arrival
at the second step. The term was first used officially in 1991 in the
Outline Eighth Five-Year Plan and the Ten-Year Guideline for Development of the National Economy and Society. The concept was brought
back into wider political discourse when it was used by Jiang Zemin in
his speech at the Sixteenth Party Congress in November 2002. The
term embraces the concepts of the level of material consumption, conditions of work, levels of social welfare, cultural and political life.

Bibliography

Anderson, P., 1974, *Lineages of the Absolutist State*, London: Verso.

Bairoch, P., 1982, 'International industrialization levels from 1750 to 1980', *Journal of European Economic History*, Fall.

Balazs, E., 1964, *Chinese Civilization and Bureaucracy*, London: Yale University Press.

Banister, J., 1987, *China's Changing Population*, Stanford: Stanford University Press.

Bank of China International (BOCI), 2002, *BOC Hong Kong (Holdings) Limited*, Hong Kong.

Berlin, I., 1969, *Four Essays on Liberty*, Oxford: Oxford University Press.

Boyd, A., 1962, *Chinese Architecture and Town Planning, 1500 BC–AD 1911*, London: Alec Tiranti.

Brooks, T., 1999, *The Confusions of Pleasure: Commerce and Culture in Ming China*, Berkeley: University of California Press.

Brzezinski, Z., 1997, *The Grand Chessboard*, New York: Basic Books.

Calavita, K., H.N. Powell and R.H. Tillman, 1997, *Big Money Crime*, London: University of California Press.

Chang, H.-J., 2002, *Kicking Away the Ladder*, London: Anthem Press.

Chi, Ch'ao-ting, 1936, *Key Economic Areas in Chinese History*, New York: Paragon Reprint.

Cipolla, C., ed., 1970, *The Economic Decline of Empires*, London: Methuen.

Comrades from the Shanghai Hutong Shipyards, and the Sixth Economic Group of the Shanghai Municipal May Seventh Cadre School, 1974, 'Two kinds of society, two kinds of wages', in M. Selden, ed., *The People's Republic of China*, New York: Monthly Review Press.

Confucius, 1979, *The Analects (Lun Yü)*, translated, with an Introduction by D.C. Lau, Harmondsworth: Penguin Books.

Council for Economic Planning and Development, 1989, *Taiwan Statistical Yearbook*, Taipei, Taiwan.

Dawson, R., 1964, 'Western conceptions of Chinese civilization', in R. Dawson, ed., *The Legacy of China*, Oxford: Oxford University Press.

Deng Xiaoping, 1979, 'The necessity of upholding the four cardinal principles in the drive for the four modernizations', in *Major Documents of the People's Republic of China*, Beijing: Foreign Languages Press.

Deng Xiaoping, 1980, 'The present situation and the tasks before us', in *Selected Works of Deng Xiaoping*, Beijing: Foreign Languages Press.

Dobb, M., 1963, *Studies in the Development of Capitalism*, London: Routledge.

Dobb, M., 1976, 'A Reply', in R. Hilton, ed., *The Transition from Feudalism to Capitalism*, London: New Left Books.

Dreze, J., and A.K. Sen, 1989, *Hunger and Public Action*, Oxford: Clarendon Press.

Eastman, L., 1988, *Families, Fields, and Ancestors*, New York: Oxford University Press.

Engels, F., 1845, *The Condition of the Working Class in England*, London: Granada Books, 1969 (first English edition, 1892).

Faure, D., 1996, 'History and Culture', in B. Hook, ed., *Guangdong, China's Promised Land*, Hong Kong: Oxford University Press.

Faure, D., 2001, 'Beyond networking: An institutional view of Chinese business', mimeo.

Feinstein, C.H., 1981, 'Capital accumulation and the industrial revolution', in R. Floud and D. McClosky, eds, *The Economic History of Britain since 1700, Vol. 1, 1700–1860*, Cambridge: Cambridge University Press.

Feuerwerker, A., 1968, *The Chinese Economy, 1911–1949*, Ann Arbor, MI: Center for Chinese Studies.

Feuerwerker, A., 1976, *State and Society in Eighteenth-Century China: The Ch'ing Empire in All Its Glory*, Ann Arbor, MI: Center for Chinese Studies.

Feuerwerker, A., 1977, *Economic Trends in the Republic of China, 1912–1949*, Ann Arbor, MI: University of Michigan Press.

Floud, R., 1981, 'Britain, 1860–1914: A survey', in R. Floud and D. McClosky, eds, *The Economic History of Britain since 1700, Vol. 2, 1860 to the 1970s*, Cambridge: Cambridge University Press.

Foner, E., 1998, *The Story of American Freedom*, New York: W.W. Norton.

Frank, A.G., 1967, *Capitalism and Underdevelopment in Latin America*, New York: Monthly Review Press.

Fromm, E., 1957, *The Art of Loving*, London: George Allen and Unwin.

Fukuyama, F., 1992, *The End of History and the Last Man*, Harmondsworth: Penguin Books.

Galbraith, J.K., 1992, *The Great Crash*, Harmondsworth: Penguin Books.

Graham, A., 1964, 'The place of reason in the Chinese philosophical tradition', in R. Dawson, ed., *The Legacy of China*, Oxford: Oxford University Press.

Gray, J., 1998, *False Dawn*, London: Granta Books.

Hahn, F., 1984, 'Reflections on the invisible hand', in *Equilibrium and Macroeconomics*, Oxford: Basil Blackwell.

Halliday, J., 1975, *A Political History of Japanese Capitalism*, London: Monthly Review Press.

Hill, C., 1961, *A Century of Revolution, 1603–1714*, Walton-on-Thames: Nelson.

Hilton, R., ed., 1976, *The Transition from Feudalism to Capitalism*, London: New Left Books.

Hirschman, A.O., 1977, *The Passions and the Interests*, Princeton: Princeton University Press.

Ho Pingti, 1959, *The Population of China*, Cambridge, MA: Harvard University Press.

Hoskins, W.G., 1976, *The Age of Plunder*, London: Longman.

Hu Jichuang, 1984, *Chinese Economic Thought before the Seventeenth Century*, Beijing: Foreign Language Press.

Hu Jintao, 2003, 'Hu Jintao's speech at the Xibaipo study meeting: Carry out the fine work style of "plain living and hard struggle" (*jianku fendou*); strive to achieve the great objective of all-roundedly establishing a small comfort (*xiaokang*) society', *Renmin ribao (People's Daily)*, 2 January.

Huang, R., 1981, *1587, A Year of No Significance*, New Haven and London: Yale University Press.

Huang, R., 1990, *China: A Macro-History*, New York: M.E. Sharpe.

Huntington, S.P., 1996, *The Clash of Civilizations and the Remaking of World Order*, New York: Simon and Schuster.

Hutton, W., 2002, *The World We're In*, London: Little Brown.

International Institute for Strategic Studies (IISS), *The Military Balance, 1998/ 99*, London: IISS.

Keynes, J.M., 1936, *The General Theory of Employment, Interest and Money*, London: Macmillan.

King, F.H., 1965, *Money and Monetary Policy in China*, Cambridge, MA: Harvard University Press.

Kornai, J., 1992, *The Socialist System*, Oxford: Clarendon Press.

Lao Zi, 1995, *The Book of Tao and the Book of Teh*, translated by Gu Zhenkun, Beijing: Peking University Press.

Lau, D.C., 1979, 'Introduction', to Confucius, *The Analects (Lun Yü)*, translated, with an Introduction by D.C. Lau, Harmondsworth: Penguin Books.

Levenson, J.R., 1968, *Confucian China and Its Modern Fate*, Berkeley: University of California Press.

Lewis, A., 1954, 'Economic development with unlimited supplies of labour', *Manchester School*, May.

Li Bozhong, 1986, *The Development of Agriculture and Industry in Jiangnan, 1644–1850: Trends and Prospects*, Hangzhou, Zhenjiang Academy of Social Sciences.

Li Bozhong, 1998, *Agricultural Development in Jiangnan, 1620–1850*, Basingstoke: Macmillan.

Li Bozhong, 2000, *The Early Industrialization of Jiangnan, 1550–1850*, Beijing: Shehui kexue wenjian Publishing House (in Chinese).

Lin Yifu, Cai Fang and Li Zhou, 1996, *The China Miracle*, Hong Kong: Chinese University Press.

Lindert, P., 1994, 'Unequal living standards', in R. Floud and D. McClosky, eds, *The Economic History of Britain since 1700, Vol. 1, 1700–1860* (second edition), Cambridge: Cambridge University Press.

Lindert, P.H., and J.G. Williamson, 1985, 'English workers' living standards during the Industrial Revolution: A new look', in J. Mokyr, ed., *The Economics of the Industrial Revolution*, London: George Allen and Unwin.

Lippitt, V., 1978, 'Economic development in Meiji Japan and contemporary China: A comparative study', *Cambridge Journal of Economics*, Vol. 2, no. 1, March.

Liu Fang and Li Zhenming, 2003, 'On the *xiao kang* society', *Guangming Ribao (Brightness Daily)*, 18 February.

Lu Xun, 1944, *Ah Q*, with woodcuts by Ding Cong, translated by Yang Xianyi and Gladys Yang, Beijing: New World Press, 2000. (Original Chinese language edition published in 1921.)

McEvedy, C., and R. Jones, 1978, *An Atlas of World Population History*, Harmondsworth: Penguin Books.

Mao Zedong (Mao Tse-tung), 1944, 'Serve the people', in *Selected Works of Mao Tse-tung*, Vol. III, Beijing: Foreign Languages Press, 1965.

Mao Zedong (Mao Tse-tung), 1949, 'Report to the Second Plenary Session of the Seventh Central Committee of the Communist Party of China', 5 March, in *Selected Works of Mao Tse-tung*, Vol. IV, Beijing: Foreign Languages Press, 1969.

Marx, K., 1853a, 'Revolution in China and Europe', in *Marx on China*, London: Lawrence and Wishart, 1968.

Marx, K., 1853b, 'The British Rule in India', in S. Aveneri, ed., *Karl Marx on Colonialism and Modernization*, New York: Anchor Books, 1969.

Marx, K., 1859, 'Trade with China', in *Marx on China*, London: Lawrence and Wishart, 1968.

Marx, K., 1887, *Capital, Vol. 1*, New York: International Publishers, 1967.

Marx, K., and F. Engels, 1848, *The Manifesto of the Communist Party*, translated by Samuel Moore, with an introduction by E. Hobsbawm, London: Verso, 1999.

Maslow, A., 1987, *Motivation and Personality* (third edition), New York: Harper and Row.

Michael, F., 1964, 'State and Society in Nineteenth-Century China', in A. Feuerwerker, ed., *Modern China*, Englewood Cliffs, NJ: Prentice Hall.

Miller, J., 1993, *Mikhail Gorbachev and the End of Soviet Power*, Basingstoke: Macmillan.

Moberg, P., 2002, *Political Turning Points: Rhetorical Analyses of Japanese Inauguration Speeches*, Gothenburg: University of Gothenburg Press.

Myers, R., 1980, *The Chinese Economy, Past and Present*, Belmont, CA: Wadsworth.

Naughton, B., 1995, *Growing Out of the Plan*, Cambridge: Cambridge University Press.

Needham, J., 1954–, *Science and Civilization in China*, Cambridge: Cambridge University Press.

Needham, J., 1965, *Science and Civilization, Vol. 4, Pt 2, Mechanical Engineering*, Cambridge: Cambridge University Press.

Nolan, P., 1988, *The Political Economy of Collective Farms*, Cambridge: Polity.

Nolan, P., 1993, *State and Market in the Chinese Economy*, Basingstoke: Macmillan.

Nolan, P., 1995, *China's Rise, Russia's Fall*, Basingstoke: Macmillan.

Nolan, P., 1998, 'The starting-point of liberalisation: China and the former USSR on the eve of reform', in J. Henderson, ed., *Industrial Transformation in Eastern Europe in the Light of the East Asian Experience*, Basingstoke: Macmillan.

Nolan, P., 2001a, *China and the Global Business Revolution*, Basingstoke: Palgrave.

Nolan, P., 2001b, *China and the Global Economy*, Basingstoke: Palgrave.

North, D.C., and R.P. Thomas, 1973, *The Rise of the Western World*, Cambridge: Cambridge University Press.

Nye, J., 2002, *The Paradox of American Power*, New York: Oxford University Press.

O'Brien, P.K., and S.L. Engerman, 1981, 'Changes in the distribution of income and its distribution during the industrial revolution', in R. Floud and D. McClosky, eds, *The Economic History of Britain since 1700, Vol. 1, 1700–1860*, Cambridge: Cambridge University Press.

Ohmae, K., 1990, The *Borderless World*, London: Collins.

Perkins, D.H., 1967, 'Government as an obstacle to industrialization: The case of nineteenth-century China', *Journal of Economic History*, Vol. 28, no. 4.

Perkins, D.H., 1968, *Agricultural Development in China, 1368–1968*, Edinburgh: Edinburgh University Press.

Polanyi, K., 1957, *The Great Transformation*, Boston: Beacon Hill.

Polo, Marco, 1974, *The Travels*, Harmondsworth: Penguin.

Putnam, R.D., 2000, *Bowling Alone*, New York: Touchstone Books.

Qu Hongbin, 2002, 'China economics: The emerging nouveaux riches', *HSBC China Monthly*.

Rodinson, M., 1974, *Islam and Capitalism*, London: Allen Lane.

Rowe, W.T., 1984, *Hankow: Commerce and Society in a Chinese City, 1796–1889*, Stanford: Stanford University Press.

Sachs, J., and W.T. Woo, 1994, 'Structural factors in the economic reforms of China, Eastern Europe and the Former Soviet Union', *Economic Policy*, Vol. 18.

Scott, M.C., 2001, *Heartland*, New York: John Wiley.

Schmitz, C.J., 1993, *The Growth of Big Business in the United States and Western Europe, 1850–1939*, London: Macmillan.

Selden, M., 1979, *The People's Republic of China*, New York: Monthly Review Press.

Sennett, R., 1998, *The Corrosion of Character*, London: Norton.

Shiba, Y., 1977, 'Ningpo and its hinterland', in G.W. Skinner, ed., *The City in Late Imperial China*, Stanford: Stanford University Press.

Shiller, R., 2001, *Irrational Exuberance*, Princeton: Princeton University Press.

Skinner, G.W., 1977, 'Regional urbanization in nineteenth-century China', in W.G. Skinner, ed., *The City in Late Imperial China*, Stanford: Stanford University Press.

Smil, V., 1993, *China's Environmental Crisis*, London: M.E. Sharpe.

Smith, Adam, 1761, *The Theory of Moral Sentiments* (revised edition), Indianapolis: Liberty Classics edition, 1982.

Smith, Adam, 1776, *The Wealth of Nations* (2 vols), Chicago: University of Chicago Press, Cannan edition, 1976.

State Statistical Bureau (SSB), various years, *Chinese Statistical Yearbook (Zhongguo tongji nianjian) (ZTN)*, Beijing: Zhongguo tongji chubanshe.

State Statistical Bureau of Guangdong (SSBG), 2001, *Guangdong Statistical Yearbook (Guangdong Tongji Nianjian) (GTN)*, Guangzhou: Tongji Chubanshe.

Steinbeck, J., 1939, *The Grapes of Wrath*, Harmondsworth: Penguin, 1992.

Sun Wu [Sun Zi or Sun Tzu], 1996, *The Essentials of War*, Beijing: New World Press.

Swamy, S., 1979, 'The response to economic challenge: A comparative economic history of China and India, 1870–1952', *Quarterly Journal of Economics*, February.

Tang, Wingshing, 2003, 'Liang Sicheng and the transformation of Beijing: A Foucault-ist analysis', University of Cambridge, PhD dissertation.

Therborn, G., 1977, 'The rule of capital and the rise of democracy', *New Left Review*, no. 104, May–June.

Toynbee, A., and Ikeda, D., 1989, *Choose Life: A Dialogue*, London: Oxford University Press.

Twohey, M., 1999, *Authority and Welfare in China*, Basingstoke: Macmillan.

UNCTAD, 2002, *World Investment Report*, Geneva: United Nations.

UNDP, various years, *Human Development Report (HDR)*, New York: Oxford University Press.

UNDP, 2000, *China: Human Development Report 1999*, New York: Oxford University Press.

Wagner, D., 1998, *The Traditional Chinese Iron Industry and its Modern Fate*, Richmond, Surrey: Curzon Press.

Wang Gungwu, 1998, *The Nanhai Trade*, Singapore: Times Academic Press.

Wang Xiaoqiang, 1998, *China's Price and Ownership Reform*, Basingstoke: Macmillan.

Wang Xiaoqiang, Deng Yingtao, Yang Shuang, and Cui Heming, 1999, *Rebuilding China*, Shanghai: Wenhui Publishers (in Chinese).

Will, P.-Ét., 1990, *Bureaucracy and Famine in Eighteenth-Century China*, Stanford: Stanford University Press.

Wittfogel, K.A., 1957, *Oriental Despotism*, London: Yale University Press.

World Bank, various years, *World Development Report* (*WDR*), Washington, DC: Oxford University Press.

World Bank, 2002, *China: National Development and Sub-national Finances*, Washington, DC: World Bank.

Xu Dixin, and Wu Chengming, 2000, *Chinese Capitalism, 1522–1840* (edited and annotated by Charles Curwen), Basingstoke: Macmillan.

Yergin, D., and J. Stanislaw, 2000, *The Commanding Heights*, New York: Touchstone Books.

Index

DATE DUE

DEMCO 38-296